The Hidden Gems

UNLOCKING THE HEALING AND METAPHYSICAL PROPERTIES OF
CRYSTALS AND ANCIENT WISDOM

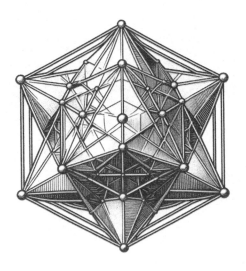

Midnight Ink Publishing

Table of Contents

CHAPTER ONE

Introduction to Gemstone Energies

Have you ever wondered why certain gemstones captivate us with their beauty and allure? Beyond their aesthetic appeal, gemstones harbor unique vibrational frequencies and energetic properties. These subtle energies interact with our own energy fields, known as auras, influencing our physical health, emotional balance, and spiritual growth. Each gemstone's energy is a product of its distinct composition, color, structure, and the geological forces that shaped it.

Explanation of What Gemstone Energies Are

The mysterious energies of gemstones originate from their intrinsic qualities. Key factors contributing to these energies include:

Chemical Composition: The minerals and elements forming a gemstone, like the silicon and oxygen in quartz, bestow it with clarity and a high vibrational frequency.

Crystalline Structure: The atomic arrangement within a gemstone, such as the piezoelectric properties of quartz and tourmaline, affects its energy absorption, storage, and transmission.

Color: The specific wavelengths of light absorbed and reflected by a gemstone give it color, each associated with different energies and chakras. For example, green stones like emerald and jade resonate with the heart chakra, promoting emotional healing.

Formation Process: Geological conditions such as heat, pressure, and time influence a gemstone's energy. Diamonds, formed under extreme pressure, are renowned for their strength and resilience."

Overview of the Concept of Energy in Gemstones

The concept of energy in gemstones is rooted in ancient traditions and modern scientific understanding:

- **Ancient Traditions:** Throughout history, various cultures have recognized the energetic properties of gemstones. Ancient Egyptians used lapis lazuli for protection and spiritual insight, while Chinese medicine incorporates jade for its balancing and healing properties.

- **Modern Science:** While not universally accepted in the scientific community, some studies suggest that gemstones can influence our energy fields. The piezoelectric and pyroelectric properties of certain crystals are evidence of their ability to generate and store energy.

- **Energy Interaction:** Gemstones are believed to interact with our energy fields in several ways:

  - **Amplification:** Some stones, like clear quartz, can amplify energy and intentions, making them powerful tools for meditation and healing.

  - **Balancing:** Stones like rose quartz and amethyst are known for their calming and balancing effects, helping to soothe emotions and promote inner peace.

  - **Protection:** Gemstones such as black tourmaline and obsidian are thought to absorb and deflect negative energies, providing a protective shield.

Basic Principles

How Gemstones Absorb, Store, and Emit Energy

- **Absorption:** Gemstones absorb energy from their surroundings, including light, heat, and even the emotions of people around them. This absorption process is influenced by their crystalline structure and the presence of certain minerals.

- **Storage:** The crystalline structure of gemstones allows them to store absorbed energy. Different gemstones have varying capacities for energy storage. For instance, quartz crystals can hold significant amounts of energy due to their stable lattice structure.

- **Emission:** Once energy is absorbed and stored, gemstones can emit this energy back into their surroundings. This emission can occur naturally or be activated through intentional practices like meditation or energy healing.

The Interaction Between Gemstones and Human Energy Fields

- **Aura Interaction:** The human aura, an electromagnetic field surrounding the body, can interact with the energies emitted by gemstones. This interaction can lead to various effects on our physical, emotional, and spiritual states.

- **Chakra Resonance:** Gemstones resonate with specific chakras, or energy centres, in the body. By placing or wearing gemstones aligned with certain chakras, individuals can influence these energy centres, promoting balance and healing.

- **Healing and Protection:** The interaction between gemstones and human energy fields can support healing by clearing blockages, enhancing energy flow, and providing protection against negative influences.

Energy and Vibration - Understanding Vibrational Frequency

- **Vibrational Properties:** Every gemstone has a unique vibrational frequency, which is determined by its physical properties such as density, composition, and structure. These vibrations can influence the energy fields they come into contact with.

- **Frequency and Healing:** Higher vibrational gemstones, like amethyst and selenite, are often associated with spiritual growth and healing, while lower vibrational stones, like hematite and garnet, are grounding and stabilising.

The Role of Vibration in Gemstone Energy

- **Energy Modulation:** The vibrational frequencies of gemstones can modulate the energies within and around us. For example, the soothing vibrations of rose quartz can help calm the heart and emotions.

- **Harmonisation:** By using gemstones with compatible vibrations, individuals can harmonise their energy fields, promoting a state of balance and well-being.

- **Amplification and Focus:** Certain gemstones can amplify the energy and intentions set by an individual, acting as a conduit to focus and enhance spiritual practices, meditations, and healing sessions.

Common Misconceptions - Debunking Myths and Misconceptions About Gemstone Energies

- **Myth: Gemstones Have Magical Powers:** While gemstones possess unique energies, they do not have magical powers. Their effects are based on natural vibrational properties and their interactions with human energy fields.

- **Myth: All Gemstones Work the Same for Everyone:** The effectiveness of gemstones can vary from person to person. Personal resonance, energetic needs, and individual sensitivity all play a role in how one experiences gemstone energies.

- **Myth: Gemstones Can Replace Medical Treatment:** Gemstones should not be used as a substitute for professional medical care. They can complement conventional treatments but should not be relied upon exclusively for healing serious health conditions.

- **Misconception: Gemstones Need Constant Cleansing:** While regular cleansing is beneficial, gemstones do not need constant cleansing. Their energy can be maintained with periodic cleansing and charging practices.

Historical Significance - Ancient Civilizations

Use of Gemstones in Ancient Egypt, Mesopotamia, India, and China

Ancient Egypt

In the land of the pharaohs, gemstones were revered not merely for their beauty but for their mystical powers. Lapis lazuli, turquoise, and carnelian adorned the jewellery, amulets, and burial masks of the elite, serving as talismans of protection and symbols of divine power. The famed burial mask of Tutankhamun, adorned with lapis lazuli, was believed to ensure safe passage to the afterlife, its deep blue hue symbolising the eternal sky and divine wisdom.

Mesopotamia

In the ancient lands of Mesopotamia, agate, jasper, and carnelian were crafted into seals and amulets, their energies believed to safeguard the bearer and confer the blessings of the gods. These stones, inscribed with sacred symbols, were tokens of protection and conduits of divine favour, connecting the earthly and the divine.

India

For millennia, the sages of India have recognized the potent energies of gemstones, integrating them into the holistic practice of Ayurvedic medicine. Rubies, sapphires, and emeralds were not merely ornaments but vital tools in balancing the body's energies and treating ailments. Ancient texts like the Vedas extol the virtues of these stones, their healing powers enshrined in the annals of history.

China

Jade, revered as the "Stone of Heaven," has held a place of honour in Chinese culture for over 5,000 years. This sacred stone, used in everything from jewellery to intricate carvings, was believed to offer protection, enhance longevity, and attract good fortune. Jade's serene green hue was a symbol of purity and moral integrity, its presence a blessing upon those who possessed it.

Gemstones in Mythology and Folklore

Greek Mythology

The ancients believed that amethyst held the power to protect against drunkenness, a belief born from the myth of Dionysus and the nymph Amethystos. Adorning oneself with amethyst was thought to keep one's mind clear and sober, a shield against the intoxicating influences of the world.

Norse Mythology

In the sagas of the Norse gods, Thor was said to wear a belt of strength adorned with powerful stones. These gemstones, seen as gifts from the gods, were imbued with protective and empowering properties, linking the mortal and the divine in a tapestry of myth and legend.

Native American Folklore

In many Native American cultures, turquoise is a sacred stone, a bridge between heaven and earth. It was believed to offer protection, health, and good fortune, its vibrant blue-green hue a symbol of life and vitality. Turquoise was woven into the fabric of ceremonial and everyday objects, a testament to its revered status.

Medieval and Renaissance Periods - Gemstones in Alchemy and Healing Practices

Alchemy

During the mediaeval period, alchemists sought to unlock the mysteries of the universe through the transformative powers of gemstones. The legendary Philosopher's Stone, central to these practices, was believed to turn base metals into gold and grant immortality. Gemstones were essential tools in the alchemist's quest, their energies harnessed in the pursuit of enlightenment and eternal life.

Healing Practices

In the Middle Ages, gemstones were integral to medical treatments, their energies believed to balance the body's humours and cure ailments. Emeralds were thought to alleviate eye strain, while rubies were used to improve circulation. These practices, rooted in both tradition and emerging science, reflected a deep belief in the healing powers of the natural world.

Symbolism and Usage in Art and Literature

Art

Renaissance artists, inspired by the mystical and symbolic properties of gemstones, incorporated them into their works to convey virtues and values. Sapphires represented purity and wisdom, while rubies symbolised passion and power. These gems, set into paintings and sculptures, added layers of meaning and depth to the artistic expression.

Literature

Gemstones frequently appeared in mediaeval and Renaissance literature, symbolising wealth, status, and moral qualities. In Chaucer's "Canterbury Tales" and Shakespeare's plays, gemstones were more than mere ornaments; they were emblems of the characters' virtues and vices, their presence a reflection of the human condition.

Modern History - Revival of Gemstone Energy Practices in the 19th and 20th Centuries

Victorian Era

The Victorians' fascination with gemstones extended beyond their aesthetic appeal to their symbolic meanings. Jewellery from this period often featured gemstones chosen for their perceived qualities, such as amethysts for piety and garnets for fidelity. This era saw a revival of interest in the metaphysical properties of gemstones, blending tradition with a burgeoning interest in spirituality.

New Age Movement

The late 20th century witnessed a resurgence of interest in gemstone energies, driven by the New Age movement. Practitioners explored the metaphysical properties of gemstones, integrating them into healing, meditation, and spiritual practices. Crystal healing became a popular holistic practice, with gemstones used to align, clear, and balance the chakras, promoting physical, emotional, and spiritual well-being.

Influence of the New Age Movement

Crystal Healing

The New Age movement popularised the use of gemstones in holistic healing practices. Crystal healers use stones to align, clear, and balance the chakras, promoting well-being. This practice, grounded in both ancient traditions and modern metaphysical beliefs, has become a cornerstone of alternative healing.

Metaphysical Stores

The rise of metaphysical stores and the availability of books and courses on gemstone energies have made the practice more accessible to the general public. These stores offer a wide variety of gemstones and resources for learning about their uses and properties, fostering a renewed interest in their mystical powers.

Popular Culture

Gemstones have also permeated popular culture, influencing fashion, interior design, and personal talismans. Their aesthetic appeal, combined with their perceived energetic properties, has made them a popular choice for jewellery, home décor, and personal items, bridging the gap between ancient traditions and contemporary trends.

Cultural Perspectives

Eastern Traditions - Gemstone Uses in Traditional Chinese Medicine (TCM)

Healing and Balancing

In the ancient practice of TCM, gemstones are revered for their ability to balance the body's energy, or Qi, and support overall health. Jade, for instance, is not only a symbol of purity but also a powerful stone used to calm the mind, promote physical healing, and ward off negative energies.

Acupuncture and Massage

Gemstones are integral to acupuncture and massage therapies in TCM. Jade rollers and gua sha tools are widely used to enhance skin health, reduce inflammation, and relieve muscle tension, channelling the stone's soothing energies directly into the body.

Feng Shui

In the art of Feng Shui, gemstones are strategically placed to harmonise the energy within living spaces. Clear quartz, citrine, and amethyst are among the crystals used to attract positive energy and improve the flow of Qi, creating environments that nurture and support those who dwell within.

Ayurvedic Practices Involving Gemstones

Dosha Balancing

Ayurveda, the ancient healing science of India, employs gemstones to balance the three doshas: Vata, Pitta, and Kapha. Pearls are used to calm the fiery Pitta, while red coral is known to stabilise the airy Vata, each stone meticulously chosen for its unique properties.

Healing Practices

In Ayurvedic healing, gemstones are worn or used in elixirs to address specific health issues. Blue sapphire, for example, is believed to enhance mental clarity and reduce anxiety, while emeralds are used to support heart health, each stone's energy aligned with the body's needs.

Chakra Healing

Ayurvedic practitioners use gemstones to align and heal the chakras. Each stone is placed on the body or worn as jewellery to target specific chakras, promoting balance and healing throughout the energy centres.

Tibetan and Himalayan Perspectives

Spiritual Tools

In Tibetan and Himalayan traditions, gemstones play a vital role in spiritual practices and religious rituals. Turquoise and coral, often used in prayer beads (mala) and protective amulets, are believed to provide spiritual protection and enhance the practitioner's connection to the divine.

Medicine Buddha

The Medicine Buddha is often depicted holding a bowl of lapis lazuli, a stone symbolising healing and wisdom. Lapis lazuli is revered as a sacred stone that enhances spiritual insight and promotes physical and emotional healing.

Mandalas and Art

Gemstones are incorporated into mandalas and other spiritual art forms, believed to channel divine energy and aid in meditation. These intricate designs, adorned with gemstones, serve as tools for spiritual growth and enlightenment.

Western Traditions - Gemstones in European Folklore and Healing

Folklore

European folklore abounds with stories of the magical properties of gemstones. Amber, for example, was believed to protect against evil spirits and bring good luck, its warm, golden glow a beacon of positive energy.

Healing Practices

In mediaeval Europe, gemstones were used in various healing practices. Physicians prescribed gemstones to be worn or taken in powdered form to treat ailments. The Doctrine of Signatures suggested that a gemstone's appearance indicated its healing properties, such as bloodstone being used for blood disorders.

Alchemy

Alchemists used gemstones in their quest for the philosopher's stone, believed to grant immortality and transform base metals into gold. They attributed mystical properties to gemstones, integral to their experiments and spiritual pursuits.

Modern Western Approaches to Gemstone Therapy

Crystal Healing

Modern crystal healing practices in the West involve using gemstones to balance energy, enhance well-being, and support healing. Practitioners place stones on the body, create crystal grids, and use gemstones in meditation to harness their specific energies.

Jewellery and Fashion

Gemstones are popular in jewellery and fashion not only for their beauty but also for their energetic properties. People wear gemstone jewellery to harness the specific energies associated with different stones, such as amethyst for tranquillity and citrine for abundance.

Mindfulness and Wellness

Gemstones are incorporated into mindfulness and wellness practices. Many people use gemstones in meditation, yoga, and personal rituals to enhance their spiritual and emotional well-being, drawing upon the ancient belief in their healing powers.

Indigenous Practices - Native American Uses of Gemstones and Crystals

Sacred Stones

Native American tribes consider certain stones, like turquoise and quartz, to be sacred. These stones are used in ceremonies, rituals, and as protective talismans, their energies believed to connect the spiritual and physical worlds.

Healing and Protection

Gemstones are used in healing practices to protect against negative energies and promote health. Shamans and healers use crystals to diagnose and treat illnesses, believing that the stones can absorb and transmute negative energy.

SymbolismEach gemstone holds specific symbolism and is used to honour the spirits and the earth. For example, turquoise is often associated with the sky and water, symbolising life and protection, its vibrant blue-green hue a link to the divine.

African and Aboriginal Gemstone Traditions

African Traditions

In various African cultures, gemstones and crystals are used in rituals, healing, and as symbols of power. Stones like malachite and carnelian are used for their protective and healing properties, their energies woven into the fabric of daily life.

Aboriginal Practices

Australian Aboriginals use gemstones such as opal in their cultural and spiritual practices. Opal is considered a powerful stone that can bring clarity, balance, and protection. Dreamtime stories often feature gemstones as gifts from the ancestors, their energies a connection to the ancient past.

Global Comparison - Similarities and Differences Across Cultures

Common Themes

Across cultures, gemstones are universally associated with healing, protection, and spiritual connection. Many cultures believe in the protective and healing properties of stones like turquoise, quartz, and jade, their energies transcending time and geography.

Cultural Variations

While the underlying beliefs about gemstone energies are similar, the specific uses and symbolic meanings can vary widely. For example, jade is highly revered in China for its protective qualities, while in Mesoamerican cultures, it is associated with fertility and abundance.

How Cultural Context Influences the Perception of Gemstone Energies

Historical Influence

The historical and cultural context in which gemstones are used significantly influences their perceived energies. Historical events, religious beliefs, and cultural practices shape how different societies view and use gemstones, each stone a reflection of the cultural tapestry.

Modern Integration

In today's globalised world, there is a blending of cultural practices related to gemstone use. Modern practices often incorporate elements from various traditions, creating a rich tapestry of beliefs and applications, each stone a bridge between the ancient and the contemporary.

CHAPTER TWO

The Science Behind Gemstone Energies

The Physics of Crystals - Crystalline Structures

Crystals are the wonders of nature, born from the dance of atoms arranged in highly ordered, repeating patterns that extend in all three spatial dimensions. This intricate arrangement bestows crystals with their unique shapes, dazzling brilliance, and mystical properties.

Types of Crystalline Structures

Crystals manifest in various forms, each with a unique structure influencing how they interact with light and energy. The main types include:

- **Cubic:** Exemplified by diamonds, these crystals possess a symmetrical, geometric elegance.

- **Hexagonal:** Quartz, a familiar and potent gemstone, forms in this structure, radiating energy from its six-sided lattice.

- **Tetragonal, Orthorhombic, Monoclinic, and Triclinic:** Each of these structures contributes distinct characteristics to the gemstones, affecting their optical properties and how they resonate with energy.

Formation of Gemstones

Geological Processes Leading to Gemstone Formation

The formation of gemstones is a saga of elemental forces, unfolding deep within the Earth's embrace.

Igneous Processes

Within the fiery depths, gemstones like diamonds and peridot are forged. As molten rock (magma) cools and crystallises in the Earth's mantle, these stones emerge, bearing the strength of their volcanic birth.

Metamorphic Processes

Gemstones such as garnet and emerald are born of transformation. Under immense pressure and heat, existing minerals undergo metamorphosis, emerging anew without melting, their crystalline hearts forever changed.

Sedimentary Processes

The gentle caress of water plays a role in the creation of opal and malachite. These gemstones form as minerals are deposited in layers from water solutions, creating beautiful, stratified treasures.

Hydrothermal Processes

In the hidden veins and cavities of rocks, gemstones like amethyst and topaz crystallise from hot, mineral-rich water solutions, emerging as radiant jewels of the Earth.

Natural vs. Synthetic Gemstones

Natural Gemstones

Formed through the Earth's timeless geological processes, natural gemstones are imbued with unique inclusions and variations, each stone telling its own ancient story.

Synthetic Gemstones

Created in the alchemical laboratories of modern times, synthetic gemstones replicate natural conditions, possessing the same chemical and physical properties as their natural counterparts but often free from inclusions and imperfections, their beauty unmarred by the hand of nature.

Properties of Crystals

Physical Properties

Hardness

Measured by the Mohs scale, which ranks minerals from 1 (softest, like talc) to 10 (hardest, like diamond), hardness affects a gemstone's durability and resistance to scratching, dictating its suitability for various uses.

Density

The mass per unit volume of a gemstone influences its heft. Denser gemstones, such as sapphire and ruby, feel weighty in the hand, their solidity a testament to their enduring nature.

Cleavage and Fracture

Cleavage describes how a gemstone breaks along specific planes, while fracture reveals its irregular breaking patterns. These properties are crucial in determining how gemstones are cut and polished, each fracture a window into the stone's crystalline soul.

Luster

The way a gemstone reflects light, ranging from metallic to dull, defines its lustre. Common lusters include vitreous (glass-like), adamantine (diamond-like), and silky, each adding to the stone's visual allure and mystical charm.

Optical Properties

Refraction

The bending of light as it passes through a gemstone, measured by the refractive index, influences the gemstone's brilliance and sparkle. Each stone bends light uniquely, creating its own dance of luminescence.

Dispersion

The separation of light into its component colours, creating a rainbow effect, is known as dispersion. High dispersion, seen in diamonds, conjures spectral wonders within the gemstone's depths.

Luminescence

The ability of a gemstone to emit light when exposed to ultraviolet light includes phenomena such as fluorescence and phosphorescence. This mystical glow, seen in some diamonds and opals, adds an ethereal quality to these stones.

Piezoelectric and Pyroelectric Effects

Introduction to Piezoelectricity and Pyroelectricity

Certain crystals possess remarkable properties that allow them to generate electric charges:

- **Piezoelectricity**

Crystals like quartz and tourmaline can generate an electric charge in response to mechanical stress. This property finds use in technologies such as quartz watches and ultrasound devices, where the crystal's stability and precision are paramount.

- **Pyroelectricity**

Some crystals can generate an electric charge in response to temperature changes. This property, observed in certain tourmalines, is harnessed in infrared sensors and other thermal detection technologies, bridging the gap between the mystical and the technological.

Examples of Gemstones Exhibiting These Effects

- **Quartz:** Renowned for its piezoelectric properties, quartz is essential in electronics and precise timekeeping, its vibrations a measure of the universe's constancy.

- **Tourmaline:** Exhibiting both piezoelectric and pyroelectric properties, tourmaline is used in pressure gauges and pyroelectric sensors, its dual nature a marvel of natural science.

Energy Storage and Transfer

How Crystals Can Store and Transfer Energy

Energy Storage

Crystals absorb and store energy from their surroundings, including light, heat, and electromagnetic energy. This stored energy can be released gradually or in response to specific stimuli, a reservoir of natural power waiting to be tapped.

Resonance and Frequency Matching

Crystals resonate at specific frequencies, which can match and influence the frequencies of other energy fields. This principle is harnessed in crystal healing to balance and align the body's energy, each stone a symphony of harmonious vibrations.

How Gemstones Interact with Human Energy Fields (Auras)

The aura is a multi-layered, electromagnetic field that surrounds the human body, shimmering with colours and patterns that reflect a person's physical, emotional, mental, and spiritual states. This subtle energy field is a mirror of our inner world, visible to those with the gift of sight.

Historical Context

The concept of the aura has roots in ancient spiritual and healing traditions. From the prismatic depictions in Hindu and Buddhist scriptures to the mystical teachings of Western esoteric practices, the aura has long been recognized as a vital component of human existence, a bridge between the corporeal and the divine.

Layers of the Aura and Their Significance

Physical Layer

The closest layer to the body, this layer reflects physical health and vitality, pulsating with the rhythm of one's corporeal being.

Etheric Layer

Connected to the physical body, the etheric layer contains the blueprint of the physical form and vital energy, a luminous template of our earthly vessel.

Emotional Layer

Reflecting the individual's emotional state and well-being, this layer is a dynamic canvas of fluctuating colours and patterns, painting a picture of the heart's current state.

Mental Layer

Representing thoughts, beliefs, and mental processes, the mental layer is typically more stable and structured, emanating the clarity or turmoil of the mind.

Astral Layer

Associated with the bridge between the physical and spiritual realms, this layer reflects higher emotions and love, a radiant field of spiritual connectivity.

Etheric Template Layer

Containing the perfect template of the physical body, this layer is involved in healing and regeneration, a reservoir of restorative energy.

Celestial Layer

Linked to higher consciousness and spiritual insight, the celestial layer often glows with the light of meditation and spiritual practices, a halo of divine wisdom.

Ketheric Template Layer

The outermost layer, representing the individual's connection to the divine and universal consciousness, this layer is a shimmering veil of cosmic unity, the final frontier of the auric field.

The Science Behind Gemstone Energies

Summary of Recent Studies on Gemstone Energies

In recent years, the scientific community has shown a growing interest in the ancient wisdom of gemstones, seeking to unravel the mysteries of their effects on human energy fields. Researchers have embarked on studies exploring the physical properties of crystals, their vibrational frequencies, and their potential therapeutic applications, blending modern science with age-old knowledge.

Key Research Areas

The primary areas of focus in gemstone research include

- **Piezoelectric and Pyroelectric Effects:** Investigating how these properties influence biological systems and energy fields.

- **Interaction with Biological Systems:** Studying the resonance and energy transfer between gemstones and human cells.

- **Psychological Impact:** Examining the psychological benefits and emotional well-being associated with gemstone use.

Key Findings and Their Implications

Resonance and Energy Transfer

Studies have shown that gemstones can resonate at specific frequencies, transferring energy to human energy fields. This interaction can potentially influence physical and emotional states, offering insights into the therapeutic use of gemstones.

Psychological Benefits

Research indicates that gemstones may provide psychological comfort and stress relief through a placebo effect. The belief in the properties of gemstones can lead to measurable improvements in mood and emotional well-being, underscoring the power of the mind in healing practices.

Biophysical Research - Studies on the Effects of Gemstones on Biological Systems

Cellular Interactions

Investigations have delved into how gemstones might affect cellular processes. For instance, studies on quartz crystals have explored their influence on cellular growth and repair, revealing a potential for promoting healing at a microscopic level.

Electromagnetic Fields

Research into how gemstones interact with the body's electromagnetic field suggests that they may alter the biofield, the subtle energy field surrounding the body. This interaction could have implications for energy balance and overall health.

Interaction of Gemstone Energies with Cellular Processes

Healing Properties

Examinations of specific gemstones, such as amethyst, have highlighted their purported detoxifying effects. These studies suggest that gemstones might promote cellular regeneration, reduce inflammation, and support the body's natural healing processes.

Energy Modulation

Studies have shown that gemstones can modulate energy at the cellular level, enhancing vitality and supporting overall health. This modulation aligns with the principles of energy medicine, where balance and harmony are key to well-being.

Psychological and Emotional Impact

Research on the Impact of Gemstones on Mental Health and Emotional Well-being

Stress Reduction

Gemstones like rose quartz and amethyst have been studied for their calming energies, with research showing they can reduce stress and promote relaxation. These findings align with the traditional use of gemstones for emotional healing.

Mood Enhancement

Research indicates that certain gemstones, such as citrine, can elevate mood and provide emotional support. Citrine, often associated with joy and positivity, has been shown to influence emotional states favourably.

Placebo Effect vs. Actual Effects

Placebo Effect

Exploration of the placebo effect reveals that the psychological benefits derived from the belief in gemstone properties are significant. Individuals who believe in the healing powers of gemstones often experience positive effects, highlighting the mind's role in healing.

Measurable Effects

Studies have documented measurable physiological changes, such as changes in heart rate, blood pressure, and stress hormone levels, when using gemstones. These findings provide empirical support for the therapeutic potential of gemstones beyond mere placebo.

Technological Applications - Use of Gemstones in Modern Technology

Electronics

Piezoelectric crystals like quartz are widely used in electronic devices, including watches, radios, and ultrasound machines. These applications leverage the stable vibrational frequencies of crystals, showcasing their practical utility in technology.

Optics

Gemstones are also used in optical devices, such as lenses and prisms, due to their unique refractive properties. Their precision and clarity make them invaluable in various technological applications.

Potential Future Applications and Innovations

Medical Devices

The potential for developing new medical technologies that utilise the energy properties of gemstones is vast. Crystals could be used in therapeutic devices to promote healing and energy balance, revolutionising medical treatments.

Sustainable Energy

Exploration of how gemstones could contribute to sustainable energy solutions is ongoing. Piezoelectric materials, for instance, might be used for energy harvesting and storage, providing innovative ways to harness natural energies.

Critiques and Controversies - Sceptical Perspectives and Scientific
Criticisms

Lack of Empirical Evidence

Despite promising findings, there remains scepticism within the scientific
community regarding the efficacy of gemstone healing. Critics point to the lack
of rigorous empirical evidence and the need for more robust studies.

Scientific Methodology

Concerns about the methodologies used in gemstone research include issues
with sample size, control groups, and reproducibility of results. These challenges
highlight the need for improved research standards.

Addressing the Challenges and Limitations of Current Research

Improving Research Standards

Recommendations for enhancing the quality and rigour of scientific studies on
gemstone energies include conducting larger, controlled studies and developing
better measurement techniques. This approach aims to provide more conclusive
evidence of gemstone effects.

Integrating Traditional Knowledge

Integrating traditional wisdom with modern scientific approaches can create a
more holistic understanding of gemstone energies. This integration honours the
rich history of gemstone use while advancing contemporary research.

Future Directions

Potential areas for future research include exploring the molecular mechanisms
behind gemstone interactions with biological systems and developing
standardised protocols for gemstone therapy. These directions promise to
deepen our understanding and application of gemstone energies.

CHAPTER THREE

Gemstone Properties and Their Energetic Effects

Colour and Vibration

The study of colour theory reveals the profound impact of colours on our perceptions and emotions. The primary colours (red, blue, yellow) blend to create secondary colours (orange, green, purple), which in turn mix to form tertiary colours. This spectrum, encompassing all visible light, resonates deeply with the human psyche and energy field.

Colour and Energy

Each colour corresponds to a specific wavelength of light, translating into unique vibrational frequencies. These vibrations interact with our energy fields, influencing our physical, emotional, and spiritual states. Understanding these connections allows us to harness the power of gemstones more effectively.

How Different Colours Correspond to Different Vibrations and Energies

Red: Energy, Passion, and Action Red, the colour of life force and vitality, pulsates with intense energy. Red gemstones such as ruby and garnet resonate with the Root Chakra, the foundation of our energetic system. These stones invigorate the body, stimulate the flow of energy, and ground us in the physical realm, providing a sense of stability and security.

- **Ruby:** Known as the stone of nobility, ruby enhances vitality and life force, inspiring courage and passion.

- **Garnet:** A stone of commitment, garnet revitalises, purifies, and balances energy, bringing serenity and inspiring love.

Orange: Creativity, Joy, and Enthusiasm

Orange, a warm and vibrant hue, embodies creativity and emotional expression. Orange gemstones like carnelian resonate with the Sacral Chakra, the seat of creativity and joy. These stones encourage emotional balance, stimulate creative thinking, and foster a sense of enthusiasm for life.

- **Carnelian:** Enhances creativity, courage, and positive life choices, banishing emotional negativity.

- **Amber:** Although technically fossilised resin, amber's rich orange glow is associated with healing, cleansing, and revitalization.

Yellow: Clarity, Confidence, and Intellect

Yellow, the colour of the sun, symbolises clarity, confidence, and intellect. Yellow gemstones like citrine are linked to the Solar Plexus Chakra, the centre of personal power. These stones boost self-confidence, enhance mental clarity, and support decision-making.

- **Citrine:** Known as the merchant's stone, citrine attracts wealth, prosperity, and success, while also encouraging generosity and sharing.

- **Yellow Topaz:** A stone of good fortune, it aids in manifesting intentions and enhancing personal power.

Green: Growth, Balance, and Healing

Green, the colour of nature, represents growth, balance, and healing. Green gemstones such as emerald and green aventurine correspond to the Heart Chakra, the centre of love and compassion. These stones promote emotional healing, enhance love and harmony, and encourage growth and renewal.

- **Emerald:** Symbolising rebirth and renewal, emerald promotes recovery, regeneration, and emotional healing.

- **Green Aventurine:** Known as the stone of opportunity, it brings good luck and abundance, enhancing growth and prosperity.

Blue: Communication, Truth, and Peace

Blue, a calming and serene colour, symbolises communication, truth, and peace. Blue gemstones like lapis lazuli and aquamarine resonate with the Throat Chakra, the centre of communication and self-expression. These stones aid in clear communication, foster self-expression, and promote inner peace.

- **Lapis Lazuli:** A stone of truth and enlightenment, lapis lazuli enhances intellectual ability and stimulates the desire for knowledge and understanding.

- **Aquamarine:** Known for its calming energies, aquamarine reduces stress, enhances communication, and brings clarity.

Indigo: Intuition, Wisdom, and Spiritual Insight

Indigo, a deep and mystical colour, is linked to intuition, wisdom, and spiritual insight. Indigo gemstones like sodalite and iolite correspond to the Third Eye Chakra, the seat of intuition and foresight. These stones enhance intuitive abilities, foster wisdom, and deepen spiritual insight.

- **Sodalite:** Enhances intuition and mental clarity, bringing insight and deeper understanding.

- **Iolite:** Also known as the Viking's compass, iolite aids in navigation and brings clarity to inner visions.

Violet: Spirituality, Enlightenment, and Transformation

Violet, a colour of spirituality and transformation, represents the highest vibrational frequency of visible light. Violet gemstones like amethyst are associated with the Crown Chakra, the gateway to higher consciousness. These stones support spiritual growth, enhance meditation, and facilitate a deeper connection to the divine.

- **Amethyst:** A powerful stone for spiritual protection and purification, amethyst aids in meditation, enhances intuition, and fosters spiritual growth.

- **Sugilite:** Known for its ability to open the Crown Chakra, sugilite enhances spiritual awareness and aligns the soul with higher realms.

By understanding the vibrational frequencies of colours and their corresponding gemstones, we can better harness the energies they offer. Each gemstone, with its unique colour and vibration, serves as a bridge between the physical and the metaphysical, guiding us toward balance, healing, and enlightenment.

Spectral Analysis - How Gemstones Absorb and Reflect Light

Light Absorption

The vibrant colours of gemstones are a result of the interaction between light and the stone's atomic structure. Gemstones absorb certain wavelengths of light while reflecting others, which gives them their distinct hues. For instance, an emerald appears green because it absorbs most wavelengths of light except green, which it reflects.

Spectroscopy

Spectroscopy is a scientific technique used to analyse the light spectra of gemstones. By studying how gemstones absorb and reflect light, scientists can identify their unique optical properties and colour characteristics. This analysis helps in understanding the precise composition and quality of the gemstones, offering insights into their energetic properties.

- **Absorption Spectrum:** Each gemstone has a characteristic absorption spectrum, a unique pattern of absorbed wavelengths, which acts like a fingerprint for identifying the stone.

- **Reflectance Spectrum:** This spectrum shows the wavelengths of light reflected by the gemstone, contributing to its visible colour and brilliance.

The Impact of Light on Gemstone Energy

Sunlight and Moonlight

Natural light sources like sunlight and moonlight play a crucial role in charging and enhancing the energies of gemstones. Sunlight, with its broad spectrum of wavelengths, can cleanse and invigorate gemstones, imbuing them with powerful solar energy. Moonlight, particularly from a full moon, offers a gentle, reflective energy that enhances the intuitive and emotional properties of gemstones.

- **Sunlight Charging:** Ideal for stones like clear quartz and citrine, sunlight can amplify their energies, making them more potent.

- **Moonlight Charging:** Suitable for sensitive stones like amethyst and moonstone, moonlight charging is a softer process that infuses calming, mystical energies.

Artificial Light

While natural light is preferred, artificial light also affects gemstones. Different types of artificial light, such as LED or incandescent, can influence the energies of gemstones in varying ways. LED lights, with their cooler, focused spectrum, may not charge gemstones as effectively as the broad, warm spectrum of incandescent lights.

- **LED Light:** May be less effective in charging gemstones but useful for highlighting specific optical properties.

- **Incandescent Light:** Mimics sunlight to some extent, providing a warmer energy that can be beneficial for certain gemstones.

Colour Healing Practices - Using Coloured Gemstones for Specific Healing Purposes

Physical Healing

Coloured gemstones are often used to target specific physical ailments, based on their vibrational properties and colour correspondences. For instance:

- **Green Stones (e.g., Emerald, Green Aventurine):** Associated with heart health, these stones are believed to support cardiovascular function and overall physical healing.

- **Red Stones (e.g., Ruby, Garnet):** Known for increasing energy levels and enhancing vitality, red stones are used to stimulate circulation and boost physical strength.

Emotional Healing

Gemstones are also powerful tools for balancing emotions and alleviating stress. The colours of the stones play a significant role in their healing properties:

- **Blue Stones (e.g., Blue Lace Agate, Aquamarine):** These calming stones help reduce anxiety and promote tranquillity, aiding in emotional balance and stress relief.

- **Pink Stones (e.g., Rose Quartz, Pink Tourmaline):** Known for fostering love and compassion, pink stones are used to heal emotional wounds and enhance feelings of self-love and acceptance.

Spiritual Healing

Enhancing spiritual practices with coloured gemstones can deepen meditation, spiritual insight, and purification:

- **Violet Stones (e.g., Amethyst, Sugilite):** These stones are ideal for deep meditation and spiritual growth, helping to connect with higher consciousness and enhance intuitive abilities.

- **White Stones (e.g., Clear Quartz, Selenite):** Used for spiritual purification and protection, white stones can cleanse the aura, remove negative energies, and connect with the divine.

By understanding and utilising the spectral properties and colour correspondences of gemstones, we can effectively harness their energies for various healing practices. Each gemstone, with its unique interaction with light and colour, serves as a powerful conduit for physical, emotional, and spiritual well-being.

Shape and Structure - Influence of Gemstone Shapes

Common Shapes and Their Specific Energetic Properties

Points

Gemstones shaped into points or wands are used to direct and focus energy. They are often employed in healing practices to channel energy into specific areas of the body, acting like a laser beam to target specific issues and promote healing.

- **Energetic Properties:** Directional energy, focus, intention

- **Uses:** Healing, energy channelling, intention setting

Spheres

Spherical gemstones emit energy evenly in all directions, making them ideal for meditation and creating a peaceful environment. They symbolise wholeness and unity, fostering harmony and balance within a space.

- **Energetic Properties:** Even energy distribution, harmony, balance

- **Uses:** Meditation, environment energy balance, holistic healing

Pyramids

Pyramid-shaped gemstones amplify and focus energy through their apex. They are used in manifesting intentions and enhancing meditation practices, drawing in energy from the base and focusing it at the point.

- **Energetic Properties:** Amplification, focus, manifestation
- **Uses:** Meditation, intention setting, energy enhancement

Cubes

Cubic gemstones ground and stabilise energy. They are associated with the Earth element and are used for grounding practices, providing a solid foundation and anchoring energies.

- **Energetic Properties:** Grounding, stability, Earth connection
- **Uses:** Grounding practices, energy stability, foundational work

Tumbled Stones

Smooth, polished gemstones that are easy to carry and use in everyday practices. They emit gentle, consistent energy and are often used in crystal grids and for carrying in pockets or pouches.

- **Energetic Properties:** Gentle energy, consistency, accessibility
- **Uses:** Everyday energy work, crystal grids, personal talismans

Clusters

Clusters contain multiple points on a single base, emitting energy in various directions. They are used to cleanse and charge other gemstones and to create a high-energy environment.

- **Energetic Properties:** Multi-directional energy, cleansing, charging
- **Uses:** Cleansing other stones, energy amplification, environmental energy enhancement

How the Shape of a Gemstone Affects Its Energy Flow

Directional Energy

The shape of a gemstone can influence how energy flows. For example, pointed crystals can direct energy precisely where needed, while spherical stones distribute energy evenly throughout a space.

Amplification and Focus

Shapes like pyramids and points can amplify and focus energy, making them powerful tools in manifestation and healing practices. The apex of a pyramid, for instance, focuses energy, intensifying its effects.

Grounding and Stability

Shapes like cubes and flat stones provide grounding and stability, helping to anchor energy and promote balance. These shapes connect us to the Earth, fostering a sense of security and solidity.

The Impact of Gemstone Cutting and Faceting on Energy - Cut and Faceting

Faceted Stones

Cutting gemstones into multiple facets enhances their brilliance and reflectivity, amplifying their energy and making them more effective in energy work. Each facet acts as a tiny mirror, reflecting light and energy, creating a dazzling interplay that magnifies the stone's inherent properties.

Raw vs. Polished Stones

- **Raw Stones:** These retain their natural energy and are often used for grounding and protection. Their unrefined state connects strongly to the Earth, providing a robust and grounding energy.

- **Polished Stones:** These are more refined and can be used for gentle, consistent energy work. The smooth surfaces allow for easier handling and integration into daily practices, enhancing their aesthetic appeal and energy flow.

Differences Between Raw and Polished Stones

Raw Stones

Uncut and unpolished, raw stones retain their natural form and energy. They are often used for grounding and protection, as they maintain a direct connection to the Earth's primal energy.

- **Uses:** Grounding, protection, deep energy work

- **Properties:** Robust, natural, unrefined energy

Polished Stones

Smoothed and shaped to enhance their appearance and energy, polished stones are used for meditation, energy healing, and as decorative pieces. Their refined surfaces allow for a gentle, consistent energy flow.

- **Uses:** Meditation, energy healing, decoration
- **Properties:** Refined, consistent, gentle energy

Sacred Geometry and Its Relation to Gemstone Shapes

Definition and Significance

Sacred geometry refers to the patterns and shapes considered fundamental to the creation and structure of the universe. These shapes carry specific vibrational frequencies and spiritual significance, influencing how energy flows and manifests.

- **Common Geometric Shapes:** Flower of Life, Metatron's Cube, Platonic Solids
- **Significance:** These shapes are believed to represent the underlying patterns of reality, carrying potent spiritual energies.

Examples of Gemstones Cut According to Sacred Geometric Principles

Merkaba

A star tetrahedron shape representing the union of body, mind, and spirit. Gemstones cut into Merkaba shapes are used for deep meditation and spiritual growth, connecting the physical and spiritual realms.

- **Uses:** Deep meditation, spiritual growth, holistic integration
- **Properties:** Union, transcendence, balance

Dodecahedron

A twelve-faced shape associated with the element of ether and higher consciousness. Dodecahedron-shaped stones are used to connect with higher realms and enhance spiritual awareness.

- **Uses:** Higher consciousness, spiritual connection, enlightenment
- **Properties:** Ether, unity, spiritual elevation

Tetrahedron

A four-faced shape representing the element of fire and dynamic energy. Tetrahedron-shaped gemstones are used to stimulate action and transformation, harnessing the power of fire for dynamic change.

- **Uses:** Action, transformation, energetic activation

- **Properties:** Fire, dynamism, transformation

Practical Applications - Choosing the Right Shape for Specific Energy Work

Healing

Use pointed or wand-shaped stones to direct healing energy to specific areas of the body. Their focused energy can target specific issues, promoting rapid and effective healing.

- **Recommended Shapes:** Points, wands

- **Uses:** Direct energy healing, targeted treatments

Meditation

Use spheres or polished stones for a calming and balanced energy flow during meditation. Their even energy distribution helps to create a serene and harmonious environment.

- **Recommended Shapes:** Spheres, polished stones

- **Uses:** Meditation, energy balance, tranquillity

Manifestation

Use pyramid-shaped stones to amplify and focus intentions for manifesting goals and desires. The shape's energy converges at the apex, intensifying the power of your intentions.

- **Recommended Shapes:** Pyramids

- **Uses:** Intention setting, manifestation, energy focus

Protection

Use raw or cluster stones to create a protective energy field around your space. Their natural energy can cleanse and shield your environment from negative influences.

- **Recommended Shapes:** Raw stones, clusters

- **Uses:** Protection, energy cleansing, environmental shielding

Integrating Shaped Gemstones into Everyday Life

Home Decor

Placing gemstone clusters or spheres in living spaces enhances the energy of the environment, promoting harmony and balance. They can act as focal points of energy, infusing your home with their unique vibrations.

- **Applications:** Living rooms, entryways, meditation spaces

- **Recommended Shapes:** Clusters, spheres

Personal Use

Carrying tumbled stones or small polished stones in pockets or wearing gemstone jewellery maintains balanced energy throughout the day. These portable stones offer continuous energetic support.

- **Applications:** Personal talismans, everyday carry, jewellery

- **Recommended Shapes:** Tumbled stones, polished stones

Workspace

Using pointed or pyramid-shaped stones on your desk enhances focus and productivity. Their energy can help clear mental blocks and boost concentration.

- **Applications:** Desks, study areas, workspaces

- **Recommended Shapes:** Points, pyramids

Chemical Composition of Gemstones

Silicates

Silicates are the most abundant group of minerals on Earth, encompassing a variety of gemstones such as quartz, amethyst, and citrine. They are composed primarily of silicon and oxygen, forming a tetrahedral structure that contributes to their high vibration and clarity.

- **Examples:** Quartz, Amethyst, Citrine

- **Composition:** Silicon and oxygen

Carbonates

Gemstones like calcite and malachite belong to the carbonate group. These stones are composed of carbon and oxygen, often forming in sedimentary environments. They are known for their grounding and stabilising properties.

- **Examples:** Calcite, Malachite

- **Composition:** Carbon and oxygen

Oxides

This group includes gemstones such as ruby, sapphire, and hematite. These stones are composed of oxygen and one or more metallic elements, offering strength and protective energies.

- **Examples:** Ruby, Sapphire, Hematite

- **Composition:** Oxygen and metallic elements

Phosphates

Gemstones like turquoise fall into the phosphate category. These are composed of phosphate groups combined with various metals, known for their healing and nurturing properties.

- **Examples:** Turquoise, Apatite

- **Composition:** Phosphate groups and metals

Halides

Gemstones like fluorite are classified as halides. They consist of halogen elements combined with metallic elements and are often used for purification and clearing negative energy.

- **Examples:** Fluorite, Halite

- **Composition:** Halogen elements and metals

How Different Elements Influence Gemstone Properties

Colour

The presence of certain elements can impart vibrant colours to gemstones. For example, chromium gives rubies their deep red colour, while copper imparts a blue-green hue to turquoise. These elements not only define the gemstone's appearance but also enhance its energetic properties.

Hardness

Certain elements influence the hardness of a gemstone. Diamonds, composed entirely of carbon, are the hardest known natural material due to their strong covalent bonds, symbolising resilience and clarity.

Reactivity

Elements within gemstones can affect their reactivity to chemicals or environmental conditions. For instance, halides like fluorite can be sensitive to acids, which must be considered when using these stones in energy work.

Mineral Families and Their Energies - Overview of Major Mineral Families

Silicates

Known for their high vibration and clarity, silicates include gemstones like quartz, amethyst, and tourmaline. They promote spiritual growth and energy amplification, making them ideal for meditation and energy healing.

Carbonates

Associated with grounding and stability, carbonates include gemstones like calcite and malachite. These stones enhance resilience and emotional balance, providing a solid foundation for personal growth.

Oxides

Linked to strength and protection, oxides include gemstones like hematite and ruby. These stones are effective for shielding against negative influences and enhancing physical endurance.

Phosphates

Known for their healing and nurturing properties, phosphates include gemstones like turquoise and apatite. These stones support emotional healing and personal growth, fostering a sense of well-being.

Halides

Often used for purification and clearing negative energy, halides include gemstones like fluorite and halite. These stones promote mental clarity and detoxification, making them excellent for cleansing spaces and individuals.

Energetic Properties Associated with Each Mineral Family

Silicates

Promote clarity, spiritual growth, and energy amplification. These stones are useful in meditation and energy healing, helping to elevate consciousness and enhance psychic abilities.

Carbonates

Provide grounding, stability, and emotional balance. Ideal for anchoring energy and enhancing resilience, these stones help to maintain equilibrium in stressful situations.

Oxides

Offer protection, strength, and vitality. Effective for shielding against negative influences, these stones enhance physical endurance and fortitude.

Phosphates

Support healing, nurturing, and emotional well-being. Beneficial for emotional healing and personal growth, these stones foster a nurturing environment.

Halides

Aid in purification, detoxification, and clearing negative energy. Excellent for cleansing spaces and promoting mental clarity, these stones help to remove energetic blockages.

The Role of Trace Elements in Modifying Gemstone Energy

Chromium

Adds a vibrant green colour to emeralds and red to rubies, enhancing their energetic properties related to the heart and passion. Chromium-infused stones are often associated with love and vitality.

Iron

Influences the colour and energy of stones like amethyst and sapphire, adding strength and protective qualities. Iron-rich stones are known for their grounding and stabilising effects.

Copper

Provides a blue-green colour to turquoise and malachite, associated with healing and communication. Copper-containing stones are believed to enhance the flow of energy and promote emotional balance.

Inclusions and Their Impact on a Gemstone's Energetic Properties

Types of Inclusions

Common inclusions include gas bubbles, liquid-filled cavities, and mineral crystals. These inclusions can significantly affect a gemstone's appearance and energy, adding unique characteristics to each stone.

Energetic Influence

Inclusions can enhance or modify a gemstone's energy. For example, rutile inclusions in quartz (rutilated quartz) are believed to amplify the stone's energy and aid in spiritual communication. Inclusions often add depth and complexity to a stone's energetic profile.

How Gemstones Relate to the Classical Elements (Earth, Air, Fire, Water, Ether)

Earth

Stones like hematite, garnet, and jasper are grounding and stabilising, connecting to the Earth element. These stones provide a solid foundation and promote physical well-being.

Air

Stones like fluorite, amethyst, and labradorite promote clarity, communication, and intellectual growth, connecting to the Air element. These stones enhance mental clarity and facilitate spiritual insight.

Fire

Stones like ruby, carnelian, and citrine enhance energy, passion, and creativity, connecting to the Fire element. These stones stimulate motivation and inspire dynamic change.

Water

Stones like aquamarine, moonstone, and turquoise promote emotional healing, intuition, and fluidity, connecting to the Water element. These stones support emotional balance and enhance intuitive abilities.

Ether

Stones like selenite, clear quartz, and moldavite support spiritual growth, higher consciousness, and connection to the divine, connecting to the Ether element. These stones facilitate spiritual enlightenment and cosmic awareness.

Using Elemental Correspondences in Energy Work and Healing

Balancing Energies

Selecting gemstones based on their elemental correspondences helps balance personal energies. For example, using Earth stones to ground excess Air energy can stabilise and harmonise one's energy field.

Enhancing Rituals

Incorporating elemental gemstones into rituals and ceremonies enhances their effectiveness and aligns with natural forces. Using Fire stones during manifestation rituals can amplify intentions and bring about dynamic change.

The Influence of a Gemstone's Geological Formation on Its Energy

Volcanic Activity

Gemstones formed through volcanic activity, such as diamonds and peridot, often carry intense, transformative energies. These stones are associated with powerful change and resilience.

Metamorphic Processes

Stones like garnet and emerald, formed through metamorphic processes, embody resilience and strength, reflecting the intense conditions of their creation. These stones promote personal growth and transformation.

Sedimentary Processes

Gemstones like opal and malachite, formed in sedimentary environments, often promote gentleness, healing, and growth, reflecting their gradual formation process. These stones support emotional healing and nurturing.

Hydrothermal Processes

Stones like amethyst and topaz, formed from hydrothermal fluids, are associated with clarity, purification, and spiritual insight. These stones facilitate mental clarity and spiritual awareness.

Examples of Gemstones Formed Under Different Geological Conditions and Their Unique Properties

Diamonds

Formed under extreme pressure and heat in the Earth's mantle, diamonds symbolise strength, clarity, and resilience. Their formation process imbues them with unparalleled durability and brilliance.

Emeralds

Formed through metamorphic processes, emeralds represent growth, healing, and compassion. These stones are known for their deep green colour and soothing energy.

Opals

Formed from sedimentary processes, opals are known for their emotional healing properties and ability to bring joy and creativity. Their unique play of colour reflects the diverse energies they hold.

Amethyst

Formed from hydrothermal processes, amethyst is associated with spiritual growth, clarity, and protection. These stones are highly regarded for their calming and meditative properties.

By understanding the composition and elemental influences of gemstones, we can better appreciate their unique properties and harness their energies for physical, emotional, and spiritual healing. Each gemstone, shaped by geological forces and infused with elemental energies, offers a powerful tool for enhancing well-being and personal growth.

CHAPTER FOUR

Chakras and Gemstones

Chakras are energy centres within the human body that regulate physical, emotional, and spiritual health. The word "chakra" comes from the ancient Sanskrit language, meaning "wheel" or "disk," a reflection of their spinning, vortex-like nature that moves energy throughout the body.

Origin

The concept of chakras originates from ancient Indian traditions, particularly detailed in the sacred texts of Hinduism and Buddhism. These energy centres have been integral to practices such as yoga, Ayurveda, and meditation for thousands of years, providing a map for spiritual development and holistic healing.

The Seven Major Chakras - Detailed Description of Each Major Chakra

Root Chakra (Muladhara)

- **Location:** Base of the spine.

- **Colour:** Red.

- **Qualities:** Grounding, survival, stability, security.

- **Gemstones:** Red Jasper, Hematite, Smoky Quartz.

- **Description:** The Root Chakra is the foundation of our energy system, connecting us to the Earth and grounding us in physical reality. It governs our basic survival instincts, physical vitality, and sense of security. A balanced Root Chakra provides stability and a sense of safety.

Sacral Chakra (Svadhisthana)

- **Location:** Below the navel.

- **Colour:** Orange.

- **Qualities:** Creativity, sexuality, pleasure, emotional balance.

- **Gemstones:** Carnelian, Orange Calcite, Moonstone.

- **Description:** The Sacral Chakra is the centre of creativity and emotional expression. It influences our capacity for pleasure, passion, and sensuality. A balanced Sacral Chakra fosters healthy relationships, creative expression, and emotional equilibrium.

Solar Plexus Chakra (Manipura)

- **Location:** Upper abdomen.

- **Colour:** Yellow.

- **Qualities:** Personal power, confidence, intellect, digestion.

- **Gemstones:** Citrine, Yellow Jasper, Tiger's Eye.

- **Description:** The Solar Plexus Chakra is the seat of personal power and self-confidence. It governs our willpower, self-esteem, and intellectual abilities. A balanced Solar Plexus Chakra empowers us to make confident decisions and take control of our lives.

Heart Chakra (Anahata)

- **Location:** Center of the chest.

- **Colour:** Green (and sometimes Pink).

- **Qualities:** Love, compassion, emotional balance, relationships.

- **Gemstones:** Rose Quartz, Green Aventurine, Jade.

- **Description:** The Heart Chakra is the bridge between the lower and upper chakras, symbolising the integration of earthly and spiritual matters. It governs love, compassion, and emotional well-being. A balanced Heart Chakra allows us to give and receive love freely and maintain harmonious relationships.

Throat Chakra (Vishuddha)

- **Location:** Throat.

- **Colour:** Blue.

- **Qualities:** Communication, self-expression, truth.

- **Gemstones:** Blue Lace Agate, Aquamarine, Lapis Lazuli.

- **Description:** The Throat Chakra is the centre of communication and self-expression. It enables us to speak our truth and articulate our thoughts clearly. A balanced Throat Chakra fosters honest communication and creative expression.

Third Eye Chakra (Ajna)

- **Location:** Between the eyebrows.

- **Colour:** Indigo.

- **Qualities:** Intuition, insight, spiritual awareness.

- **Gemstones:** Amethyst, Sodalite, Labradorite.

- **Description:** The Third Eye Chakra is the gateway to inner vision and higher consciousness. It governs intuition, insight, and spiritual awareness. A balanced Third Eye Chakra enhances psychic abilities and deepens our understanding of the spiritual realms.

Crown Chakra (Sahasrara)

- **Location:** Top of the head.

- **Colour:** Violet or White.

- **Qualities:** Spirituality, enlightenment, connection to the divine.

- **Gemstones:** Clear Quartz, Amethyst, Selenite.

- **Description:** The Crown Chakra is the centre of spirituality and enlightenment. It connects us to the divine and universal consciousness. A balanced Crown Chakra opens us to higher states of awareness and spiritual transcendence.

Minor Chakras and Energy Centres - Overview of Lesser-Known Chakras and Secondary Energy Centers

Earth Star Chakra

- **Location:** Below the feet.

- **Associated with:** Deep grounding and connection to the Earth's core.

- **Significance:** Anchors one's energy to the Earth, providing stability and grounding.

Higher Heart Chakra (Thymic Chakra)

- **Location:** Between the Heart and Throat Chakras.

- **Associated with:** Compassion, forgiveness, higher love.

- **Significance:** Bridges the emotional and spiritual aspects of love, promoting empathy and universal compassion.

Soul Star Chakra

- **Location:** Above the head.

- **Associated with:** Spiritual transcendence and connection to higher realms.

- **Significance:** Facilitates spiritual ascension and connection with one's higher self and the cosmos.

Hand and Foot Chakras

- **Location:** Palms and soles.

- **Associated with:** Energy flow and healing abilities.

- **Significance:** Enable energy transfer and reception, important for healers and those who work with energy.

Their Roles and Significance in the Energy Body

Earth Star Chakra

Anchors one's energy deeply into the Earth, providing a foundation for spiritual and physical stability. It connects us to the Earth's nurturing energies, fostering a sense of belonging and security.

Higher Heart Chakra

Acts as a bridge between the physical and spiritual dimensions of love. It enhances our capacity for compassion and forgiveness, helping to heal emotional wounds and promote universal love.

Soul Star Chakra

Acts as a gateway to higher consciousness, facilitating spiritual growth and connection to the divine. It helps us access higher wisdom and align with our true purpose.

Hand and Foot Chakras

Play a crucial role in the circulation of energy throughout the body. They are essential for healing practices, allowing energy to flow in and out, enhancing our ability to give and receive healing.

Chakra System in Different Traditions

Hindu Tradition

The primary source of the chakra system, detailing seven main chakras along the spine. Each chakra is associated with specific deities, elements, and mantras. The Hindu tradition provides a comprehensive framework for understanding the chakras' roles in physical, emotional, and spiritual health.

Buddhist Tradition

Focuses on energy centres called "chakras" or "wheels" of energy, integrated into practices like Tibetan Buddhism and Tantric rituals. Buddhist teachings emphasise the chakras' role in achieving spiritual enlightenment and balance.

New Age Tradition

Incorporates traditional chakra concepts with additional chakras and energy centres. Emphasises personal development and holistic health, blending ancient wisdom with modern practices. The New Age tradition often expands the chakra system to include additional energy centres like the Earth Star and Soul Star chakras.

Similarities and Differences Across Cultures

Similarities

- **Energy Centers:** Common themes of energy centres that influence physical, emotional, and spiritual health.

- **Alignment:** Major chakras are typically aligned along the spine, from the base to the crown.

- **Attributes:** Association of colours, elements, and specific qualities with each chakra.

Differences

- **Number and Location:** Variations in the number and precise location of chakras.

- **Qualities and Functions:** Different qualities and functions attributed to each chakra across traditions.

- **Integration:** Integration of chakras into spiritual practices and healing modalities varies, reflecting cultural and doctrinal differences.

By exploring the rich tapestry of chakra systems and their associated gemstones, we gain a deeper understanding of how these energy centres influence our overall well-being. Each chakra, with its unique attributes and associated gemstones, offers a pathway to balance and harmony, guiding us on our journey toward spiritual enlightenment and holistic health.

Matching Gemstones to Chakras

Root Chakra (Muladhara)

Gemstones Associated

- **Red Jasper:** Known for its grounding properties, Red Jasper provides stability and balance, enhancing endurance and strength. It is a stone of empowerment, bringing courage and insight into difficult situations.

- **Hematite:** This stone is effective in grounding and protecting. It harmonises mind, body, and spirit, dissolves negativity, and prevents the absorption of negative energies. Hematite boosts self-esteem and survivability.

- **Smoky Quartz:** Helps to ground and neutralise negative vibrations, enhancing survival instincts and bringing emotional calmness. It is a powerful detoxifier and protector.

Energetic Properties and Healing Benefits

- **Grounding and Stability:** These stones help connect the wearer to the Earth, promoting feelings of safety and security.

- **Physical Health:** They support physical health by enhancing vitality and strengthening the immune system.

- **Emotional Balance:** These stones help release fear, anxiety, and feelings of ungroundedness.

Sacral Chakra (Svadhisthana)

Gemstones Associated

- **Carnelian:** Enhances creativity, courage, and motivation. It is a stone of action, helping to overcome procrastination and instilling a love of life.

- **Orange Calcite:** Known for its ability to cleanse and energise the sacral chakra, boosting creativity and healing emotional issues. It dispels fear and balances emotions.

- **Moonstone:** Associated with feminine energy and intuition, Moonstone helps balance emotions and enhances emotional intelligence. It promotes inner growth and strength.

Energetic Properties and Healing Benefits

- **Creativity and Passion:** These stones stimulate creativity and passion, aiding in artistic expression and sexual health.

- **Emotional Healing:** They help to release emotional blockages and trauma, promoting a healthy emotional balance.

- **Enhancing Joy and Pleasure:** These gemstones bring joy, pleasure, and a sense of well-being.

Solar Plexus Chakra (Manipura)

Gemstones Associated

- **Citrine:** Known as the "merchant's stone," Citrine attracts wealth, success, and prosperity. It enhances self-confidence and personal power.

- **Yellow Jasper:** Provides protection and absorbs negative energy. It stimulates the solar plexus chakra, promoting vitality and self-confidence.

- **Tiger's Eye:** Combines the grounding properties of the earth with the uplifting energies of the sun, enhancing personal power, courage, and integrity.

Energetic Properties and Healing Benefits

- **Personal Power and Confidence:** These stones boost self-esteem, confidence, and personal power, helping to overcome fear and self-doubt.

- **Mental Clarity and Focus:** They enhance mental clarity and focus, aiding in decision-making and problem-solving.

- **Abundance and Prosperity:** These gemstones attract abundance and success, promoting a positive attitude towards wealth and prosperity.

Heart Chakra (Anahata)

Gemstones Associated

- **Rose Quartz:** Known as the stone of unconditional love, Rose Quartz promotes love, compassion, and emotional healing. It opens the heart to all types of love.

- **Green Aventurine:** Brings luck, abundance, and success. It comforts, harmonises, and protects the heart.

- **Jade:** Symbolises purity and serenity. It increases love and nurturing, protecting the wearer from harm and bringing harmony.

Energetic Properties and Healing Benefits

- **Love and Compassion:** These stones open the heart to love, fostering compassion and kindness towards oneself and others.

- **Emotional Healing:** They help heal emotional wounds and traumas, promoting forgiveness and emotional balance.

- **Harmony and Peace:** These gemstones bring a sense of inner peace and harmony, reducing stress and anxiety.

Throat Chakra (Vishuddha)

Gemstones Associated

- **Blue Lace Agate:** Known for its calming and soothing properties, Blue Lace Agate aids in communication and self-expression.

- **Aquamarine:** Enhances clarity of thought, courage, and self-expression. It is associated with the calming and cleansing properties of the sea.

- **Lapis Lazuli:** Promotes truth, wisdom, and communication. It enhances intellectual ability and stimulates the desire for knowledge.

Energetic Properties and Healing Benefits

- **Communication and Self-Expression:** These stones enhance the ability to communicate clearly and effectively, promoting honesty and truthfulness.

- **Calming and Soothing:** They have calming properties that help reduce stress and anxiety, promoting a sense of peace and tranquillity.

- **Intellectual Clarity:** These gemstones enhance intellectual abilities and stimulate a desire for knowledge and understanding.

Third Eye Chakra (Ajna)

Gemstones Associated

- **Amethyst:** Known for its spiritual properties, Amethyst enhances intuition, meditation, and spiritual growth.

- **Sodalite:** Promotes rational thought, objectivity, and truth. It enhances self-esteem, self-acceptance, and self-trust.

- **Labradorite:** Enhances intuition, psychic abilities, and spiritual awareness. It is known as the stone of transformation.

Energetic Properties and Healing Benefits

- **Intuition and Insight:** These stones enhance intuition, psychic abilities, and spiritual insight, promoting a deeper understanding of oneself and the universe.

- **Mental Clarity:** They help clear the mind of clutter and confusion, enhancing mental clarity and focus.

- **Spiritual Growth:** These gemstones support spiritual growth and transformation, aiding in meditation and connecting with higher realms.

Crown Chakra (Sahasrara)

Gemstones Associated

- **Clear Quartz:** Known as the "master healer," Clear Quartz amplifies energy and thought, enhancing spiritual growth and connection.

- **Amethyst:** Promotes spiritual awareness, intuition, and psychic abilities. It enhances meditation and spiritual growth.

- **Selenite:** Promotes purity, honesty, and spiritual connection. It clears negative energy and enhances mental clarity.

Energetic Properties and Healing Benefits

- **Spiritual Connection:** These stones enhance spiritual connection, promoting enlightenment and higher consciousness.

- **Mental Clarity and Focus:** They help clear the mind of negative thoughts and distractions, enhancing mental clarity and focus.

- **Purification and Protection:** These gemstones purify and protect the energy field, promoting a sense of peace and tranquillity.

Choosing the Right Gemstone

How to Intuitively Select Gemstones for Chakra Work

- **Personal Resonance:** Choose stones that you feel naturally drawn to. Trust your intuition and the energy you feel from the stone.

- **Current Energetic State:** Consider your current emotional and physical state and select stones that address your specific needs and imbalances.

Factors to Consider

- **Colour Correspondence:** Select stones that match the colour of the chakra you want to work on.

- **Energetic Properties:** Consider the specific properties and benefits of the stone and how they align with your intentions.

- **Personal Preference:** Choose stones that you find aesthetically pleasing and that you feel comfortable using.

By matching gemstones to the appropriate chakras, we can harness their specific energies to balance and enhance our physical, emotional, and spiritual well-being. Each gemstone, with its unique properties and vibrational frequencies, serves as a powerful tool for healing and transformation, guiding us toward a more harmonious and enlightened existence.

Balancing Chakras with Gemstones

Identifying Chakra Imbalances - Common Signs and Symptoms of Imbalanced Chakras

Root Chakra

- **Signs:** Feelings of insecurity, financial instability, physical ailments in the lower body, anxiety, and fear.

- **Symptoms:** Fatigue, lower back pain, leg and feet issues, frequent colds or illnesses.

Sacral Chakra

- **Signs:** Creative blocks, sexual dysfunction, emotional instability, addiction issues, and lack of passion.

- **Symptoms:** Lower abdominal pain, urinary problems, reproductive issues, emotional swings.

Solar Plexus Chakra

- **Signs:** Low self-esteem, lack of confidence, digestive issues, and difficulty making decisions.

- **Symptoms:** Stomach ulcers, indigestion, liver problems, chronic fatigue.

Heart Chakra

- **Signs:** Emotional distress, difficulty in relationships, feelings of loneliness, and physical heart problems.

- **Symptoms:** Heart palpitations, high blood pressure, asthma, and immune system disorders.

Throat Chakra

- **Signs:** Difficulty expressing oneself, sore throat, thyroid issues, and fear of public speaking.

- **Symptoms:** Throat infections, hoarseness, neck and shoulder pain, hormonal imbalances.

Third Eye Chakra

- **Signs:** Lack of intuition, difficulty concentrating, headaches, and feeling disconnected from inner wisdom.

- **Symptoms:** Vision problems, sinus issues, insomnia, and headaches.

Crown Chakra

- **Signs:** Feeling disconnected from spirituality, lack of purpose, depression, and confusion.

- **Symptoms:** Migraines, neurological disorders, depression, and chronic fatigue.

Self-Assessment Techniques and Tools

Meditation and Introspection

- **Method:** Spend quiet time in meditation to reflect on any areas of life where you feel imbalances.
- **Practice:** Focus on each chakra, noticing any physical sensations or emotional responses that arise.

Physical Symptoms

- **Method:** Note any recurring physical symptoms that may be linked to specific chakras.
- **Practice:** Keep a health journal to track patterns and identify potential chakra imbalances.

Emotional Patterns

- **Method:** Identify emotional patterns and triggers that could indicate chakra imbalances.
- **Practice:** Reflect on your emotional reactions to situations and consider which chakra might be involved.

Chakra Assessment Tools

- **Method:** Use tools like pendulums, muscle testing, or professional chakra assessment questionnaires to identify imbalances.
- **Practice:** Consult with a healer or use self-assessment techniques to gain insights into your chakra health.

Methods for Balancing Chakras - Placing Gemstones on Chakras During Meditation

Preparation

- **Steps:** Find a quiet, comfortable space and gather the gemstones you need. Cleanse and charge the stones before use.
- **Tools:** Use sage, incense, or saltwater to cleanse the stones; sunlight or moonlight to charge them.

Placement

- **Steps:** Lie down and place the corresponding gemstones on each chakra. Focus on your breath and visualise the energy of the stones balancing the chakras.

- **Techniques:** Use visualisation or guided imagery to enhance the experience.

Visualisation

- **Steps:** Visualise each chakra as a spinning wheel of light. See the gemstone's energy merging with the chakra, clearing any blockages and restoring balance.

- **Techniques:** Imagine the colour of each chakra growing brighter and more vibrant.

Wearing Gemstone Jewelry for Continuous Support

Necklaces and Pendants

- **Purpose:** Wear gemstones close to the corresponding chakras for continuous energy support.

- **Examples:** Wear a Rose Quartz pendant for heart chakra support or a Lapis Lazuli necklace for throat chakra enhancement.

Bracelets and Anklets

- **Purpose:** Wear gemstone bracelets or anklets to support specific chakras and maintain a balanced energy flow throughout the day.

- **Examples:** Tiger's Eye bracelet for solar plexus chakra strength or Carnelian anklet for sacral chakra vitality.

Rings and Earrings

- **Purpose:** Use rings and earrings to focus on specific chakras like the Throat, Third Eye, and Crown Chakras.

- **Examples:** Amethyst ring for third eye clarity or Clear Quartz earrings for crown chakra enlightenment.

Creating Chakra Crystal Grids

Designing the Grid

- **Steps:** Choose gemstones for each chakra and arrange them in a geometric pattern. Use a central stone to anchor the grid and enhance its power.

- **Tools:** Use a grid template or create a unique design.

Activation

- **Steps:** Set your intention for the grid and use a crystal wand or your hands to activate it. Visualise the energy of the stones harmonising and balancing the chakras.

- **Techniques:** Perform a brief meditation or use affirmations to energise the grid.

Maintenance

- **Steps:** Regularly cleanse and recharge the stones and revisit the grid to reinforce your intentions.

- **Tools:** Use moonlight or sunlight for recharging and sage or sound for cleansing.

Chakra Healing Practices

Guided Meditations with Gemstones for Each Chakra

- **Root Chakra Meditation:** Visualise red energy flowing from the Earth into the Root Chakra, grounding and stabilising your energy. Use Red Jasper.

- **Sacral Chakra Meditation:** Imagine a warm, orange light flowing into the Sacral Chakra, igniting creativity and passion. Use Carnelian.

- **Solar Plexus Chakra Meditation:** Visualise a bright, yellow sun radiating from the Solar Plexus Chakra, filling you with confidence and personal power. Use Citrine.

- **Heart Chakra Meditation:** Picture a green or pink light expanding from the Heart Chakra, filling you with love and compassion. Use Rose Quartz.

- **Throat Chakra Meditation:** Visualise a blue light radiating from the Throat Chakra, clearing communication pathways and promoting self-expression. Use Aquamarine.

- **Third Eye Chakra Meditation:** Imagine an indigo light shining from the Third Eye Chakra, enhancing intuition and spiritual insight. Use Amethyst.

- **Crown Chakra Meditation:** Picture a violet or white light flowing from the Crown Chakra, connecting you to higher consciousness and spiritual enlightenment. Use Clear Quartz.

Using Gemstone Elixirs for Chakra Alignment

Preparation

- **Steps:** Create gemstone elixirs by placing cleansed gemstones in water to absorb their energy. Use indirect methods for stones that are not water-safe.

- **Tools:** Use glass containers and ensure stones are cleansed.

Consumption

- **Steps:** Drink the elixir or use it topically to balance specific chakras. Set an intention for the elixir to enhance its effectiveness.

- **Techniques:** Use affirmations or meditative focus while consuming the elixir.

Chakra Sprays

- **Steps:** Create chakra sprays by adding gemstone elixirs to a spray bottle with essential oils. Spray the elixir around your energy field to balance and align chakras.

- **Tools:** Use high-quality essential oils and distilled water.

Combining Gemstones with Other Healing Modalities:

Reiki

- **Method:** Use gemstones in conjunction with Reiki sessions to enhance the flow of healing energy. Place stones on the chakras during treatments.

- **Techniques:** Allow the Reiki practitioner to guide the placement and energy flow.

Sound Therapy

- **Method:** Incorporate gemstones with sound healing tools like singing bowls, tuning forks, or chimes. The combination of sound vibrations and gemstone energy can deepen the healing experience.

- **Techniques:** Place stones around the body or hold them while using sound tools.

Yoga and Movement

- **Method:** Use gemstones during yoga practice to enhance the connection between the physical body and the chakras. Place stones on the mat or wear gemstone jewellery while practising.

- **Techniques:** Focus on chakra-aligned poses and breathwork.

Maintaining Chakra Health - Daily Practices for Chakra Maintenance

Meditation

- **Practice:** Regularly meditate with gemstones to keep chakras balanced and aligned.

- **Techniques:** Use guided meditations or silent contemplation with your chosen stones.

Affirmations

- **Practice:** Use positive affirmations associated with each chakra to reinforce balance and health.

- **Examples:** "I am grounded and safe" for the Root Chakra or "I express my truth clearly" for the Throat Chakra.

Breathwork

- **Practice:** Practise deep breathing exercises to enhance energy flow and maintain chakra health.

- **Techniques:** Focus on deep, rhythmic breathing to clear and balance each chakra.

Regular Cleansing and Recharging of Gemstones

- **Steps:** Cleanse gemstones regularly using methods like smudging, running water, moonlight, or sound.

- **Tools:** Use sage, Palo Santo, or singing bowls for cleansing.

Recharging

- **Steps:** Recharge gemstones by placing them in sunlight, moonlight, or on a selenite charging plate.

- **Tools:** Utilise natural elements or selenite plates for effective recharging.

Integrating Gemstone Work into a Holistic Wellness Routine

- **Practice:** Combine gemstone work with other wellness practices like healthy eating, exercise, mindfulness, and self-care.

- **Techniques:** Create a balanced routine that incorporates physical, emotional, and spiritual practices.

Consistent Practice

- **Practice:** Make gemstone work a regular part of your daily routine to maintain overall well-being and energetic balance.

- **Techniques:** Use gemstones in morning rituals, meditation, or evening relaxation practices.

Journaling

- **Practice:** Keep a journal to track your experiences with gemstones and chakra work, noting any changes in your physical, emotional, and spiritual health.

- **Techniques:** Reflect on your progress and insights gained from your gemstone practices.

By identifying chakra imbalances and applying the appropriate methods to balance them, we can enhance our overall well-being. Each gemstone, with its unique properties, serves as a powerful ally in maintaining the harmony and health of our chakras, guiding us toward a more balanced and fulfilling life.

CHAPTER FIVE

Quartz Family: Clear Quartz, Rose Quartz, Amethyst

Clear Quartz: The Master Healer

Appearance

Clear Quartz is a transparent to translucent crystal that often exhibits a vitreous lustre, giving it a glass-like appearance. It can appear in various forms, including single terminated points, clusters, geodes, and tumbled stones. Some Clear Quartz crystals contain internal fractures or inclusions, which can create beautiful rainbows within the stone.

Varieties

There are several notable varieties of Clear Quartz, each with unique features:

- **Milky Quartz**: Opaque and white, caused by tiny inclusions of gas or liquid.

- **Rutilated Quartz**: Contains needle-like inclusions of rutile, which can be gold, silver, or red.

- **Phantom Quartz**: Displays ghost-like inclusions within the crystal, representing its growth stages.

- **Smoky Quartz**: A grey, brown, or black variety of quartz that gets its colour from natural irradiation.

Arcane Energetic Properties Amplification: Clear Quartz is renowned for its ability to amplify energy and thought. It can enhance the effect of other crystals, making it a powerful stone for healing and spiritual work.

Clarity and Focus: This crystal is excellent for enhancing mental clarity, focus, and concentration. It can help clear the mind of distractions and aid in decision-making.

Energy Balancing: Clear Quartz is versatile and can balance and align all the chakras, promoting overall energy harmony and healing on all levels—physical, emotional, and spiritual.

Uses and Applications Meditation: Clear Quartz is commonly used in meditation practices. Meditators hold the crystal or place it nearby to enhance spiritual connection, clarity, and insight.

Energy Grids: It is often used in crystal grids to amplify the energy of the entire arrangement and to strengthen the intention of the grid.

Healing: Healers use Clear Quartz to amplify the energy and effectiveness of other healing stones. It is placed on or around the body to facilitate energy flow and remove blockages.

Manifestation: Clear Quartz can be programmed with specific intentions and goals, making it a valuable tool for manifestation practices.

Chakra Alignment Crown Chakra: Clear Quartz is primarily associated with the Crown Chakra, located at the top of the head. It enhances spiritual connection, enlightenment, and the ability to receive guidance from higher realms.

Historical and Cultural Significance Ancient Cultures: Clear Quartz has been used for thousands of years by various cultures for its healing and spiritual properties. Ancient Egyptians believed it could channel energy and light, while the Greeks thought it was eternal ice sent by the gods. In many Native American traditions, Clear Quartz is considered a sacred stone with powerful spiritual significance.

Modern Mysticism: Today, Clear Quartz is widely used in contemporary healing practices, energy work, and spiritual rituals. It is valued for its versatility, powerful energy, and ability to amplify the effects of other crystals.

Scientific Properties Chemical Composition: Clear Quartz is composed of silicon dioxide (SiO_2). It is one of the most abundant minerals on Earth.

Hardness: It has a Mohs hardness rating of 7, making it a durable stone suitable for various applications.

Piezoelectricity: Clear Quartz has piezoelectric properties, meaning it can generate an electric charge in response to mechanical stress. This property is utilised in many technological applications, such as watches, microphones, and radio transmitters.

Ritual Care and Cleansing Cleansing Methods: Clear Quartz should be cleansed regularly to maintain its energetic purity. Methods include rinsing with water, smudging with sage or palo santo, placing in moonlight, or using sound vibrations.

Recharging: To recharge Clear Quartz, place it in sunlight or moonlight, or on a selenite charging plate. Some prefer to bury it in the earth overnight to restore its natural energy.

Mystical Practical Tips Daily Empowerment: Carry a small Clear Quartz crystal in your pocket or wear it as jewellery to benefit from its amplifying and balancing properties throughout the day.

Sanctified Spaces: Place Clear Quartz in your home or workspace to create a balanced and harmonious environment. It can also be placed near electronic devices to neutralise electromagnetic frequencies (EMFs).

Meditative Practices: Keep a Clear Quartz crystal in your meditation space to enhance your practice and deepen your connection to higher consciousness.

Rose Quartz: The Stone of Universal Love

Appearance

Rose Quartz is characterised by its gentle pink colour, which can range from pale to deep rose. It often appears translucent with a vitreous lustre. The colour is due to trace amounts of titanium, iron, or manganese. Rose Quartz can be found in raw chunks, tumbled stones, beads, and carved into various shapes like hearts and spheres.

Varieties

Includes star rose quartz, which displays a star-like pattern (asterism) due to microscopic inclusions of rutile needles.

Arcane Energetic Properties Love and Compassion: Known as the "Stone of Universal Love," Rose Quartz promotes unconditional love, compassion, and emotional healing. It encourages self-love, fosters harmonious relationships, and opens the heart to all forms of love.

Emotional Balance: Helps to soothe and calm emotions, fostering a sense of inner peace and tranquillity. It is particularly effective for healing emotional wounds and traumas, promoting forgiveness and acceptance.

Heart Healing: Assists in healing the heart on both a physical and emotional level. It can help alleviate heartache and grief, encouraging feelings of joy and emotional rejuvenation.

Uses and Applications Heart Chakra Healing: Place Rose Quartz on the Heart Chakra to open and balance emotional energy. It can be used in crystal healing layouts, worn as jewellery, or carried close to the heart.

Meditation: Use during meditation to cultivate self-love and compassion. Hold the stone or place it nearby to enhance the meditation experience and deepen emotional healing.

Home Decor: Place in the home to create a loving and harmonious environment. Common placements include the bedroom to enhance romantic relationships and the living room to promote family harmony.

Skin Care: Some use Rose Quartz facial rollers and gua sha tools for their purported benefits in enhancing skin health and promoting a youthful appearance.

Chakra Alignment Heart Chakra: Strongly associated with the Heart Chakra, Rose Quartz helps to open, activate, and heal this energy centre, promoting love, compassion, and emotional well-being.

Historical and Cultural Significance Ancient Cultures: Rose Quartz has been revered since ancient times. The ancient Egyptians believed it could prevent ageing, and they used it in facial masks. The Romans and Greeks used Rose Quartz as a seal to signify ownership and ensure fidelity in relationships. In Chinese culture, it was used as a token of love.

Modern Mysticism: In modern crystal healing practices, Rose Quartz is widely used to attract love, promote self-love, and enhance emotional healing. It is also a popular stone in New Age and holistic healing communities for its gentle and nurturing energy.

Scientific Properties Chemical Composition: Rose Quartz is composed of silicon dioxide (SiO_2), like all varieties of quartz. The pink colour comes from trace amounts of titanium, iron, or manganese.

Hardness: It has a Mohs hardness rating of 7, making it relatively durable for various uses.

Piezoelectricity: Like other quartz crystals, Rose Quartz exhibits piezoelectric properties, allowing it to generate an electric charge under mechanical stress.

Ritual Care and Cleansing Cleansing Methods: Rose Quartz should be cleansed regularly to maintain its energetic purity. Effective methods include rinsing with water, smudging with sage or palo santo, placing in moonlight, or using sound vibrations.

Recharging: To recharge Rose Quartz, place it in sunlight or moonlight, or on a selenite charging plate. Avoid prolonged exposure to direct sunlight to prevent colour fading.

Mystical Practical Tips Daily Empowerment: Carry a small Rose Quartz crystal in your pocket or wear it as jewellery to benefit from its loving and soothing properties throughout the day.

Sanctified Spaces: Place Rose Quartz in your home or workspace to create a loving and harmonious environment. It can be placed in areas where relationships and communication are important.

Gift Giving: Rose Quartz makes a thoughtful gift for loved ones, symbolising love, compassion, and emotional support.

Amethyst: The Stone of Spirituality

Appearance: Amethyst is a variety of quartz characterised by its stunning purple colour, which can range from light lavender to deep violet. It is often transparent to translucent with a vitreous lustre. Amethyst can be found in geodes, clusters, single points, and tumbled stones.

Varieties

Includes notable types such as:

- **Chevron Amethyst:** Features a distinctive V-shaped banding pattern with white quartz.

- **Brandberg Amethyst**: Known for its exceptional clarity and unique colour zoning.

- **Ametrine**: A naturally occurring combination of amethyst and citrine, showcasing both purple and yellow hues.

Arcane Energetic Properties Spiritual Awareness: Known as the "Stone of Spirituality," Amethyst enhances spiritual awareness and intuition. It is believed to connect the physical realm with the higher planes of existence.

Calming and Soothing: Promotes calmness and relaxation, making it an excellent stone for stress relief and meditation. It can help soothe the mind and emotions, providing a sense of tranquillity.

Protection: Offers protective qualities, shielding against negative energies, psychic attacks, and harmful environmental influences. It is often used for cleansing and purifying the aura.

Uses and Applications Meditation: Use Amethyst during meditation to enhance spiritual growth, deepen intuitive insights, and achieve a higher state of consciousness. It can be held, placed on the Third Eye Chakra, or used in a meditation space.

Sleep Aid: Place Amethyst under the pillow or on the nightstand to promote restful sleep, prevent nightmares, and enhance dream recall.

Healing: Use in healing practices to calm the mind, balance emotions, and support the immune system. It is often used in energy healing sessions to cleanse and stabilise the aura.

Jewellery: Wearing Amethyst jewellery helps maintain its calming and protective energy throughout the day, making it a popular choice for pendants, rings, and bracelets.

Chakra Alignment Third Eye Chakra: Amethyst is strongly associated with the Third Eye Chakra, located between the eyebrows. It enhances intuition, psychic abilities, and spiritual insight.

Crown Chakra: Also associated with the Crown Chakra, located at the top of the head. It promotes spiritual awareness, enlightenment, and connection to the divine.

Historical and Cultural Significance Ancient Cultures: Amethyst has been revered since ancient times for its beauty and spiritual properties. The ancient Greeks and Romans believed it could prevent drunkenness and promote clarity of mind. It was often carved into drinking vessels and worn as amulets.

Medieval and Renaissance Europe: Amethyst was considered a symbol of royalty and power, often used in ecclesiastical and royal jewellery. It was believed to provide protection against evil and to bring wisdom and humility.

Modern Mysticism: In contemporary crystal healing practices, Amethyst is widely used for its calming and protective properties. It is a popular stone in New Age and holistic healing communities for enhancing spiritual growth and intuition.

Scientific Properties Chemical Composition: Amethyst is composed of silicon dioxide (SiO_2), like all varieties of quartz. Its purple colour is due to trace amounts of iron and natural irradiation.

Hardness: It has a Mohs hardness rating of 7, making it durable and suitable for various applications.

Piezoelectricity: Like other quartz crystals, Amethyst exhibits piezoelectric properties, allowing it to generate an electric charge under mechanical stress.

Ritual Care and Cleansing Cleansing Methods: Amethyst should be cleansed regularly to maintain its energetic purity. Effective methods include rinsing with water, smudging with sage or palo santo, placing in moonlight, or using sound vibrations.

Recharging: To recharge Amethyst, place it in moonlight or on a selenite charging plate. Avoid prolonged exposure to direct sunlight to prevent colour fading.

Mystical Practical Tips Daily Empowerment: Carry a small Amethyst crystal in your pocket or wear it as jewellery to benefit from its calming and protective properties throughout the day.

Sanctified Spaces: Place Amethyst in your home or workspace to create a peaceful and harmonious environment. It can be placed in areas where relaxation and focus are needed.

Meditation Space: Keep an Amethyst crystal in your meditation space to enhance your practice and deepen your spiritual connection.

CHAPTER SIX

Protective Stones: Black Tourmaline, Hematite, Obsidian

Black Tourmaline: The Guardian Stone

Appearance Black Tourmaline is characterised by its deep black colour and often striated surface. It can appear opaque with a slightly glossy to matte finish. Black Tourmaline is commonly found in rod-like or columnar crystal formations and can also be tumbled or carved into various shapes.

Varieties: While Black Tourmaline (Schörl) is the most well-known, Tourmaline comes in a variety of colours. However, this section focuses on the properties unique to Black Tourmaline.

Arcane Energetic Properties Protection: Black Tourmaline is renowned for its strong protective qualities. It is believed to create an energetic shield around the user, deflecting and absorbing negative energies, psychic attacks, and harmful electromagnetic radiation (EMF).

Grounding: This stone is excellent for grounding, helping to anchor energy to the Earth and promoting a sense of stability and security. It is particularly useful for those who feel scattered or disconnected.

Purification: Black Tourmaline is also known for its ability to purify and cleanse the energy field. It can transform dense, stagnant energies into lighter, more positive vibrations.

Uses and Applications Personal Protection: Carry Black Tourmaline in your pocket or wear it as jewellery to protect against negative influences and environmental stressors. It can also be placed in bags or vehicles for on-the-go protection.

Home and Workspace: Place Black Tourmaline in your home or workspace, particularly near electronic devices, to reduce EMF exposure and create a protective barrier. It can be placed at entry points to block negative energies from entering the space.

Meditation: Use Black Tourmaline during meditation to enhance grounding and protection. Holding the stone or placing it near the base of the spine can help anchor your energy and promote a deeper state of relaxation.

Chakra Alignment Root Chakra: Black Tourmaline is strongly associated with the Root Chakra, located at the base of the spine. It promotes grounding, security, and a sense of physical and emotional stability.

Historical and Cultural Significance Ancient Cultures: Black Tourmaline has been used for centuries by various cultures for protection and grounding. Ancient African tribes used it in healing rituals and as protective talismans.

Modern Mysticism: Today, Black Tourmaline is widely used in contemporary crystal healing practices for its protective and grounding properties. It is popular in holistic health and wellness communities as a tool for energy purification and protection against environmental stressors.

Scientific Properties Chemical Composition: Black Tourmaline is a complex borosilicate mineral with the chemical formula $NaFe_3+3Al6(BO_3)_3Si6O18(OH)_4$.

Hardness: It has a Mohs hardness rating of 7-7.5, making it a relatively hard and durable stone.

Piezoelectricity: Black Tourmaline exhibits piezoelectric properties, meaning it can generate an electric charge under mechanical stress, contributing to its protective qualities against EMFs.

Ritual Care and Cleansing Cleansing Methods: Black Tourmaline should be cleansed regularly to maintain its protective and grounding properties. Effective methods include rinsing with water, smudging with sage or palo santo, burying in the earth, or using sound vibrations.

Recharging: To recharge Black Tourmaline, place it in sunlight or moonlight, or on a selenite charging plate. Earth recharging, by burying it in the soil for a day or night, is particularly effective for grounding stones.

Mystical Practical Tips Daily Empowerment: Carry a small Black Tourmaline crystal in your pocket or wear it as jewellery to benefit from its protective and grounding properties throughout the day.

Sanctified Spaces: Place Black Tourmaline in strategic locations around your home or workspace to create a protective and grounded environment. Near electronic devices, it can help mitigate EMF exposure.

Meditation Space: Keep Black Tourmaline in your meditation space to enhance grounding and protection during your practice, helping to deepen your connection to the Earth.

Hematite: The Stone of the Mind

Appearance Hematite is a striking stone with a metallic sheen, ranging from dark grey to black. It is opaque and has a high iron content, which gives it its characteristic metallic lustre. Hematite is often found in polished form, such as tumbled stones, beads, and carved shapes like hearts and spheres.

Varieties While Hematite is primarily known for its metallic appearance, it can also appear in a reddish-brown form when oxidised. The polished variety is the most commonly used in jewellery and decorative items.

Arcane Energetic Properties Grounding: Hematite is one of the most effective grounding stones. It helps to anchor the user's energy to the Earth, promoting feelings of safety and stability.

Protection: Hematite creates a protective shield around the user, deflecting negative energies and environmental stressors. It is particularly effective for shielding against electromagnetic frequencies (EMFs).

Mental Clarity: Hematite enhances mental organisation, concentration, and focus. It helps to clear confusion and supports logical thinking and problem-solving.

Uses and Applications Personal Protection: Carry Hematite in your pocket or wear it as jewellery to benefit from its grounding and protective properties throughout the day. It is especially useful in environments with high EMF exposure, such as offices with numerous electronic devices.

Home and Workspace: Place Hematite in your home or workspace to create a grounded and protected environment. It can be particularly effective near electronic devices to mitigate EMF exposure.

Meditation: Use Hematite during meditation to enhance grounding and focus. Hold the stone or place it at the base of the spine to anchor your energy and deepen your meditation practice.

Chakra Alignment Root Chakra: Hematite is strongly associated with the Root Chakra, located at the base of the spine. It promotes grounding, stability, and a sense of security, making it an excellent stone for balancing this energy centre.

Historical and Cultural Significance Ancient Cultures: Hematite has been used for thousands of years for its grounding and protective properties. Ancient Egyptians used it as a talisman for protection and to prevent bleeding. It was also used by Native American tribes for body paint and in spiritual ceremonies.

Modern Mysticism: In contemporary crystal healing practices, Hematite is widely used for its grounding and protective qualities. It is popular in holistic health and wellness communities as a tool for enhancing mental clarity and shielding against negative influences.

Scientific Properties Chemical Composition: Hematite is an iron oxide with the chemical formula Fe_2O_3. Its high iron content gives it a metallic sheen and makes it a dense and heavy stone.

Hardness: It has a Mohs hardness rating of 5.5-6.5, making it relatively durable but susceptible to scratches.

Magnetic Properties: While Hematite itself is not strongly magnetic, synthetic Hematite (sometimes called Hematine) can exhibit magnetic properties due to the manufacturing process.

Ritual Care and Cleansing Cleansing Methods: Hematite should be cleansed regularly to maintain its energetic purity. Effective methods include rinsing with water, smudging with sage or palo santo, and using sound vibrations. Avoid using saltwater, as it can damage the stone's surface.

Recharging: To recharge Hematite, place it in sunlight or moonlight, or on a selenite charging plate. Burying it in the earth overnight can also help to restore its grounding energy.

Mystical Practical Tips Daily Empowerment: Carry a small Hematite crystal in your pocket or wear it as jewellery to benefit from its grounding and protective properties throughout the day. It is particularly useful during stressful situations or in high-energy environments.

Sanctified Spaces: Place Hematite in strategic locations around your home or workspace to create a grounded and protected environment. Near electronic devices, it can help mitigate EMF exposure and enhance focus.

Meditation Space: Keep Hematite in your meditation space to enhance grounding and focus during your practice. It can help to anchor your energy and promote a deeper state of relaxation.

Obsidian: The Mirror Stone

Appearance Obsidian is a volcanic glass, typically appearing black but can also come in other colours like brown, green, and even rainbow. It has a smooth, glassy texture and can be opaque or slightly translucent. Obsidian is often found in raw chunks, polished stones, and carved shapes such as spheres and arrowheads.

Varieties Notable types of Obsidian include:

- **Black Obsidian:** The most common variety, known for its deep black colour and mirror-like surface when polished.

- **Snowflake Obsidian:** Features white or grey inclusions resembling snowflakes, providing a unique pattern.

- **Mahogany Obsidian**: Exhibits reddish-brown and black banding, resembling mahogany wood.

- **Rainbow Obsidian**: Displays a spectrum of colours, typically seen when light reflects off its surface.

- **Gold and Silver Sheen Obsidian**: Exhibits a shimmering effect due to inclusions of tiny gas bubbles.

Arcane Energetic Properties Protection: Obsidian is renowned for its powerful protective qualities. It forms a shield against negativity, psychic attacks, and harmful environmental influences.

Grounding: This stone is excellent for grounding, helping to anchor energy to the Earth and providing stability during turbulent times.

Emotional Healing: Obsidian can bring hidden emotions and traumas to the surface, allowing for deep emotional healing. It helps to release negative patterns and encourages growth and transformation.

Clarity and Truth: Known as a "stone of truth," Obsidian helps reveal hidden truths and promotes clarity of mind. It encourages honest self-reflection and supports personal growth.

Uses and Applications Personal Protection: Carry Obsidian in your pocket or wear it as jewellery to benefit from its protective properties throughout the day. It is particularly useful in environments with high stress or negative energy.

Home and Workspace: Place Obsidian in your home or workspace to create a protective and grounded environment. It can be placed at entry points or near electronic devices to reduce EMF exposure.

Meditation: Use Obsidian during meditation to enhance grounding, protection, and emotional healing. Hold the stone or place it at the base of the spine to anchor your energy and deepen your meditation practice.

Emotional Healing: Incorporate Obsidian into emotional healing practices to release negative emotions and patterns. It can be used in crystal layouts or placed on the body during energy healing sessions.

Chakra Alignment Root Chakra: Obsidian is strongly associated with the Root Chakra, located at the base of the spine. It promotes grounding, stability, and a sense of security, making it an excellent stone for balancing this energy centre.

Historical and Cultural Significance Ancient Cultures: Obsidian has been used for thousands of years by various cultures for its protective and healing properties. Ancient Mesoamerican civilizations, such as the Aztecs and Mayans, used Obsidian for making tools, weapons, and mirrors. It was also considered a powerful stone for divination and scrying.

Modern Mysticism: In contemporary crystal healing practices, Obsidian is widely used for its protective and grounding qualities. It is popular in holistic health and wellness communities as a tool for emotional healing and personal growth.

Scientific Properties Chemical Composition: Obsidian is an igneous rock composed primarily of silica (SiO_2). It is formed from rapidly cooling lava, which prevents the formation of a crystalline structure, giving it a glassy texture.

Hardness: It has a Mohs hardness rating of 5-5.5, making it relatively brittle and prone to breaking if not handled carefully.

Fracture: Obsidian fractures conchoidally, meaning it breaks with smooth, curved surfaces. This property made it valuable for crafting sharp tools and weapons in ancient times.

Ritual Care and Cleansing Cleansing Methods: Obsidian should be cleansed regularly to maintain its protective and grounding properties. Effective methods include rinsing with water, smudging with sage or palo santo, and using sound vibrations. Avoid using saltwater, as it can damage the stone's surface.

Recharging: To recharge Obsidian, place it in sunlight or moonlight, or on a selenite charging plate. Burying it in the earth overnight can also help to restore its grounding energy.

Mystical Practical Tips Daily Empowerment: Carry a small Obsidian crystal in your pocket or wear it as jewellery to benefit from its protective and grounding properties throughout the day. It is particularly useful during stressful situations or in high-energy environments.

Sanctified Spaces: Place Obsidian in strategic locations around your home or workspace to create a grounded and protected environment. Near electronic devices, it can help mitigate EMF exposure and enhance focus.

Meditation Space: Keep Obsidian in your meditation space to enhance grounding and protection during your practice. It can help to anchor your energy and promote a deeper state of relaxation.

CHAPTER SEVEN

Healing Stones: Lapis Lazuli, Malachite, Fluorite

Lapis Lazuli: The Stone of Wisdom

Appearance Lapis Lazuli is a deep blue metamorphic rock often flecked with gold pyrite and white calcite. Its rich, royal blue colour has made it a highly sought-after gemstone for centuries. Lapis Lazuli is typically opaque and has a matte to slightly glossy finish when polished.

Varieties High-quality Lapis Lazuli has a vibrant blue colour with minimal calcite and pyrite inclusions. Lower-grade stones may have more white and less intense blue.

Arcane Energetic Properties Spiritual Insight: Known as the "Stone of Wisdom," Lapis Lazuli enhances intellectual ability and stimulates the desire for knowledge and understanding. It aids in the development of intuition and spiritual insight.

Truth and Communication: Lapis Lazuli promotes honesty, self-awareness, and the expression of one's truth. It helps in clear communication and can be particularly beneficial for writers, speakers, and those in leadership roles.

Emotional Healing: This stone has calming energy that can soothe the mind and release stress. It encourages self-awareness and self-expression, helping to confront and overcome past traumas and emotional blockages.

Uses and Applications Meditation: Use Lapis Lazuli during meditation to enhance spiritual growth and intuitive abilities. Place the stone on the Third Eye Chakra or hold it in your hand to deepen your meditative state.

Personal Empowerment: Wear Lapis Lazuli jewellery, such as pendants or rings, to boost self-confidence, self-expression, and inner power throughout the day.

Home and Workspace: Place Lapis Lazuli in your home or workspace to create an environment of wisdom and clear communication. It can be particularly effective in study areas or offices.

Healing Practices: Use Lapis Lazuli in energy healing sessions to balance the Third Eye and Throat Chakras, promoting mental clarity and emotional healing.

Chakra Alignment Third Eye Chakra: Lapis Lazuli is strongly associated with the Third Eye Chakra, located between the eyebrows. It enhances intuition, psychic abilities, and spiritual insight.

Throat Chakra: Also associated with the Throat Chakra, located at the throat, Lapis Lazuli promotes clear communication, truth, and self-expression.

Historical and Cultural Significance Ancient Cultures: Lapis Lazuli has been highly valued since ancient times. The ancient Egyptians used it in jewellery, amulets, and as a pigment for cosmetics and tomb paintings. It was also used to adorn statues of the gods and was considered a sacred stone. In ancient Mesopotamia, it was believed to contain the essence of the gods, and in mediaeval Europe, it was ground into powder to create ultramarine, a precious blue pigment used in artwork.

Modern Mysticism: Today, Lapis Lazuli is widely used in contemporary crystal healing practices for its spiritual and communicative properties. It is popular in holistic health and wellness communities for enhancing mental clarity and emotional healing.

Scientific Properties Chemical Composition: Lapis Lazuli is composed of several minerals, primarily lazurite (a sodium calcium aluminosilicate) along with calcite, pyrite, and minor amounts of other minerals.

Hardness: It has a Mohs hardness rating of 5-6, making it relatively soft and susceptible to scratches and abrasions.

Formation: Lapis Lazuli forms in metamorphic rocks, often through the contact metamorphism of limestone.

Ritual Care and Cleansing Cleansing Methods: Lapis Lazuli should be cleansed regularly to maintain its energetic purity. Effective methods include smudging with sage or palo santo, using sound vibrations, and placing in moonlight. Avoid using water or saltwater, as it can damage the stone.

Recharging: To recharge Lapis Lazuli, place it in moonlight or on a selenite charging plate. Avoid prolonged exposure to direct sunlight to prevent colour fading.

Mystical Practical Tips Daily Empowerment: Carry a small Lapis Lazuli crystal in your pocket or wear it as jewellery to benefit from its intellectual and communicative properties throughout the day. It is particularly useful during study sessions, meetings, or any situation that requires clear thinking and communication.

Sanctified Spaces: Place Lapis Lazuli in strategic locations around your home or workspace to create an environment of wisdom and clear communication. It can be placed in study areas, offices, or near communication devices.

Meditation Space: Keep Lapis Lazuli in your meditation space to enhance spiritual growth and intuitive abilities during your practice. It can help to open the Third Eye and Throat Chakras, promoting deeper meditation and clearer insight.

Malachite: The Stone of Transformation

Appearance Malachite is a striking green mineral with distinctive banding patterns in varying shades of green, ranging from dark forest green to light, almost pastel green. It often forms botryoidal, fibrous, or stalagmitic masses and is usually opaque with a silky to vitreous lustre when polished.

Varieties Malachite can occur in different forms, including fibrous aggregates, stalactitic formations, and massive chunks. High-quality malachite has vibrant colour and well-defined banding patterns.

Arcane Energetic Properties Transformation: Known as a "Stone of Transformation," Malachite assists in changing situations and providing support during times of change. It encourages risk-taking and the embracing of new opportunities.

Emotional Healing: Malachite is a powerful stone for emotional healing. It helps to release past traumas and suppressed emotions, promoting emotional balance and well-being.

Protection: This stone provides strong protective energy, particularly for travellers and those who are exposed to negative energies. It absorbs negative energies and pollutants from the environment and the body.

Uses and Applications Personal Transformation: Carry Malachite or wear it as jewellery to support personal growth and transformation. It can help to overcome fear and encourage positive changes.

Emotional Healing: Use Malachite in energy healing sessions to release emotional blockages and promote emotional balance. It can be placed on the heart or solar plexus chakras during healing sessions.

Protection: Place Malachite in your home or workspace to create a protective environment. It is particularly useful near entry points to prevent negative energies from entering.

Meditation: Use Malachite during meditation to enhance insight and understanding of personal growth and transformation. Hold the stone or place it on the heart chakra to deepen emotional healing.

Chakra Alignment Heart Chakra: Malachite is strongly associated with the Heart Chakra, promoting love, compassion, and emotional balance. It helps to heal the heart and enhance emotional well-being.

Solar Plexus Chakra: Also associated with the Solar Plexus Chakra, Malachite enhances personal power, confidence, and the ability to make positive changes.

Historical and Cultural Significance Ancient Cultures: Malachite has been used since ancient times for its protective and healing properties. The ancient Egyptians used it as a protective amulet, and it was ground into powder for use as eye makeup. The Greeks and Romans also used Malachite for jewellery and decorative purposes, believing it could protect against the evil eye.

Modern Mysticism: Today, Malachite is widely used in contemporary crystal healing practices for its transformative and protective qualities. It is popular in holistic health and wellness communities for supporting personal growth and emotional healing.

Scientific Properties Chemical Composition: Malachite is a copper carbonate hydroxide mineral with the chemical formula $Cu_2CO_3(OH)_2$. Its vibrant green colour is due to its high copper content.

Hardness: It has a Mohs hardness rating of 3.5-4, making it relatively soft and susceptible to scratches and damage if not handled carefully.

Formation: Malachite forms through the weathering and oxidation of copper ore deposits, often found in association with azurite, another copper carbonate mineral.

Ritual Care and Cleansing Cleansing Methods: Malachite should be cleansed regularly to maintain its energetic purity. Effective methods include smudging with sage or palo santo, using sound vibrations, and placing in moonlight. Avoid using water or saltwater, as it can damage the stone.

Recharging: To recharge Malachite, place it in moonlight or on a selenite charging plate. Avoid prolonged exposure to direct sunlight to prevent colour fading.

Mystical Practical Tips Daily Empowerment: Carry a small Malachite crystal in your pocket or wear it as jewellery to benefit from its transformative and protective properties throughout the day. It is particularly useful during times of change or emotional stress.

Sanctified Spaces: Place Malachite in strategic locations around your home or workspace to create a protective and supportive environment. Near entry points, it can help to prevent negative energies from entering.

Meditation Space: Keep Malachite in your meditation space to enhance personal growth and emotional healing during your practice. It can help to open the Heart and Solar Plexus Chakras, promoting deeper meditation and greater insight.

Fluorite: The Stone of Mental Clarity

Appearance Fluorite is a colourful mineral that comes in a range of colours, including purple, green, blue, yellow, and clear. It often displays a striking banded or zoned pattern and can be transparent to translucent with a vitreous lustre. Fluorite can be found in various forms, such as cubes, octahedrons, clusters, and tumbled stones.

Varieties Notable varieties of Fluorite include:

- **Rainbow Fluorite:** Exhibits multiple colours within a single stone, often displaying beautiful banding patterns.

- **Green Fluorite:** Known for its calming and healing energy.

- **Purple Fluorite**: Associated with spiritual development and protection.

- **Blue Fluorite**: Linked to clear communication and inner peace.

Arcane Energetic Properties Clarity and Focus: Fluorite is renowned for its ability to enhance mental clarity and focus. It helps to clear confusion, sharpen concentration, and promote quick thinking.

Protection: This stone offers strong protective energies, particularly on a psychic level. It shields against negative energies and can help to ward off psychic attacks.

Emotional Healing: Fluorite aids in emotional stability and balance. It helps to soothe and calm the mind, reducing stress and anxiety.

Spiritual Growth: Fluorite is a powerful stone for spiritual development. It enhances intuition, fosters spiritual insight, and promotes a deeper connection to higher consciousness.

Uses and Applications Mental Clarity: Use Fluorite in study or work environments to enhance concentration, organisation, and decision-making. It is particularly useful during exams or complex tasks.

Protection: Carry Fluorite or place it in your home or workspace to create a protective shield against negative energies and psychic attacks. It is especially effective near computers and other electronic devices to reduce electromagnetic stress.

Emotional Healing: Use Fluorite in energy healing sessions to balance emotions and promote mental clarity. Place it on the Third Eye or Heart Chakras during healing sessions.

Meditation: Use Fluorite during meditation to deepen spiritual insight and enhance intuitive abilities. Hold the stone or place it on the Third Eye Chakra to facilitate a deeper meditative state.

Chakra Alignment Third Eye Chakra: Fluorite is strongly associated with the Third Eye Chakra, enhancing intuition, psychic abilities, and mental clarity.

Heart Chakra: Green Fluorite, in particular, is associated with the Heart Chakra, promoting emotional healing and balance.

Throat Chakra: Blue Fluorite is linked to the Throat Chakra, supporting clear communication and self-expression.

Historical and Cultural Significance Ancient Cultures: Fluorite has been used since ancient times for its protective and healing properties. The ancient Romans believed it could protect against evil spirits and enhance mental clarity. It was also used in carvings, sculptures, and as a source of fluorine in metallurgy.

Modern Mysticism: Today, Fluorite is widely used in contemporary crystal healing practices for its mental clarity, protective, and spiritual qualities. It is popular in holistic health and wellness communities for supporting emotional balance and spiritual growth.

Scientific Properties Chemical Composition: Fluorite is a calcium fluoride mineral with the chemical formula CaF_2. Its vibrant colours are due to trace impurities and structural defects.

Hardness: It has a Mohs hardness rating of 4, making it relatively soft and susceptible to scratches.

Fluorescence: Fluorite is known for its fluorescent properties under ultraviolet (UV) light, often glowing a bright blue or other colours.

Ritual Care and Cleansing Cleansing Methods: Fluorite should be cleansed regularly to maintain its energetic purity. Effective methods include rinsing with water, smudging with sage or palo santo, and using sound vibrations. Avoid prolonged exposure to water, as Fluorite can be sensitive to moisture.

Recharging: To recharge Fluorite, place it in moonlight or on a selenite charging plate. Avoid prolonged exposure to direct sunlight to prevent colour fading.

Mystical Practical Tips Daily Empowerment: Carry a small Fluorite crystal in your pocket or wear it as jewellery to benefit from its mental clarity and protective properties throughout the day. It is particularly useful during study sessions, meetings, or any situation that requires clear thinking and focus.

Sanctified Spaces: Place Fluorite in strategic locations around your home or workspace to create a protective and focused environment. Near electronic devices, it can help mitigate EMF exposure and enhance concentration.

Meditation Space: Keep Fluorite in your meditation space to enhance spiritual growth and intuitive abilities during your practice. It can help to open the Third Eye, Heart, and Throat Chakras, promoting deeper meditation and clearer insight.

CHAPTER EIGHT

Calming Stones: Blue Lace Agate, Lepidolite, Angelite

Blue Lace Agate: The Stone of Calm Communication

Appearance Blue Lace Agate is a beautiful light blue variety of agate characterised by delicate, lace-like bands of white and blue. It has a soft, soothing appearance and a waxy lustre. The stone is typically translucent to opaque and can be found in various forms, such as tumbled stones, beads, and carved shapes.

Varieties While Blue Lace Agate is the most well-known form of this stone, it is part of the broader agate family, which includes many other varieties with different colours and patterns.

Arcane Energetic Properties Calming and Soothing: Blue Lace Agate is renowned for its gentle, calming energy. It helps to soothe an overactive mind, reduce stress, and promote relaxation.

Communication: This stone enhances communication, especially when expressing thoughts and emotions. It encourages truthful and clear communication, making it an excellent stone for public speakers and those who struggle with verbal expression.

Emotional Healing: Blue Lace Agate supports emotional healing by bringing a sense of peace and tranquillity. It helps to release suppressed emotions and promotes emotional balance and stability.

Uses and Applications Stress Relief: Carry Blue Lace Agate or wear it as jewellery to benefit from its calming properties throughout the day. It is particularly useful during stressful situations or when feeling overwhelmed.

Enhanced Communication: Use Blue Lace Agate in settings where clear and effective communication is needed, such as meetings, presentations, or difficult conversations. Place it near the Throat Chakra during speaking engagements.

Emotional Healing: Use Blue Lace Agate in energy healing sessions to soothe emotional distress and promote a sense of peace. Place it on the Heart or Throat Chakras during healing sessions.

Meditation: Incorporate Blue Lace Agate into meditation practices to enhance relaxation and emotional healing. Hold the stone or place it nearby to deepen your meditative state and promote inner calm.

Chakra Alignment Throat Chakra: Blue Lace Agate is strongly associated with the Throat Chakra, located at the throat. It promotes clear communication, self-expression, and emotional release.

Heart Chakra: Also associated with the Heart Chakra, Blue Lace Agate helps to soothe emotional wounds and promote inner peace and harmony.

Historical and Cultural Significance Ancient Cultures: Agate has been used for thousands of years for its protective and healing properties. The ancient Egyptians used agate for amulets and talismans, believing it could provide protection and bring good fortune. In ancient Rome, agate was used to make seals and signet rings.

Modern Mysticism: Today, Blue Lace Agate is widely used in contemporary crystal healing practices for its calming and communicative properties. It is popular in holistic health and wellness communities for promoting relaxation and emotional healing.

Scientific Properties Chemical Composition: Blue Lace Agate is a variety of chalcedony, a type of microcrystalline quartz with the chemical formula SiO_2. Its blue colour is due to the presence of trace amounts of copper and other minerals.

Hardness: It has a Mohs hardness rating of 6.5-7, making it relatively durable and suitable for various uses.

Formation: Blue Lace Agate forms in volcanic rocks and is created through the deposition of silica-rich solutions in cavities. Over time, these deposits form the characteristic banded patterns.

Ritual Care and Cleansing Cleansing Methods: Blue Lace Agate should be cleansed regularly to maintain its energetic purity. Effective methods include rinsing with water, smudging with sage or palo santo, and using sound vibrations. Avoid using saltwater, as it can damage the stone.

Recharging: To recharge Blue Lace Agate, place it in moonlight or on a selenite charging plate. Avoid prolonged exposure to direct sunlight to prevent colour fading.

Mystical Practical Tips Daily Empowerment: Carry a small Blue Lace Agate crystal in your pocket or wear it as jewellery to benefit from its calming and communicative properties throughout the day. It is particularly useful during stressful situations or when clear communication is needed.

Sanctified Spaces: Place Blue Lace Agate in strategic locations around your home or workspace to create a calming and harmonious environment. Near communication areas, it can help to enhance clarity and understanding.

Meditation Space: Keep Blue Lace Agate in your meditation space to enhance relaxation and emotional healing during your practice. It can help to open the Throat and Heart Chakras, promoting deeper meditation and clearer insight.

Lepidolite: The Stone of Peace and Transition

Appearance Lepidolite is a lilac-grey or rose-coloured member of the mica group of minerals. It often exhibits a sparkling, glittery appearance due to its high mica content. Lepidolite can be found in raw chunks, polished stones, and carved shapes such as hearts and spheres. It has a vitreous to pearly lustre.

Varieties While Lepidolite is typically lavender to pink, it can also appear in grey, white, or yellow, depending on the trace elements present.

Arcane Energetic Properties Calming and Stress Relief: Lepidolite is known for its strong calming and stress-relief properties. It helps to reduce anxiety, depression, and other stress-related disorders.

Emotional Balance: This stone supports emotional healing and balance. It helps to stabilise mood swings, promote inner peace, and relieve emotional suffering.

Spiritual Growth: Lepidolite aids in spiritual growth and transformation. It enhances meditation, promotes spiritual insight, and facilitates connection to higher consciousness.

Uses and Applications Stress Relief: Carry Lepidolite or wear it as jewellery to benefit from its calming properties throughout the day. It is particularly useful during stressful situations or when dealing with anxiety.

Emotional Healing: Use Lepidolite in energy healing sessions to release emotional blockages and promote emotional balance. Place it on the Heart or Crown Chakras during healing sessions.

Meditation: Incorporate Lepidolite into meditation practices to enhance relaxation and spiritual growth. Hold the stone or place it nearby to deepen your meditative state and promote inner peace.

Sleep Aid: Place Lepidolite under your pillow or on your nightstand to promote restful sleep and prevent nightmares. Its calming energy can help to reduce insomnia and promote deep, restorative sleep.

Chakra Alignment Heart Chakra: Lepidolite is associated with the Heart Chakra, promoting emotional healing, love, and compassion. It helps to open and balance this energy centre, fostering emotional well-being.

Crown Chakra: Also associated with the Crown Chakra, Lepidolite enhances spiritual growth, intuition, and connection to higher consciousness.

Historical and Cultural Significance Ancient Cultures: Lepidolite has been used for its healing properties for centuries. While it was not specifically identified by ancient cultures due to its similarity to other mica minerals, it has been valued for its calming and emotional healing properties in modern times.

Modern Mysticism: Today, Lepidolite is widely used in contemporary crystal healing practices for its calming, emotional healing, and spiritual properties. It is popular in holistic health and wellness communities for supporting mental health and spiritual growth.

Scientific Properties Chemical Composition: Lepidolite is a lithium-rich mica mineral with the chemical formula $K(Li,Al)_3(Al,Si,Rb)_4O_{10}(F,OH)_2$. Its lavender colour is due to the presence of lithium, manganese, and other trace elements.

Hardness: It has a Mohs hardness rating of 2.5-3, making it relatively soft and delicate. Care should be taken when handling Lepidolite to avoid damage.

Formation: Lepidolite forms in granite pegmatites through the crystallisation of lithium-bearing minerals. It is often found in association with other lithium minerals such as spodumene and tourmaline.

Ritual Care and Cleansing Cleansing Methods: Lepidolite should be cleansed regularly to maintain its energetic purity. Effective methods include smudging with sage or palo santo, using sound vibrations, and placing in moonlight. Avoid prolonged exposure to water, as it can damage the stone.

Recharging: To recharge Lepidolite, place it in moonlight or on a selenite charging plate. Avoid prolonged exposure to direct sunlight to prevent colour fading.

Mystical Practical Tips Daily Empowerment: Carry a small Lepidolite crystal in your pocket or wear it as jewellery to benefit from its calming and emotional healing properties throughout the day. It is particularly useful during stressful situations or when dealing with anxiety or emotional turmoil.

Sanctified Spaces: Place Lepidolite in strategic locations around your home or workspace to create a calming and harmonious environment. Near your bed, it can help to promote restful sleep and reduce insomnia.

Meditation Space: Keep Lepidolite in your meditation space to enhance relaxation and spiritual growth during your practice. It can help to open the Heart and Crown Chakras, promoting deeper meditation and greater insight.

Angelite: The Stone of Angelic Communication

Appearance Angelite is a soft blue to bluish-grey variety of anhydrite. It often has a matte finish with a waxy lustre and can appear slightly translucent to opaque. Angelite is typically found in tumbled stones, raw chunks, and carved shapes such as spheres and angel figurines.

Varieties While Angelite itself is a specific variety of anhydrite, it is closely related to other forms of anhydrite and gypsum. However, its unique blue colour distinguishes it from other minerals in this group.

Arcane Energetic Properties Calming and Soothing: Angelite is renowned for its gentle, calming energy. It helps to soothe an overactive mind, reduce stress, and promote inner peace.

Spiritual Connection: This stone enhances spiritual awareness and facilitates connection with higher realms, spirit guides, and angels. It promotes a sense of serenity and spiritual well-being.

Communication: Angelite supports clear and compassionate communication. It encourages expressing thoughts and emotions with honesty and empathy, making it an excellent stone for improving interpersonal relationships.

Uses and Applications Stress Relief: Carry Angelite or wear it as jewellery to benefit from its calming properties throughout the day. It is particularly useful during stressful situations or when feeling overwhelmed.

Enhanced Communication: Use Angelite in settings where clear and compassionate communication is needed, such as meetings, counselling sessions, or personal conversations. Place it near the Throat Chakra during speaking engagements.

Spiritual Practices: Use Angelite during meditation, prayer, or spiritual rituals to enhance your connection with higher realms and spirit guides. Hold the stone or place it nearby to deepen your spiritual practice.

Emotional Healing: Incorporate Angelite into energy healing sessions to soothe emotional distress and promote a sense of peace. Place it on the Throat or Crown Chakras during healing sessions.

Chakra Alignment Throat Chakra: Angelite is strongly associated with the Throat Chakra, located at the throat. It promotes clear communication, self-expression, and emotional release.

Crown Chakra: Also associated with the Crown Chakra, Angelite enhances spiritual awareness, connection to higher realms, and a sense of serenity.

Historical and Cultural Significance Modern Mysticism: Angelite is a relatively new discovery in the mineral world, found in the late 20th century. It has quickly gained popularity in contemporary crystal healing practices for its calming and spiritual properties. It is widely used in holistic health and wellness communities for promoting relaxation, spiritual growth, and improved communication.

Scientific Properties Chemical Composition: Angelite is a variety of anhydrite, a calcium sulphate mineral with the chemical formula $CaSO_4$. It is formed through the dehydration of gypsum.

Hardness: It has a Mohs hardness rating of 3-3.5, making it relatively soft and susceptible to scratches and damage if not handled carefully.

Formation: Angelite forms through the evaporation of seawater in sedimentary basins. Over time, the gypsum dehydrates to form anhydrite, which can take on the characteristic blue colour of Angelite through trace mineral inclusions.

Ritual Care and Cleansing Cleansing Methods: Angelite should be cleansed regularly to maintain its energetic purity. Effective methods include smudging with sage or palo santo, using sound vibrations, and placing in moonlight. Avoid using water or saltwater, as it can damage the stone.

Recharging: To recharge Angelite, place it in moonlight or on a selenite charging plate. Avoid prolonged exposure to direct sunlight to prevent colour fading.

Mystical Practical Tips Daily Empowerment: Carry a small Angelite crystal in your pocket or wear it as jewellery to benefit from its calming and communicative properties throughout the day. It is particularly useful during stressful situations or when clear communication is needed.

Sanctified Spaces: Place Angelite in strategic locations around your home or workspace to create a calming and harmonious environment. Near communication areas, it can help to enhance clarity and understanding.

Meditation Space: Keep Angelite in your meditation space to enhance spiritual connection and emotional healing during your practice. It can help to open the Throat and Crown Chakras, promoting deeper meditation and greater insight.

CHAPTER NINE

Energising Stones: Citrine, Carnelian, Sunstone

Citrine: The Merchant's Stone

Appearance Citrine is a variety of quartz that ranges in colour from pale yellow to deep amber. It often exhibits a transparent to translucent clarity with a vitreous lustre. Citrine can be found in various forms, including tumbled stones, clusters, and points.

Varieties Citrine can occur naturally or be heat-treated. Natural Citrine typically has a pale to golden yellow colour, while heat-treated Citrine, often derived from amethyst, has a deeper orange or reddish hue.

Arcane Energetic Properties Abundance and Prosperity: Known as the "Merchant's Stone," Citrine is associated with wealth, success, and abundance. It attracts prosperity and helps to manifest financial and business goals.

Positive Energy: Citrine carries the energy of the sun, promoting joy, enthusiasm, and a positive outlook on life. It helps to dispel negative energies and protect against emotional stress.

Confidence and Personal Power: This stone enhances self-confidence, personal power, and creativity. It supports the Solar Plexus Chakra, empowering individuals to take decisive action and achieve their goals.

Uses and Applications Manifestation: Use Citrine to set and achieve financial and business goals. Place it in a cash register, wallet, or business area to attract prosperity and success.

Personal Empowerment: Carry Citrine or wear it as jewellery to boost self-confidence, creativity, and personal power throughout the day. It is particularly useful during challenging situations or when starting new projects.

Energy Cleansing: Citrine can be used to cleanse and purify the energy of a space. Place it in your home or workspace to maintain a positive and vibrant atmosphere.

Meditation: Incorporate Citrine into meditation practices to enhance joy, positivity, and personal empowerment. Hold the stone or place it on the Solar Plexus Chakra to deepen your meditative state and support manifestation.

Chakra Alignment Solar Plexus Chakra: Citrine is strongly associated with the Solar Plexus Chakra, located in the upper abdomen. It enhances personal power, confidence, and the ability to manifest goals.

Sacral Chakra: Also associated with the Sacral Chakra, Citrine promotes creativity, joy, and emotional balance.

Historical and Cultural Significance Ancient Cultures: Citrine has been used for thousands of years for its protective and healing properties. The ancient Greeks and Romans believed it could protect against evil thoughts and snake venom. It was also used as a decorative stone in jewellery and amulets.

Modern Mysticism: Today, Citrine is widely used in contemporary crystal healing practices for its energising and manifesting properties. It is popular in holistic health and wellness communities for attracting abundance and enhancing personal power.

Scientific Properties Chemical Composition: Citrine is composed of silicon dioxide (SiO_2), like all varieties of quartz. Its yellow to amber colour is due to trace amounts of iron.

Hardness: It has a Mohs hardness rating of 7, making it durable and suitable for various uses.

Formation: Citrine forms in igneous and metamorphic rocks, often in association with amethyst, smoky quartz, and other quartz varieties. Natural Citrine is relatively rare, with most commercial Citrine being heat-treated amethyst.

Ritual Care and Cleansing Cleansing Methods: Citrine should be cleansed regularly to maintain its energetic purity. Effective methods include rinsing with water, smudging with sage or palo santo, and using sound vibrations. Avoid prolonged exposure to water, as it can damage the stone.

Recharging: To recharge Citrine, place it in sunlight or moonlight, or on a selenite charging plate. Avoid prolonged exposure to direct sunlight to prevent colour fading.

Mystical Practical Tips Daily Empowerment: Carry a small Citrine crystal in your pocket or wear it as jewellery to benefit from its energising and manifesting properties throughout the day. It is particularly useful during stressful situations or when clear communication is needed.

Sanctified Spaces: Place Citrine in strategic locations around your home or workspace to create an energising and prosperous environment. Near communication areas, it can help to enhance clarity and understanding.

Meditation Space: Keep Citrine in your meditation space to enhance joy, positivity, and personal empowerment during your practice. It can help to open the Solar Plexus and Sacral Chakras, promoting deeper meditation and greater insight.

Carnelian: The Stone of Motivation

Appearance Carnelian is a vibrant orange to red variety of chalcedony, a type of microcrystalline quartz. It often exhibits a translucent to opaque appearance with a vitreous to waxy lustre. Carnelian can be found in various forms, including tumbled stones, cabochons, beads, and carved shapes.

Varieties The colour of Carnelian can range from pale orange to deep reddish-brown, depending on the amount of iron oxide present. High-quality Carnelian typically has a rich, uniform colour without too many inclusions.

Arcane Energetic Properties Vitality and Motivation: Known as a stone of motivation and endurance, Carnelian boosts physical energy, vitality, and motivation. It helps to overcome procrastination and stimulates action.

Creativity and Passion: Carnelian enhances creativity, passion, and artistic expression. It is particularly beneficial for artists, writers, and anyone engaged in creative pursuits.

Courage and Confidence: This stone promotes courage, confidence, and self-esteem. It helps to dispel fears and overcome challenges, making it an excellent stone for public speaking and leadership.

Uses and Applications Boosting Energy: Carry Carnelian or wear it as jewellery to benefit from its energising properties throughout the day. It is particularly useful during periods of low energy or when undertaking demanding tasks.

Enhancing Creativity: Use Carnelian in creative spaces to stimulate artistic expression and innovation. Place it in your studio, workspace, or near your tools to boost creativity and inspiration.

Personal Empowerment: Wear Carnelian jewellery or carry a stone in your pocket to enhance courage and confidence. It is especially useful for public speaking, presentations, and leadership roles.

Meditation: Incorporate Carnelian into meditation practices to enhance motivation, creativity, and personal empowerment. Hold the stone or place it on the Sacral Chakra to deepen your meditative state and support manifestation.

Chakra Alignment Sacral Chakra: Carnelian is strongly associated with the Sacral Chakra, located below the navel. It enhances creativity, passion, and emotional balance.

Root Chakra: Also associated with the Root Chakra, Carnelian promotes grounding, stability, and physical vitality.

Historical and Cultural Significance Ancient Cultures: Carnelian has been used for thousands of years for its protective and energising properties. The ancient Egyptians used it in jewellery, amulets, and seals, believing it could protect against evil and bring good fortune. In ancient Rome, Carnelian was used to make signet rings and was associated with courage and leadership.

Modern Mysticism: Today, Carnelian is widely used in contemporary crystal healing practices for its energising and motivating properties. It is popular in holistic health and wellness communities for supporting creativity, courage, and personal empowerment.

Scientific Properties Chemical Composition: Carnelian is a variety of chalcedony, composed of silicon dioxide (SiO_2). Its orange to red colour is due to the presence of iron oxide.

Hardness: It has a Mohs hardness rating of 6.5-7, making it relatively durable and suitable for various uses.

Formation: Carnelian forms in volcanic and sedimentary rocks through the deposition of silica-rich solutions in cavities and fissures. Over time, the silica crystallises and incorporates iron oxide, giving the stone its characteristic colour.

Ritual Care and Cleansing Cleansing Methods: Carnelian should be cleansed regularly to maintain its energetic purity. Effective methods include rinsing with water, smudging with sage or palo santo, and using sound vibrations. Avoid prolonged exposure to water, as it can damage the stone.

Recharging: To recharge Carnelian, place it in sunlight or moonlight, or on a selenite charging plate. Avoid prolonged exposure to direct sunlight to prevent colour fading.

Mystical Practical Tips Daily Empowerment: Carry a small Carnelian crystal in your pocket or wear it as jewellery to benefit from its energising and motivating properties throughout the day. It is particularly useful during stressful situations or when clear communication is needed.

Sanctified Spaces: Place Carnelian in strategic locations around your home or workspace to create an energising and creative environment. Near communication areas, it can help to enhance clarity and understanding.

Meditation Space: Keep Carnelian in your meditation space to enhance motivation, creativity, and personal empowerment during your practice. It can help to open the Sacral and Root Chakras, promoting deeper meditation and greater insight.

Sunstone: The Stone of Joy

Appearance Sunstone is a feldspar mineral known for its warm, shimmering appearance, often displaying a sparkling effect called aventurescence. The colours range from pale yellow and orange to deep red and brown, with flashes of gold, red, or copper. Sunstone can be found in various forms, including tumbled stones, cabochons, beads, and carved shapes.

Varieties Sunstone's aventurescence is caused by inclusions of hematite or goethite. High-quality Sunstone exhibits a strong, visible shimmer with vibrant, uniform colour.

Arcane Energetic Properties Joy and Positivity: Known as a stone of joy, Sunstone carries the energy of the sun, promoting positivity, happiness, and an optimistic outlook on life.

Empowerment and Confidence: Sunstone enhances personal power, confidence, and leadership abilities. It helps to dispel self-doubt and promotes a positive self-image.

Vitality and Motivation: This stone boosts physical energy, vitality, and motivation. It helps to overcome procrastination and encourages action and progress.

Uses and Applications Enhancing Positivity: Carry Sunstone or wear it as jewellery to benefit from its uplifting properties throughout the day. It is particularly useful during periods of stress or negativity.

Boosting Confidence: Use Sunstone to enhance self-confidence and personal power. Place it in areas where you need a boost in confidence, such as your workspace or personal study area.

Increasing Vitality: Keep Sunstone nearby during activities that require physical energy and motivation. It is especially useful for athletes, performers, and anyone engaged in high-energy tasks.

Meditation: Incorporate Sunstone into meditation practices to enhance joy, positivity, and personal empowerment. Hold the stone or place it on the Solar Plexus Chakra to deepen your meditative state and support manifestation.

Chakra Alignment Solar Plexus Chakra: Sunstone is strongly associated with the Solar Plexus Chakra, located in the upper abdomen. It enhances personal power, confidence, and vitality.

Sacral Chakra: Also associated with the Sacral Chakra, Sunstone promotes creativity, joy, and emotional balance.

Historical and Cultural Significance Ancient Cultures: Sunstone has been used for centuries for its energising and protective properties. The Vikings are believed to have used Sunstone as a navigational tool, utilising its ability to polarise light. In Native American cultures, Sunstone was used in ceremonial practices to call upon the power of the sun.

Modern Mysticism: Today, Sunstone is widely used in contemporary crystal healing practices for its uplifting and empowering properties. It is popular in holistic health and wellness communities for promoting positivity, confidence, and vitality.

Scientific Properties Chemical Composition: Sunstone is a variety of feldspar, typically composed of sodium calcium aluminium silicate. Its aventurescence is due to inclusions of hematite or goethite.

Hardness: It has a Mohs hardness rating of 6-6.5, making it relatively durable and suitable for various uses.

Formation: Sunstone forms in plutonic and volcanic rocks through the slow cooling of molten rock, which allows the formation of its characteristic inclusions and shimmer.

Ritual Care and Cleansing Cleansing Methods: Sunstone should be cleansed regularly to maintain its energetic purity. Effective methods include rinsing with water, smudging with sage or palo santo, and using sound vibrations. Avoid prolonged exposure to water, as it can damage the stone.

Recharging: To recharge Sunstone, place it in sunlight or moonlight, or on a selenite charging plate. Avoid prolonged exposure to direct sunlight to prevent colour fading.

Mystical Practical Tips Daily Empowerment: Carry a small Sunstone crystal in your pocket or wear it as jewellery to benefit from its energising and empowering properties throughout the day. It is particularly useful during stressful situations or when clear communication is needed.

Sanctified Spaces: Place Sunstone in strategic locations around your home or workspace to create an energising and positive environment. Near communication areas, it can help to enhance clarity and understanding.

Meditation Space: Keep Sunstone in your meditation space to enhance joy, positivity, and personal empowerment during your practice. It can help to open the Solar Plexus and Sacral Chakras, promoting deeper meditation and greater insight.

CHAPTER TEN

Precious Stones: Diamond, Sapphire, Ruby, Emerald

Diamond: The Stone of Invincibility

Appearance Diamonds are renowned for their brilliant sparkle and unparalleled hardness. They are typically clear and colourless but can also come in a variety of colours, including blue, yellow, green, pink, and even black. Diamonds have a high refractive index, which gives them their characteristic brilliance and fire. They are often found in raw, uncut forms or as finely cut and polished gems in various shapes like round, princess, emerald, and pear.

Varieties Diamonds can be categorised based on their colour and clarity. Fancy-coloured diamonds (e.g., blue, pink, yellow) are highly prized for their rarity and vibrant hues. Colourless diamonds are graded on a scale from D (colourless) to Z (light yellow or brown), and clarity ranges from Flawless (no inclusions or blemishes visible under 10x magnification) to Included (inclusions and/or blemishes visible to the naked eye).

Arcane Energetic Properties Amplification: Diamonds are powerful amplifiers of energy. They enhance the energy of other stones and can intensify one's thoughts and intentions.

Clarity and Purity: Known as a symbol of clarity and purity, diamonds promote mental clarity, truth, and spiritual insight. They help to clear away emotional and mental fog, allowing for better decision-making and a clear path forward.

Strength and Resilience: Diamonds symbolise strength, resilience, and invincibility. They encourage courage, perseverance, and the ability to withstand adversity.

Uses and Applications Personal Empowerment: Wear diamond jewellery to benefit from its amplifying and strengthening properties throughout the day. It enhances personal power, confidence, and resilience.

Meditation and Spiritual Practices: Use diamonds during meditation to enhance spiritual insight, clarity, and connection to higher realms. Hold the stone or place it nearby to deepen your meditative state.

Healing Practices: Incorporate diamonds into energy healing sessions to amplify the effects of other stones and promote overall well-being. Place the diamond on any chakra to clear blockages and enhance energy flow.

Chakra Alignment Crown Chakra: Diamonds are strongly associated with the Crown Chakra, located at the top of the head. They promote spiritual awakening, enlightenment, and a deep connection to the divine.

Historical and Cultural Significance Ancient Cultures: Diamonds have been cherished for thousands of years for their beauty, rarity, and perceived mystical properties. In ancient India, diamonds were used in religious icons and believed to bring strength, courage, and invincibility. In ancient Greece, diamonds were thought to be tears of the gods or splinters from falling stars.

Modern Mysticism: Today, diamonds are widely used in jewellery and are a symbol of love, commitment, and purity, often featured in engagement rings. They are also used in industrial applications due to their unmatched hardness.

Scientific Properties Chemical Composition: Diamonds are composed of pure carbon (C) arranged in a crystal lattice structure. This structure gives diamonds their extraordinary hardness.

Hardness: Diamonds have a Mohs hardness rating of 10, making them the hardest natural substance on Earth.

Formation: Diamonds form under high-pressure, high-temperature conditions deep within the Earth's mantle. They are brought to the surface through volcanic eruptions, forming kimberlite and lamproite pipes.

Ritual Care and Cleansing Cleansing Methods: Diamonds should be cleansed regularly to maintain their energetic purity. Effective methods include rinsing with water, smudging with sage or palo santo, and using sound vibrations. Diamonds can also be cleansed using ultrasonic cleaners, though care should be taken to ensure they are securely set in jewellery.

Recharging: To recharge diamonds, place them in sunlight or moonlight, or on a selenite charging plate. Their natural brilliance and resilience mean they rarely need intensive recharging.

Mystical Practical Tips Daily Empowerment: Wear diamond jewellery or carry a small diamond to benefit from its amplifying and strengthening properties throughout the day. It is particularly useful during important events or challenging situations.

Sanctified Spaces: Place diamonds in strategic locations around your home or workspace to create a clear, focused, and resilient environment. Near communication areas, they can help to enhance clarity and understanding.

Meditation Space: Keep diamonds in your meditation space to enhance spiritual insight and clarity during your practice. They can help to open the Crown Chakra, promoting deeper meditation and greater connection to higher consciousness.

Sapphire: The Stone of Wisdom

Appearance Sapphires are a variety of corundum and come in a wide range of colours, although the most recognized is the deep blue variety. Sapphires can also be found in pink, yellow, green, purple, and even colourless. The blue sapphire's colour is due to trace amounts of iron and titanium. They have a vitreous lustre and are typically transparent to translucent. Sapphires are often cut into faceted gemstones, cabochons, or polished into beads.

Varieties Notable varieties of sapphire include:

- **Blue Sapphire:** The most iconic type, ranging from light to deep blue.

- **Star Sapphire:** Exhibits a star-like pattern (asterism) due to rutile inclusions.

- **Padparadscha**: A rare pinkish-orange sapphire highly prized for its unique colour.

- **Fancy Sapphires**: Includes all other colours of sapphires, such as yellow, green, and purple.

Arcane Energetic Properties Wisdom and Insight: Known as the "Stone of Wisdom," sapphires enhance mental clarity, focus, and insight. They aid in accessing deeper levels of consciousness and understanding.

Protection: Sapphires provide strong protective energies, shielding against negative energies and psychic attacks. They help to maintain a calm and composed state of mind.

Spiritual Growth: This stone supports spiritual awakening and growth. It enhances intuition, meditation, and connection to higher realms.

Uses and Applications Enhancing Wisdom: Wear sapphire jewellery or carry a sapphire stone to benefit from its wisdom-enhancing properties. It is particularly useful for students, scholars, and those engaged in intellectual pursuits.

Protection: Use sapphires for protection against negative energies and psychic attacks. Place them in your home or workspace to create a protective barrier.

Meditation and Spiritual Practices: Incorporate sapphires into meditation to enhance spiritual growth, intuition, and insight. Hold the stone or place it on the Third Eye Chakra to deepen your meditative state.

Healing Practices: Use sapphires in energy healing sessions to clear blockages and enhance the flow of energy. Place them on any chakra to balance and align the energy centres.

Chakra Alignment Third Eye Chakra: Sapphires are strongly associated with the Third Eye Chakra, located between the eyebrows. They enhance intuition, psychic abilities, and spiritual insight.

Throat Chakra: Also associated with the Throat Chakra, sapphires promote clear communication, self-expression, and truth.

Historical and Cultural Significance Ancient Cultures: Sapphires have been cherished for thousands of years for their beauty and protective properties. Ancient Persians believed that the sky was painted blue by the reflection of sapphires. In mediaeval Europe, clergy wore sapphires to symbolise heaven and protect against envy and harm. They were also believed to protect the wearer from poisoning.

Modern Mysticism: Today, sapphires are widely used in jewellery and are a symbol of wisdom, virtue, and good fortune. They are popular in engagement rings and are often used in high-end watches and other luxury items.

Scientific Properties Chemical Composition: Sapphires are composed of aluminium oxide (Al_2O_3) and belong to the corundum family. The presence of trace elements such as iron, titanium, and chromium gives sapphires their various colours.

Hardness: Sapphires have a Mohs hardness rating of 9, making them one of the hardest gemstones, second only to diamonds.

Formation: Sapphires form in metamorphic and igneous rocks, often found in alluvial deposits. They are typically mined from secondary deposits in riverbeds and gravel beds.

Ritual Care and Cleansing Cleansing Methods: Sapphires should be cleansed regularly to maintain their energetic purity. Effective methods include rinsing with water, smudging with sage or palo santo, and using sound vibrations. Sapphires can also be cleaned using ultrasonic cleaners and steam cleaners.

Recharging: To recharge sapphires, place them in sunlight or moonlight, or on a selenite charging plate. Their natural hardness and durability mean they can withstand most cleansing and recharging methods.

Mystical Practical Tips Daily Empowerment: Wear sapphire jewellery or carry a small sapphire stone to benefit from its wisdom-enhancing and protective properties throughout the day. It is particularly useful during intellectual or stressful activities.

Sanctified Spaces: Place sapphires in strategic locations around your home or workspace to create a protective and insightful environment. Near communication areas, they can help to enhance clarity and understanding.

Meditation Space: Keep sapphires in your meditation space to enhance spiritual growth, intuition, and insight during your practice. They can help to open the Third Eye and Throat Chakras, promoting deeper meditation and greater connection to higher consciousness.

Ruby: The Stone of Passion

Appearance Rubies are a variety of corundum, known for their vibrant red colour, which ranges from pinkish-red to deep crimson. This rich colour is due to the presence of chromium. Rubies are typically transparent to translucent with a vitreous lustre and are often cut into faceted gemstones, cabochons, and beads.

Varieties Rubies can vary in hue, saturation, and tone. The most sought-after rubies are known as "pigeon blood" rubies, which exhibit a deep red colour with a hint of blue. Star rubies display a star-like pattern (asterism) due to rutile inclusions.

Arcane Energetic Properties Vitality and Energy: Known as a stone of passion and vitality, rubies are believed to boost energy levels, increase stamina, and promote a zest for life. They help to overcome lethargy and stimulate motivation.

Courage and Confidence: Rubies enhance courage, confidence, and leadership qualities. They help to dispel fear and anxiety, promoting a positive and assertive attitude.

Love and Passion: This stone is associated with love and passion, enhancing romantic relationships and emotional connections. It promotes a deep sense of commitment and loyalty.

Uses and Applications Enhancing Vitality: Wear ruby jewellery or carry a ruby stone to benefit from its energising properties throughout the day. It is particularly useful during physically demanding activities or when feeling fatigued.

Boosting Confidence: Use rubies to enhance self-confidence and courage. Place them in areas where you need a boost in confidence, such as your workspace or personal study area.

Promoting Love: Incorporate rubies into your romantic relationships to enhance love and passion. Place them in your bedroom or wear them as jewellery to promote emotional connection and intimacy.

Meditation: Use rubies during meditation to enhance vitality, courage, and emotional healing. Hold the stone or place it on the Heart or Root Chakra to deepen your meditative state.

Chakra Alignment Root Chakra: Rubies are strongly associated with the Root Chakra, located at the base of the spine. They promote grounding, stability, and physical vitality.

Heart Chakra: Also associated with the Heart Chakra, rubies enhance love, passion, and emotional well-being.

Historical and Cultural Significance Ancient Cultures: Rubies have been cherished for thousands of years for their beauty and powerful properties. Ancient Burmese warriors believed that rubies made them invincible in battle. In India, rubies were considered the "king of gemstones" and were used in religious offerings. Mediaeval Europeans believed that rubies could bring good fortune, health, and wisdom.

Modern Mysticism: Today, rubies are widely used in jewellery and are a symbol of love, passion, and prosperity. They are popular in engagement rings and are often used to celebrate milestones such as anniversaries and birthdays.

Scientific Properties Chemical Composition: Rubies are composed of aluminium oxide (Al_2O_3) with trace amounts of chromium, which gives them their red colour.

Hardness: Rubies have a Mohs hardness rating of 9, making them one of the hardest gemstones, second only to diamonds.

Formation: Rubies form in metamorphic and igneous rocks, often found in alluvial deposits. They are typically mined from secondary deposits in riverbeds and gravel beds.

Ritual Care and Cleansing Cleansing Methods: Rubies should be cleansed regularly to maintain their energetic purity. Effective methods include rinsing with water, smudging with sage or palo santo, and using sound vibrations. Rubies can also be cleaned using ultrasonic cleaners and steam cleaners.

Recharging: To recharge rubies, place them in sunlight or moonlight, or on a selenite charging plate. Their natural hardness and durability mean they can withstand most cleansing and recharging methods.

Mystical Practical Tips Daily Empowerment: Wear ruby jewellery or carry a small ruby stone to benefit from its energising and confidence-boosting properties throughout the day. It is particularly useful during physically demanding or stressful situations.

Sanctified Spaces: Place rubies in strategic locations around your home or workspace to create an energising and positive environment. Near communication areas, they can help to enhance clarity and understanding.

Meditation Space: Keep rubies in your meditation space to enhance vitality, courage, and emotional healing during your practice. They can help to open the Root and Heart Chakras, promoting deeper meditation and greater insight.

Emerald: The Stone of Successful Love

Appearance Emeralds are a variety of beryl and are known for their vibrant green colour, which can range from light green to deep, rich green. This coloration is due to trace amounts of chromium and sometimes vanadium. Emeralds typically have a vitreous lustre and are often transparent to translucent, with some inclusions common. They are often cut into faceted gemstones, cabochons, and beads.

Varieties The quality of emeralds can vary significantly based on colour, clarity, and cut. The most prized emeralds are those with a deep, vivid green colour and high transparency. Emeralds with fewer inclusions, known as "jardin," are considered more valuable.

Arcane Energetic Properties Love and Compassion: Known as the "Stone of Successful Love," emeralds open and nurture the heart. They promote unconditional love, compassion, and emotional balance.

Growth and Abundance: Emeralds symbolise growth, renewal, and abundance. They encourage personal growth, prosperity, and the manifestation of goals.

Healing and Protection: This stone is believed to have strong healing and protective energies. It supports physical healing, emotional recovery, and shields against negative energies.

Uses and Applications Enhancing Love: Wear emerald jewellery or carry an emerald stone to benefit from its love-enhancing properties throughout the day. It is particularly useful for strengthening romantic relationships and fostering deeper emotional connections.

Promoting Growth: Use emeralds to encourage personal and spiritual growth. Place them in areas where you focus on personal development, such as a study or meditation space.

Supporting Healing: Incorporate emeralds into healing practices to support physical and emotional recovery. Place them on the Heart Chakra during healing sessions to promote balance and well-being.

Meditation: Use emeralds during meditation to enhance love, compassion, and growth. Hold the stone or place it on the Heart Chakra to deepen your meditative state and support emotional healing.

Chakra Alignment Heart Chakra: Emeralds are strongly associated with the Heart Chakra, located at the centre of the chest. They promote love, compassion, and emotional balance.

Third Eye Chakra: Also associated with the Third Eye Chakra, emeralds enhance intuition, insight, and spiritual growth.

Historical and Cultural Significance Ancient Cultures: Emeralds have been cherished for thousands of years for their beauty and perceived mystical properties. In ancient Egypt, emeralds were associated with fertility and rebirth and were favoured by Cleopatra. The Incas and Aztecs of South America, where many of the finest emeralds are found, used them in religious ceremonies and as symbols of wealth and power. In ancient Rome, emeralds were dedicated to the goddess Venus, symbolising love and beauty.

Modern Mysticism: Today, emeralds are widely used in jewellery and are a symbol of love, growth, and prosperity. They are popular in engagement rings and other fine jewellery pieces, often given as gifts to symbolise enduring love and commitment.

Scientific Properties Chemical Composition: Emeralds are composed of beryllium aluminium silicate ($Be_3Al_2(SiO_3)6$) with trace amounts of chromium and sometimes vanadium, which give them their green colour.

Hardness: Emeralds have a Mohs hardness rating of 7.5-8, making them relatively hard but more susceptible to chipping and cracking due to their natural inclusions.

Formation: Emeralds form in hydrothermal veins and pegmatites, often in association with quartz, feldspar, and other minerals. They are primarily mined in Colombia, Zambia, Brazil, and Zimbabwe.

Ritual Care and Cleansing Cleansing Methods: Emeralds should be cleansed regularly to maintain their energetic purity. Effective methods include rinsing with water, smudging with sage or palo santo, and using sound vibrations. Avoid using ultrasonic cleaners or steam cleaners, as the inclusions in emeralds can make them more fragile.

Recharging: To recharge emeralds, place them in sunlight or moonlight, or on a selenite charging plate. Their natural durability and vibrancy mean they can withstand most cleansing and recharging methods.

Mystical Practical Tips Daily Empowerment: Wear emerald jewellery or carry a small emerald stone to benefit from its love-enhancing and growth-promoting properties throughout the day. It is particularly useful during periods of personal development or emotional healing.

Sanctified Spaces: Place emeralds in strategic locations around your home or workspace to create a loving and growth-oriented environment. Near communication areas, they can help to enhance understanding and compassion.

Meditation Space: Keep emeralds in your meditation space to enhance love, compassion, and personal growth during your practice. They can help to open the Heart and Third Eye Chakras, promoting deeper meditation and greater insight.

CHAPTER ELEVEN

Semi-Precious Stones: Agate, Jasper, Malachite, etc.

Agate: The Stone of Grounding and Stability

Appearance Agate is a variety of chalcedony, a microcrystalline form of quartz. It is known for its wide range of colours and unique banding patterns, which can include stripes, swirls, and specks. Agates can be found in many colours, including red, blue, green, yellow, brown, and multicoloured varieties. They often have a waxy lustre and can be translucent to opaque. Agate is commonly found in geodes, nodules, and as tumbled stones, cabochons, and beads.

Varieties There are many types of agate, each with its unique appearance and properties:

- **Blue Lace Agate**: Light blue with white lace-like patterns.

- **Moss Agate**: Contains green, moss-like inclusions.

- **Fire Agate**: Displays iridescent colours due to limonite inclusions.

- **Dendritic Agate**: Features tree or fern-like inclusions.

Arcane Energetic Properties Stability and Grounding: Agate is known for its grounding and stabilising properties. It helps to centre and stabilise physical energy, providing a sense of security and balance.

Emotional Healing: Agate aids in emotional healing, helping to overcome negativity and bitterness. It promotes love, courage, and emotional strength.

Cognitive Function: This stone enhances mental function by improving concentration, perception, and analytical abilities. It helps to overcome negativity and foster a positive mindset.

Uses and Applications Grounding and Stability: Carry agate or wear it as jewellery to benefit from its grounding and stabilising properties throughout the day. It is particularly useful during stressful situations or when feeling overwhelmed.

Emotional Healing: Use agate in energy healing sessions to support emotional healing and balance. Place it on the Heart Chakra to promote emotional strength and stability.

Enhancing Focus: Incorporate agate into your workspace or study area to enhance concentration and analytical abilities. It can help to improve focus and cognitive function.

Meditation: Use agate during meditation to enhance grounding and emotional healing. Hold the stone or place it on any chakra to deepen your meditative state.

Chakra Alignment Root Chakra: Agate is strongly associated with the Root Chakra, located at the base of the spine. It promotes grounding, stability, and security.

Other Chakras: Different types of agate can be associated with various chakras depending on their colour and properties. For example, Blue Lace Agate is associated with the Throat Chakra for communication, and Moss Agate is associated with the Heart Chakra for emotional balance.

Historical and Cultural Significance Ancient Cultures: Agate has been used for thousands of years for its protective and healing properties. The ancient Greeks and Romans used agate in jewellery and amulets, believing it could protect against danger and bring good fortune. In ancient Egypt, agate was used in talismans and as a decorative stone.

Modern Mysticism: Today, agate is widely used in contemporary crystal healing practices for its grounding, stabilising, and healing properties. It is popular in holistic health and wellness communities for promoting balance and emotional well-being.

Scientific Properties Chemical Composition: Agate is composed of silicon dioxide (SiO_2) and is a variety of chalcedony, a microcrystalline form of quartz.

Hardness: It has a Mohs hardness rating of 6.5-7, making it relatively durable and suitable for various uses.

Formation: Agate forms in volcanic and metamorphic rocks through the deposition of silica-rich solutions in cavities. Over time, the silica crystallises, forming the characteristic banded patterns.

Ritual Care and Cleansing Cleansing Methods: Agate should be cleansed regularly to maintain its energetic purity. Effective methods include rinsing with water, smudging with sage or palo santo, and using sound vibrations. Agate can also be cleansed using mild soap and water.

Recharging: To recharge agate, place it in sunlight or moonlight, or on a selenite charging plate. Avoid prolonged exposure to direct sunlight to prevent colour fading.

Mystical Practical Tips Daily Empowerment: Carry a small agate crystal in your pocket or wear it as jewellery to benefit from its grounding and stabilising properties throughout the day. It is particularly useful during stressful situations or when needing to enhance focus.

Sanctified Spaces: Place agate in strategic locations around your home or workspace to create a balanced and stable environment. Near communication areas, it can help to enhance clarity and understanding.

Meditation Space: Keep agate in your meditation space to enhance grounding and emotional healing during your practice. It can help to open the Root Chakra and other chakras, promoting deeper meditation and greater insight.

Jasper: The Supreme Nurturer

Appearance Jasper is an opaque variety of chalcedony and comes in a wide range of colours and patterns. It is known for its rich, earthy tones, including red, yellow, brown, green, and blue. Jasper often exhibits unique patterns such as stripes, spots, or swirls, giving each piece a distinctive look. It is commonly found in tumbled stones, cabochons, beads, and carved shapes.

Varieties There are many types of jasper, each with unique appearances and properties:

- **Red Jasper:** Known for its deep red colour and grounding properties.

- **Yellow Jasper:** Exhibits yellow hues and is associated with clarity and confidence.

- **Green Jasper:** Promotes healing and balance with its green colour.

- **Picture Jasper:** Displays intricate patterns that resemble landscapes or pictures.

- **Ocean Jasper:** Features orbs and wavy patterns in a variety of colours.

Arcane Energetic Properties Grounding and Stability: Jasper is known as the "Supreme Nurturer." It provides grounding and stability, helping to anchor energy and promote a sense of calm and balance.

Emotional Healing: Jasper supports emotional healing by providing strength and comfort. It helps to alleviate stress, anxiety, and emotional turmoil.

Physical Vitality: This stone boosts physical energy and vitality. It promotes endurance, stamina, and overall well-being.

Uses and Applications Grounding and Stability: Carry jasper or wear it as jewellery to benefit from its grounding and stabilising properties throughout the day. It is particularly useful during stressful situations or when feeling unbalanced.

Emotional Healing: Use jasper in energy healing sessions to support emotional healing and balance. Place it on the Heart Chakra to promote emotional strength and stability.

Enhancing Vitality: Incorporate jasper into your daily routine to boost physical energy and vitality. It can be used in physical activities or during times of fatigue.

Meditation: Use jasper during meditation to enhance grounding and emotional healing. Hold the stone or place it on any chakra to deepen your meditative state.

Chakra Alignment Root Chakra: Jasper is strongly associated with the Root Chakra, located at the base of the spine. It promotes grounding, stability, and physical vitality.

Other Chakras: Different types of jasper can be associated with various chakras depending on their colour and properties. For example, Red Jasper is associated with the Root Chakra, Yellow Jasper with the Solar Plexus Chakra, and Green Jasper with the Heart Chakra.

Historical and Cultural Significance Ancient Cultures: Jasper has been used for thousands of years for its protective and healing properties. Ancient Egyptians used jasper for amulets and jewellery, believing it could protect against danger and promote fertility. In ancient Greece, jasper was considered a stone of protection and endurance.

Modern Mysticism: Today, jasper is widely used in contemporary crystal healing practices for its grounding, stabilising, and healing properties. It is popular in holistic health and wellness communities for promoting balance and emotional well-being.

Scientific Properties Chemical Composition: Jasper is composed of silicon dioxide (SiO_2) and is a variety of chalcedony, a microcrystalline form of quartz.

Hardness: It has a Mohs hardness rating of 6.5-7, making it relatively durable and suitable for various uses.

Formation: Jasper forms in sedimentary and volcanic rocks through the deposition of silica-rich solutions. Over time, the silica crystallises, incorporating various impurities that give jasper its distinctive colours and patterns.

Ritual Care and Cleansing Cleansing Methods: Jasper should be cleansed regularly to maintain its energetic purity. Effective methods include rinsing with water, smudging with sage or palo santo, and using sound vibrations. Jasper can also be cleansed using mild soap and water.

Recharging: To recharge jasper, place it in sunlight or moonlight, or on a selenite charging plate. Avoid prolonged exposure to direct sunlight to prevent colour fading.

Mystical Practical Tips Daily Empowerment: Carry a small jasper crystal in your pocket or wear it as jewellery to benefit from its grounding and stabilising properties throughout the day. It is particularly useful during stressful situations or when needing to enhance focus.

Sanctified Spaces: Place jasper in strategic locations around your home or workspace to create a balanced and stable environment. Near communication areas, it can help to enhance clarity and understanding.

Meditation Space: Keep jasper in your meditation space to enhance grounding and emotional healing during your practice. It can help to open the Root Chakra and other chakras, promoting deeper meditation and greater insight.

Malachite: The Stone of Transformation

Appearance Malachite is a striking green mineral known for its vibrant, banded patterns in varying shades of green. It often displays a silky to vitreous lustre and can be translucent to opaque. Malachite is typically found in raw chunks, polished stones, cabochons, and beads.

Varieties While malachite itself is a specific mineral, it can form in various patterns and structures, including botryoidal, fibrous, and stalactitic formations. The most prized malachite has vivid colour contrasts and intricate banding.

Arcane Energetic Properties Transformation and Change: Known as the "Stone of Transformation," malachite assists in changing situations and provides support during times of change. It encourages risk-taking and embracing new opportunities.

Emotional Healing: Malachite is a powerful stone for emotional healing. It helps to release past traumas and suppressed emotions, promoting emotional balance and well-being.

Protection: This stone provides strong protective energy, particularly for travellers and those exposed to negative energies. It absorbs negative energies and pollutants from the environment and the body.

Uses and Applications Personal Transformation: Carry malachite or wear it as jewellery to support personal growth and transformation. It can help to overcome fear and encourage positive changes.

Emotional Healing: Use malachite in energy healing sessions to release emotional blockages and promote emotional balance. Place it on the Heart or Solar Plexus Chakras during healing sessions.

Protection: Place malachite in your home or workspace to create a protective environment. It is particularly useful near entry points to prevent negative energies from entering.

Meditation: Use malachite during meditation to enhance insight and understanding of personal growth and transformation. Hold the stone or place it on the Heart Chakra to deepen emotional healing.

Chakra Alignment Heart Chakra: Malachite is strongly associated with the Heart Chakra, promoting love, compassion, and emotional balance. It helps to heal the heart and enhance emotional well-being.

Solar Plexus Chakra: Also associated with the Solar Plexus Chakra, malachite enhances personal power, confidence, and the ability to make positive changes.

Historical and Cultural Significance Ancient Cultures: Malachite has been used since ancient times for its protective and healing properties. The ancient Egyptians used it as a protective amulet and ground it into powder for use as eye makeup. The Greeks and Romans also used malachite for jewellery and decorative purposes, believing it could protect against the evil eye.

Modern Mysticism: Today, malachite is widely used in contemporary crystal healing practices for its transformative and protective qualities. It is popular in holistic health and wellness communities for supporting personal growth and emotional healing.

Scientific Properties Chemical Composition: Malachite is a copper carbonate hydroxide mineral with the chemical formula $Cu_2CO_3(OH)_2$. Its vibrant green colour is due to its high copper content.

Hardness: It has a Mohs hardness rating of 3.5-4, making it relatively soft and susceptible to scratches and damage if not handled carefully.

Formation: Malachite forms through the weathering and oxidation of copper ore deposits, often found in association with azurite, another copper carbonate mineral.

Ritual Care and Cleansing Cleansing Methods: Malachite should be cleansed regularly to maintain its energetic purity. Effective methods include smudging with sage or palo santo, using sound vibrations, and placing in moonlight. Avoid using water or saltwater, as it can damage the stone.

Recharging: To recharge malachite, place it in moonlight or on a selenite charging plate. Avoid prolonged exposure to direct sunlight to prevent colour fading.

Mystical Practical Tips Daily Empowerment: Carry a small malachite crystal in your pocket or wear it as jewellery to benefit from its transformative and protective properties throughout the day. It is particularly useful during times of change or emotional stress.

Sanctified Spaces: Place malachite in strategic locations around your home or workspace to create a protective and supportive environment. Near entry points, it can help to prevent negative energies from entering.

Meditation Space: Keep malachite in your meditation space to enhance personal growth and emotional healing during your practice. It can help to open the Heart and Solar Plexus Chakras, promoting deeper meditation and greater insight.

Moonstone: The Stone of Intuition and Balance

Appearance Moonstone is a variety of feldspar that exhibits a unique optical phenomenon known as adularescence, which is a soft, billowy sheen that moves across the stone as the light changes. It can be found in various colours, including white, grey, peach, and blue. Moonstone is typically translucent to opaque and has a pearly to vitreous lustre. It is often cut into cabochons, tumbled stones, and beads.

Varieties Notable types of moonstone include:

- **Rainbow Moonstone:** Displays a variety of colours in the sheen, often with a blue or rainbow-like play of colour.

- **White Moonstone:** Known for its milky white appearance and classic adularescence.

- **Peach Moonstone:** Exhibits warm peach or pink hues with a soft glow.

- **Gray Moonstone:** Features a more muted colour with a subtle sheen.

Arcane Energetic Properties Emotional Balance: Moonstone is known for its soothing and calming energy. It helps to stabilise emotions, reduce stress, and promote a sense of peace and tranquillity.

Intuition and Insight: This stone enhances intuition, psychic abilities, and spiritual insight. It is particularly beneficial for meditation and spiritual practices.

Feminine Energy: Moonstone is associated with feminine energy, supporting the reproductive system, hormonal balance, and fertility. It also promotes self-discovery and inner growth.

Uses and Applications Emotional Healing: Carry moonstone or wear it as jewellery to benefit from its calming and soothing properties throughout the day. It is particularly useful during times of emotional stress or instability.

Enhancing Intuition: Use moonstone to enhance intuition and psychic abilities. Place it in areas where you practise meditation or spiritual work to deepen your connection to higher consciousness.

Feminine Health: Incorporate moonstone into healing practices to support feminine health and hormonal balance. It can be used in energy healing sessions or placed on the body during meditation.

Meditation: Use moonstone during meditation to enhance emotional balance and spiritual insight. Hold the stone or place it on the Third Eye or Crown Chakra to deepen your meditative state.

Chakra Alignment Crown Chakra: Moonstone is strongly associated with the Crown Chakra, located at the top of the head. It promotes spiritual awakening, enlightenment, and connection to higher realms.

Third Eye Chakra: Also associated with the Third Eye Chakra, moonstone enhances intuition, psychic abilities, and spiritual insight.

Historical and Cultural Significance Ancient Cultures: Moonstone has been used for centuries for its mystical and healing properties. In ancient Rome, it was believed to be formed from moonlight and was associated with the lunar deities. In India, moonstone is considered sacred and is often used in traditional jewellery.

Modern Mysticism: Today, moonstone is widely used in contemporary crystal healing practices for its calming, intuitive, and feminine properties. It is popular in holistic health and wellness communities for promoting emotional balance and spiritual growth.

Scientific Properties Chemical Composition: Moonstone is a variety of feldspar, specifically orthoclase or albite, with the chemical formula $(K,Na)AlSi_3O8$.

Hardness: It has a Mohs hardness rating of 6-6.5, making it relatively durable but susceptible to scratches and abrasions.

Formation: Moonstone forms in igneous and metamorphic rocks through the slow cooling of molten rock, which allows the formation of its characteristic adularescence.

Ritual Care and Cleansing Cleansing Methods: Moonstone should be cleansed regularly to maintain its energetic purity. Effective methods include rinsing with water, smudging with sage or palo santo, and using sound vibrations. Avoid prolonged exposure to water, as it can damage the stone.

Recharging: To recharge moonstone, place it in moonlight or on a selenite charging plate. Avoid prolonged exposure to direct sunlight to prevent colour fading.

Mystical Practical Tips Daily Empowerment: Carry a small moonstone crystal in your pocket or wear it as jewellery to benefit from its calming and intuitive properties throughout the day. It is particularly useful during times of emotional stress or when needing to enhance intuition.

Sanctified Spaces: Place moonstone in strategic locations around your home or workspace to create a calming and harmonious environment. Near communication areas, it can help to enhance clarity and understanding.

Meditation Space: Keep moonstone in your meditation space to enhance emotional balance and spiritual insight during your practice. It can help to open the Crown and Third Eye Chakras, promoting deeper meditation and greater connection to higher consciousness.

Tiger's Eye: The Stone of Protection and Confidence

Description and Appearance Appearance: Tiger's Eye is a variety of quartz known for its distinct golden to reddish-brown colour and silky lustre. It exhibits a unique chatoyancy, or "cat's eye" effect, which gives it a shimmering, reflective quality. Tiger's Eye is typically found in tumbled stones, cabochons, beads, and carved shapes.

Varieties There are different types of Tiger's Eye, including:

- **Golden Tiger's Eye**: Exhibits golden yellow to brown stripes.

- **Red Tiger's Eye**: Achieved through gentle heating, it shows shades of red and brown.

- **Blue Tiger's Eye (Hawk's Eye)**: Displays shades of blue and grey with the same chatoyant effect.

Arcane Energetic Properties Protection and Grounding: Tiger's Eye is known for its protective qualities. It helps to ground and stabilise the user, offering protection from negative energies and promoting a sense of security.

Confidence and Courage: This stone enhances confidence, courage, and personal power. It helps to overcome fear and anxiety, encouraging decisive action and assertiveness.

Focus and Clarity: Tiger's Eye aids in improving focus, mental clarity, and decision-making. It helps to resolve inner conflicts and balance emotional extremes.

Uses and Applications Personal Protection: Carry Tiger's Eye or wear it as jewellery to benefit from its protective and grounding properties throughout the day. It is particularly useful in high-stress environments or when facing challenging situations.

Boosting Confidence: Use Tiger's Eye to enhance self-confidence and courage. Place it in areas where you need a boost in confidence, such as your workspace or personal study area.

Improving Focus: Incorporate Tiger's Eye into your daily routine to enhance focus and mental clarity. It can be used during study sessions or important decision-making processes.

Meditation: Use Tiger's Eye during meditation to enhance grounding, focus, and personal empowerment. Hold the stone or place it on the Solar Plexus Chakra to deepen your meditative state.

Chakra Alignment Solar Plexus Chakra: Tiger's Eye is strongly associated with the Solar Plexus Chakra, located in the upper abdomen. It enhances personal power, confidence, and vitality.

Root Chakra: Also associated with the Root Chakra, Tiger's Eye promotes grounding, stability, and security.

Historical and Cultural Significance Ancient Cultures: Tiger's Eye has been used for centuries for its protective and grounding properties. The ancient Egyptians believed it provided the wearer with the protection of the sun and earth combined. Roman soldiers carried Tiger's Eye to be brave in battle.

Modern Mysticism: Today, Tiger's Eye is widely used in contemporary crystal healing practices for its protective, grounding, and confidence-boosting properties. It is popular in holistic health and wellness communities for promoting balance and emotional stability.

Scientific Properties Chemical Composition: Tiger's Eye is a variety of quartz with the chemical formula SiO_2. The chatoyancy effect is caused by fibrous inclusions of crocidolite (blue asbestos) that have been replaced by silica.

Hardness: It has a Mohs hardness rating of 6.5-7, making it relatively durable and suitable for various uses.

Formation: Tiger's Eye forms in metamorphic rocks through the alteration of crocidolite fibres. The silica replacement process gives Tiger's Eye its distinctive golden to reddish-brown colour and chatoyancy.

Ritual Care and Cleansing Cleansing Methods: Tiger's Eye should be cleansed regularly to maintain its energetic purity. Effective methods include rinsing with water, smudging with sage or palo santo, and using sound vibrations. Tiger's Eye can also be cleansed using mild soap and water.

Recharging: To recharge Tiger's Eye, place it in sunlight or moonlight, or on a selenite charging plate. Avoid prolonged exposure to direct sunlight to prevent colour fading.

Mystical Practical Tips Daily Empowerment: Carry a small Tiger's Eye crystal in your pocket or wear it as jewellery to benefit from its protective and grounding properties throughout the day. It is particularly useful during stressful situations or when needing to enhance focus.

Sanctified Spaces: Place Tiger's Eye in strategic locations around your home or workspace to create a balanced and stable environment. Near communication areas, it can help to enhance clarity and understanding.

Meditation Space: Keep Tiger's Eye in your meditation space to enhance grounding and personal empowerment during your practice. It can help to open the Solar Plexus and Root Chakras, promoting deeper meditation and greater insight.

Turquoise: The Stone of Healing and Protection

Description and Appearance Appearance: Turquoise is a blue to green mineral that is prized for its distinct colour and unique patterns. It often exhibits a waxy to vitreous lustre and can be opaque or slightly translucent. The colour of turquoise ranges from sky blue to green, often with veins of other minerals such as limonite or pyrite, creating a spiderweb pattern. Turquoise is commonly found in cabochons, beads, and carved shapes.

Varieties The quality of turquoise can vary significantly based on colour, matrix patterns, and overall appearance. High-quality turquoise is usually more uniform in colour and has fewer matrix veins.

Arcane Energetic Properties Healing and Protection: Known as a master healing stone, turquoise provides a strong protective shield. It is believed to absorb negative energies and pollutants, promoting overall well-being.

Communication and Expression: This stone enhances communication, self-expression, and creativity. It helps to articulate thoughts and emotions clearly and effectively.

Calming and Balancing: Turquoise has calming and balancing properties, promoting inner peace and emotional stability. It helps to alleviate stress, anxiety, and mood swings.

Uses and Applications Healing and Protection: Carry turquoise or wear it as jewellery to benefit from its healing and protective properties throughout the day. It is particularly useful during times of stress or when facing negative environments.

Enhancing Communication: Use turquoise to improve communication and self-expression. Place it in areas where clear and effective communication is needed, such as workspaces or meeting rooms.

Promoting Calm: Incorporate turquoise into your daily routine to promote calm and balance. It can be used during meditation or relaxation practices to enhance inner peace.

Meditation: Use turquoise during meditation to enhance spiritual growth, communication, and emotional balance. Hold the stone or place it on the Throat Chakra to deepen your meditative state.

Chakra Alignment Throat Chakra: Turquoise is strongly associated with the Throat Chakra, located at the throat. It promotes clear communication, self-expression, and emotional release.

Heart Chakra: Also associated with the Heart Chakra, turquoise enhances love, compassion, and emotional balance.

Historical and Cultural Significance Ancient Cultures: Turquoise has been valued for thousands of years for its beauty and healing properties. Ancient Egyptians used turquoise in jewellery and amulets, believing it could protect against harm. Native American cultures consider turquoise sacred and use it in ceremonial rituals, jewellery, and tools. In ancient Persia, turquoise was worn to protect against the evil eye.

Modern Mysticism: Today, turquoise is widely used in contemporary crystal healing practices for its protective, healing, and calming properties. It is popular in holistic health and wellness communities for promoting balance and emotional well-being.

Scientific Properties Chemical Composition: Turquoise is a hydrated phosphate of copper and aluminium with the chemical formula $CuAl6(PO4)4(OH)8 \cdot 4H2O$. Its blue to green colour is due to the presence of copper.

Hardness: It has a Mohs hardness rating of 5-6, making it relatively soft and susceptible to scratches and damage if not handled carefully.

Formation: Turquoise forms in arid regions through the weathering and oxidation of copper-rich minerals. It is typically found in nodules, veins, and as crusts on the host rock.

Ritual Care and Cleansing Cleansing Methods: Turquoise should be cleansed regularly to maintain its energetic purity. Effective methods include smudging with sage or palo santo, using sound vibrations, and placing in moonlight. Avoid prolonged exposure to water, as it can damage the stone.

Recharging: To recharge turquoise, place it in moonlight or on a selenite charging plate. Avoid prolonged exposure to direct sunlight to prevent colour fading.

Mystical Practical Tips Daily Empowerment: Carry a small turquoise crystal in your pocket or wear it as jewellery to benefit from its healing and protective properties throughout the day. It is particularly useful during stressful situations or when clear communication is needed.

Sanctified Spaces: Place turquoise in strategic locations around your home or workspace to create a calming and balanced environment. Near communication areas, it can help to enhance clarity and understanding.

Meditation Space: Keep turquoise in your meditation space to enhance spiritual growth and emotional balance during your practice. It can help to open the Throat and Heart Chakras, promoting deeper meditation and greater insight.

CHAPTER TWELVE

Rare and Exotic Stones

Moldavite: The Stone of Transformation and Spiritual Awakening

Description and Appearance Appearance: Moldavite is a green, translucent stone with a unique, pitted surface that is often compared to melted glass. Its colour ranges from a deep forest green to a lighter, olive green, and it typically has a vitreous to resinous lustre. Moldavite is usually found in irregular shapes and forms, often as natural fragments, tumbled stones, or faceted gemstones.

Varieties There are no distinct varieties of moldavite, but its appearance can vary based on the region it was found in. The most prized moldavite is the clear, vibrant green variety with minimal inclusions.

Arcane Energetic Properties Spiritual Growth: Moldavite is renowned for its ability to accelerate spiritual growth and transformation. It is often used to expand consciousness and facilitate profound spiritual experiences.

Psychic Abilities: This stone enhances psychic abilities, intuition, and sensitivity to the spiritual realm. It helps to open and activate the Third Eye and Crown Chakras, promoting clairvoyance and other psychic skills.

Transformation: Moldavite is a powerful stone for transformation, aiding in the release of old patterns, beliefs, and behaviours that no longer serve one's highest good. It supports the process of personal and spiritual evolution.

Uses and Applications Meditation: Use moldavite during meditation to deepen spiritual awareness, enhance intuition, and facilitate transformative experiences. Hold the stone or place it on the Third Eye or Heart Chakra to intensify the meditative state.

Spiritual Awakening: Carry moldavite or wear it as jewellery to support ongoing spiritual growth and awakening. It is particularly useful during times of significant change or personal transformation.

Enhancing Intuition: Incorporate moldavite into practices that develop and enhance psychic abilities and intuition. It can be used in conjunction with other stones to amplify their energies and promote deeper insights.

Chakra Alignment Heart Chakra: Moldavite is associated with the Heart Chakra, located at the centre of the chest. It promotes emotional healing, compassion, and love, helping to open the heart to higher vibrations.

Third Eye Chakra: Also associated with the Third Eye Chakra, moldavite enhances intuition, psychic abilities, and spiritual insight. It aids in accessing higher realms of consciousness and spiritual wisdom.

Historical and Cultural Significance Extraterrestrial Origin: Moldavite is believed to have formed from a meteorite impact in southern Germany around 15 million years ago. This event created a unique form of natural glass, making moldavite one of the few gemstones with extraterrestrial origins. It has been highly valued for its transformative properties and mystical significance.

Modern Mysticism: Today, moldavite is widely used in contemporary crystal healing practices for its powerful spiritual and transformative properties. It is popular in holistic health and wellness communities for promoting spiritual growth, intuition, and personal transformation.

Scientific Properties Chemical Composition: Moldavite is a type of tektite, primarily composed of silicon dioxide (SiO_2) with traces of aluminium oxide (Al_2O_3) and other minerals. Its unique green colour is due to the presence of iron and other trace elements.

Hardness: It has a Mohs hardness rating of 5.5-7, making it relatively durable but susceptible to damage if not handled carefully.

Formation: Moldavite formed from the intense heat and pressure of a meteorite impact, which melted terrestrial rock and meteorite material, creating a unique form of natural glass.

Ritual Care and Cleansing Cleansing Methods: Moldavite should be cleansed regularly to maintain its energetic purity. Effective methods include rinsing with water, smudging with sage or palo santo, and using sound vibrations. Avoid using harsh chemicals or prolonged exposure to water, as it can damage the stone.

Recharging: To recharge moldavite, place it in moonlight or on a selenite charging plate. Avoid prolonged exposure to direct sunlight to prevent colour fading.

Mystical Practical Tips Daily Empowerment: Carry a small moldavite crystal in your pocket or wear it as jewellery to benefit from its transformative and spiritual properties throughout the day. It is particularly useful during times of significant change or when seeking spiritual connection.

Sanctified Spaces: Place moldavite in strategic locations around your home or workspace to create a spiritually uplifting and transformative environment. Near your meditation area, it can help to enhance spiritual practices and insights.

Meditation Space: Keep moldavite in your meditation space to enhance spiritual growth, intuition, and transformation during your practice. It can help to open the Heart and Third Eye Chakras, promoting deeper meditation and greater spiritual connection.

Larimar: The Stone of Serenity and Communication

Description and Appearance Appearance: Larimar is a rare blue variety of the mineral pectolite, characterised by its light blue to blue-green colour, often with white patterns that resemble ocean waves or sky reflections. It is typically opaque to translucent with a silky to vitreous lustre. Larimar is most commonly found in cabochons, beads, and polished stones.

Varieties Larimar's colour intensity can range from pale blue to deep blue. The most sought-after pieces have a vibrant blue colour with minimal white veining and a high degree of translucence.

Arcane Energetic Properties Calm and Relaxation: Larimar is known for its calming and soothing energy. It helps to reduce stress, anxiety, and emotional turmoil, promoting a sense of tranquillity and relaxation.

Emotional Healing: This stone supports emotional balance and healing. It helps to release pent-up emotions, alleviate fears, and promote self-nurturing and inner peace.

Enhancing Communication: Larimar enhances communication and self-expression, particularly in expressing emotions and thoughts. It encourages clear and compassionate communication, making it an excellent stone for those who struggle with articulating their feelings.

Uses and Applications Stress Relief: Carry larimar or wear it as jewellery to benefit from its calming and stress-relieving properties throughout the day. It is particularly useful during times of high stress or emotional upheaval.

Emotional Balance: Use larimar in energy healing sessions to support emotional balance and healing. Place it on the Heart or Throat Chakras during healing sessions to promote emotional well-being and clear communication.

Enhancing Communication: Incorporate larimar into practices that require clear and compassionate communication. Place it in areas where open and honest communication is needed, such as workspaces or meeting rooms.

Meditation: Use larimar during meditation to enhance relaxation, emotional healing, and spiritual growth. Hold the stone or place it on the Throat Chakra to deepen your meditative state.

Chakra Association Throat Chakra: Larimar is strongly associated with the Throat Chakra, located at the throat. It promotes clear communication, self-expression, and emotional release.

Heart Chakra: Also associated with the Heart Chakra, larimar enhances love, compassion, and emotional balance.

Historical and Cultural Significance Discovery and Mythology: Larimar was discovered in the Dominican Republic in the 1970s. It is often associated with the mythical Atlantis, leading to its nickname "The Atlantis Stone." Local legends suggest that the stone has spiritual connections to the lost civilization of Atlantis and holds significant metaphysical properties.

Modern Mysticism: Today, larimar is widely used in contemporary crystal healing practices for its calming, emotional, and communicative properties. It is popular in holistic health and wellness communities for promoting relaxation, emotional balance, and clear communication.

Scientific Properties Chemical Composition: Larimar is a variety of pectolite, composed of sodium calcium silicate hydroxide with the chemical formula $NaCa_2Si_3O_8(OH)$. Its blue colour is due to the presence of copper.

Hardness: It has a Mohs hardness rating of 4.5-5, making it relatively soft and susceptible to scratches and damage if not handled carefully.

Formation: Larimar forms in cavities within basaltic lava flows through hydrothermal activity. It is typically found in volcanic regions, particularly in the Dominican Republic.

Ritual Care and Cleansing Cleansing Methods: Larimar should be cleansed regularly to maintain its energetic purity. Effective methods include smudging with sage or palo santo, using sound vibrations, and placing in moonlight. Avoid using water or saltwater, as it can damage the stone.

Recharging: To recharge larimar, place it in moonlight or on a selenite charging plate. Avoid prolonged exposure to direct sunlight to prevent colour fading.

Mystical Practical Tips Daily Empowerment: Carry a small larimar crystal in your pocket or wear it as jewellery to benefit from its calming and communicative properties throughout the day. It is particularly useful during stressful situations or when clear communication is needed.

Sanctified Spaces: Place larimar in strategic locations around your home or workspace to create a calming and balanced environment. Near communication areas, it can help to enhance clarity and understanding.

Meditative Practices: Keep larimar in your meditation space to enhance relaxation, emotional healing, and spiritual growth during your practice. It can help to open the Throat and Heart Chakras, promoting deeper meditation and greater insight.

Tanzanite: The Stone of Transformation and Spiritual Insight

Description and Appearance Appearance: Tanzanite is a variety of the mineral zoisite and is known for its stunning blue to violet colour, which can vary depending on the angle of the light and the presence of trace elements. Tanzanite has a vitreous lustre and is typically transparent. It is often found in faceted gemstones, tumbled stones, and beads.

Varieties Tanzanite can range in colour from a deep, rich blue to a lighter blue with violet hues. High-quality tanzanite displays a vivid blue or violet colour with high transparency and minimal inclusions.

Arcane Energetic Properties Communication: Tanzanite enhances communication and self-expression, particularly in spiritual and intuitive contexts. It helps to articulate thoughts and emotions clearly and effectively.

Spiritual Awareness: This stone promotes spiritual growth, awareness, and insight. It aids in connecting with higher consciousness and facilitates deeper meditation and spiritual practices.

Transformation: Tanzanite is known for its transformative properties, aiding in personal and spiritual evolution. It helps to release old patterns and beliefs that no longer serve one's highest good, encouraging growth and positive change.

Uses and Applications Enhancing Communication: Use tanzanite to improve communication and self-expression. Place it in areas where clear and effective communication is needed, such as workspaces or meeting rooms.

Spiritual Growth: Carry tanzanite or wear it as jewellery to support ongoing spiritual growth and awareness. It is particularly useful during meditation and other spiritual practices.

Meditation: Use tanzanite during meditation to enhance spiritual awareness, communication, and transformation. Hold the stone or place it on the Third Eye or Throat Chakra to deepen your meditative state.

Chakra Association Third Eye Chakra: Tanzanite is strongly associated with the Third Eye Chakra, located between the eyebrows. It enhances intuition, psychic abilities, and spiritual insight.

Throat Chakra: Also associated with the Throat Chakra, tanzanite promotes clear communication, self-expression, and emotional release.

Historical and Cultural Significance Discovery and Rarity: Tanzanite was discovered in the Mererani Hills of Northern Tanzania in the 1960s and is named after the country of its origin. It is a relatively new gemstone in the world of crystal healing but has quickly gained popularity due to its stunning colour and powerful energetic properties.

Modern Uses: Today, tanzanite is widely used in contemporary crystal healing practices for its transformative, spiritual, and communicative properties. It is popular in holistic health and wellness communities for promoting spiritual growth, intuition, and personal transformation.

Scientific Properties Chemical Composition: Tanzanite is a blue to violet variety of zoisite, with the chemical formula $Ca_2Al_3(SiO_4)_3(OH)$. Its colour is due to trace amounts of vanadium.

Hardness: It has a Mohs hardness rating of 6-7, making it relatively durable but susceptible to scratches and damage if not handled carefully.

Formation: Tanzanite forms in metamorphic rocks through the heat and pressure associated with tectonic processes. It is typically found in Tanzania and is considered one of the rarest gemstones in the world.

Ritual Care and Cleansing Cleansing Methods: Tanzanite should be cleansed regularly to maintain its energetic purity. Effective methods include smudging with sage or palo santo, using sound vibrations, and placing in moonlight. Avoid using harsh chemicals or prolonged exposure to water, as it can damage the stone.

Recharging: To recharge tanzanite, place it in moonlight or on a selenite charging plate. Avoid prolonged exposure to direct sunlight to prevent colour fading.

Mystical Practical Tips Daily Use: Carry a small tanzanite crystal in your pocket or wear it as jewellery to benefit from its communicative and spiritual properties throughout the day. It is particularly useful during stressful situations or when seeking spiritual connection.

Sanctified Spaces: Place tanzanite in strategic locations around your home or workspace to create a calming and spiritually uplifting environment. Near your meditation area, it can help to enhance spiritual practices and insights.

Meditative Practices: Keep tanzanite in your meditation space to enhance spiritual growth, communication, and transformation during your practice. It can help to open the Third Eye and Throat Chakras, promoting deeper meditation and greater spiritual connection.

Sugilite: The Stone of Spiritual Awakening and Emotional Healing

Description and Appearance Appearance: Sugilite is a rare mineral that ranges in colour from light pink to deep purple. It can be opaque to translucent, often exhibiting a waxy to vitreous lustre. Sugilite is typically found in massive form, but can also occur as tiny prismatic crystals. It is often seen in cabochons, tumbled stones, beads, and carved shapes.

Varieties: The colour intensity of sugilite can vary, with deep, rich purple being the most prized. Some sugilite may have black or white veining due to the presence of other minerals.

Energetic Properties

- **Spiritual Growth**: Sugilite is known for its strong spiritual properties.

It promotes spiritual growth, awakening, and a deeper connection to higher consciousness.

- **Emotional Healing**: This stone supports emotional healing and balance. It helps to alleviate feelings of grief, fear, and despair, promoting a sense of peace and well-being.

- **Protection**: Sugilite provides powerful protection against negative energies and psychic attacks. It helps to cleanse and shield the aura, creating a protective barrier around the user.

Uses and Applications

- **Spiritual Practices**: Use sugilite to enhance meditation, spiritual growth, and psychic abilities. Place it in your meditation space or hold it during meditation to deepen your spiritual practice.

- **Emotional Healing**: Carry sugilite or wear it as jewellery to benefit from its emotional healing properties throughout the day. It is particularly useful during times of emotional stress or when seeking inner peace.

- **Protection**: Use sugilite for protection against negative energies and psychic attacks. Place it in your home or workspace to create a protective shield.

Chakra Association

- **Third Eye Chakra**: Sugilite is strongly associated with the Third Eye Chakra, located between the eyebrows. It enhances intuition, psychic abilities, and spiritual insight.

- **Crown Chakra**: Also associated with the Crown Chakra, sugilite promotes spiritual awakening, enlightenment, and a deep connection to higher realms.

Historical and Cultural Significance

- **Discovery and Origins**: Sugilite was first discovered in Japan in 1944 by Ken-ichi Sugi, after whom it is named. Significant deposits were later found in South Africa. Sugilite has gained popularity in the crystal healing community for its deep spiritual and healing properties.

- **Modern Uses**: Today, sugilite is widely used in contemporary crystal healing practices for its spiritual, protective, and healing properties. It is popular in holistic health and wellness communities for promoting spiritual growth, emotional balance, and protection from negativity.

Scientific Properties

- **Chemical Composition**: Sugilite is a potassium sodium lithium iron manganese aluminium silicate with the chemical formula $KNa_2(Fe,Mn,Al)_2Li_3Si_{12}O_{30}$.

- **Hardness**: It has a Mohs hardness rating of 5.5-6.5, making it relatively durable but susceptible to scratches and damage if not handled carefully.

- **Formation**: Sugilite forms in manganese-rich metamorphic rocks, typically in association with other manganese minerals. It is primarily found in Japan and South Africa.

Care and Cleansing

- **Cleansing Methods**: Sugilite should be cleansed regularly to maintain its energetic purity. Effective methods include smudging with sage or palo santo, using sound vibrations, and placing in moonlight. Avoid using harsh chemicals or prolonged exposure to water, as it can damage the stone.

- **Recharging**: To recharge sugilite, place it in moonlight or on a selenite charging plate. Avoid prolonged exposure to direct sunlight to prevent colour fading.

Practical Tips

- **Daily Use**: Carry a small sugilite crystal in your pocket or wear it as jewellery to benefit from its spiritual and protective properties throughout the day. It is particularly useful during stressful situations or when seeking spiritual connection.

- **Home and Workspace**: Place sugilite in strategic locations around your home or workspace to create a spiritually uplifting and protective environment. Near your meditation area, it can help to enhance spiritual practices and insights.

- **Meditation Space**: Keep sugilite in your meditation space to enhance spiritual growth, emotional healing, and protection during your practice. It can help to open the Third Eye and Crown Chakras, promoting deeper meditation and greater spiritual connection.

Phenacite: The Stone of Spiritual Awakening and Clarity

Description and Appearance Appearance: Phenacite is a rare beryllium silicate mineral that can be colourless, white, yellow, or occasionally pink. It is known for its high transparency and brilliant sparkle, often resembling quartz or diamond. Phenacite typically forms in prismatic, tabular, or rhombohedral crystals and is often found as faceted gemstones or small raw crystals.

Varieties: Phenacite's appearance can vary depending on the location and specific conditions under which it formed. Clear, high-quality phenacite is the most prized, especially when cut into gemstones.

Energetic Properties

- **Spiritual Awakening:** Phenacite is known for its ability to accelerate spiritual awakening and development. It enhances one's connection to higher consciousness and promotes profound spiritual insights.

- **Clarity and Focus**: This stone helps to clear mental fog and enhance focus, making it easier to achieve clarity in thoughts and actions. It supports clear decision-making and intellectual pursuits.

- **Healing and Protection**: Phenacite is believed to have strong healing properties, aiding in physical, emotional, and spiritual healing. It also provides a protective shield against negative energies.

Uses and Applications

- **Meditation**: Use phenacite during meditation to enhance spiritual awakening and connection to higher consciousness. Hold the stone or place it on the Crown Chakra to deepen your meditative state.

- **Enhancing Clarity**: Carry phenacite or place it in areas where mental clarity and focus are needed, such as study spaces or work areas. It can help to clear the mind and promote productive thinking.

- **Healing Practices**: Incorporate phenacite into healing sessions to support physical, emotional, and spiritual healing. Place it on any chakra to balance and align the energy centres.

Chakra Association

- **Crown Chakra**: Phenacite is strongly associated with the Crown Chakra, located at the top of the head. It promotes spiritual awakening, enlightenment, and a deep connection to higher realms.

- **Third Eye Chakra**: Also associated with the Third Eye Chakra, phenacite enhances intuition, psychic abilities, and spiritual insight.

Historical and Cultural Significance

- **Modern Discovery**: Phenacite was first discovered in the Ural Mountains of Russia in the 19th century. It has since been found in other locations, including Brazil, Madagascar, and the United States. Despite being a relatively modern discovery, it has quickly gained a reputation for its powerful energetic properties.

- **Modern Uses**: Today, phenacite is widely used in contemporary crystal healing practices for its spiritual, healing, and clarity-enhancing properties. It is popular in holistic health and wellness communities for promoting spiritual growth, mental clarity, and protection.

Scientific Properties

- **Chemical Composition**: Phenacite is a beryllium silicate with the chemical formula Be_2SiO_4. Its high refractive index gives it a brilliant sparkle, similar to that of a diamond.

- **Hardness**: It has a Mohs hardness rating of 7.5-8, making it relatively durable and suitable for various uses.

- **Formation**: Phenacite forms in pegmatites and hydrothermal veins through the cooling and crystallisation of silica-rich solutions. It is often found in association with other minerals such as quartz, beryl, and topaz.

Care and Cleansing

- **Cleansing Methods**: Phenacite should be cleansed regularly to maintain its energetic purity. Effective methods include rinsing with water, smudging with sage or palo santo, and using sound vibrations. Avoid using harsh chemicals or prolonged exposure to water, as it can damage the stone.

- **Recharging**: To recharge phenacite, place it in moonlight or on a selenite charging plate. Avoid prolonged exposure to direct sunlight to prevent colour fading.

Practical Tips

- **Daily Use**: Carry a small phenacite crystal in your pocket or wear it as jewellery to benefit from its clarity and spiritual properties throughout the day. It is particularly useful during periods of study or when seeking spiritual connection.

- **Home and Workspace**: Place phenacite in strategic locations around your home or workspace to create a mentally stimulating and spiritually uplifting environment. Near your meditation area, it can help to enhance spiritual practices and insights.

- **Meditation Space**: Keep phenacite in your meditation space to enhance spiritual growth, clarity, and healing during your practice. It can help to open the Crown and Third Eye Chakras, promoting deeper meditation and greater spiritual connection.

Danburite: The Stone of Spiritual Enlightenment and Clarity

Description and Appearance Appearance: Danburite is a transparent to translucent mineral, often colourless or light yellow, but it can also be found in shades of pink, brown, and grey. It has a vitreous lustre and is typically found in prismatic, striated crystals that can be quite large. Danburite is often cut into faceted gemstones or polished into cabochons and tumbled stones.

Varieties: The most common variety of danburite is colourless, but the pink variety, often referred to as "pink danburite," is particularly prized for its gentle energy and aesthetic appeal.

Energetic Properties

- **Spiritual Enlightenment**: Danburite is known for its ability to connect with higher realms and facilitate spiritual enlightenment. It aids in accessing higher states of consciousness and spiritual insight.

- **Emotional Healing**: This stone supports emotional healing and balance. It helps to release stress, anxiety, and past traumas, promoting a sense of peace and well-being.

- **Clarity and Purity**: Danburite promotes mental clarity and purity. It helps to clear mental fog and enhance focus, making it easier to achieve clarity in thoughts and actions.

Uses and Applications

- **Meditation**: Use danburite during meditation to enhance spiritual enlightenment and connection to higher realms. Hold the stone or place it on the Crown Chakra to deepen your meditative state.

- **Emotional Healing**: Carry danburite or wear it as jewellery to benefit from its emotional healing properties throughout the day. It is particularly useful during times of stress or emotional turmoil.

- **Enhancing Clarity**: Use danburite to improve mental clarity and focus. Place it in areas where clear thinking and decision-making are needed, such as workspaces or study areas.

Chakra Association

- **Crown Chakra**: Danburite is strongly associated with the Crown Chakra, located at the top of the head. It promotes spiritual enlightenment, higher consciousness, and a deep connection to the divine.

- **Heart Chakra**: Also associated with the Heart Chakra, danburite enhances emotional healing, love, and compassion.

Historical and Cultural Significance

- **Discovery and Origins**: Danburite was first discovered in Danbury, Connecticut, in the 19th century, from which it derives its name. Despite being a relatively modern discovery, it has gained popularity for its powerful energetic properties and beautiful appearance.

- **Modern Uses**: Today, danburite is widely used in contemporary crystal healing practices for its spiritual, emotional, and clarity-enhancing properties. It is popular in holistic health and wellness communities for promoting spiritual growth, emotional balance, and mental clarity.

Scientific Properties

- **Chemical Composition**: Danburite is a calcium boron silicate with the chemical formula $CaB_2(SiO_4)_2$. Its crystal structure is orthorhombic, which gives it its characteristic prismatic form.

- **Hardness**: It has a Mohs hardness rating of 7-7.5, making it relatively durable and suitable for various uses.

- **Formation**: Danburite forms in metamorphic and hydrothermal environments, often found in association with other minerals such as quartz, calcite, and tourmaline. It is primarily found in Mexico, Japan, and the United States.

Care and Cleansing

- **Cleansing Methods**: Danburite should be cleansed regularly to maintain its energetic purity. Effective methods include rinsing with water, smudging with sage or palo santo, and using sound vibrations. Avoid using harsh chemicals or prolonged exposure to water, as it can damage the stone.

- **Recharging**: To recharge danburite, place it in moonlight or on a selenite charging plate. Avoid prolonged exposure to direct sunlight to prevent colour fading.

Practical Tips

- **Daily Use**: Carry a small danburite crystal in your pocket or wear it as jewellery to benefit from its clarity and spiritual properties throughout the day. It is particularly useful during periods of stress or when seeking spiritual connection.

- **Home and Workspace**: Place danburite in strategic locations around your home or workspace to create a mentally stimulating and spiritually uplifting environment. Near your meditation area, it can help to enhance spiritual practices and insights.

- **Meditation Space**: Keep danburite in your meditation space to enhance spiritual growth, emotional healing, and clarity during your practice. It can help to open the Crown and Heart Chakras, promoting deeper meditation and greater spiritual connection.

Kyanite: The Stone of Alignment and Communication

Description and Appearance Appearance: Kyanite is a unique gemstone that can be blue, black, green, or orange. The most common variety is blue, which ranges from pale to deep blue and often has white streaks running through it. Kyanite has a vitreous to pearly lustre and is typically found in long, bladed crystals or as tumbled stones. Its transparency ranges from transparent to translucent.

Varieties:

- **Blue Kyanite:** Known for its blue colour and common associations with the Throat Chakra.

- **Black Kyanite:** Exhibits a fan-like formation and is known for grounding and protective properties.

- **Green Kyanite:** Found in shades of green and associated with the Heart Chakra.

- **Orange Kyanite:** Less common and known for its associations with the Sacral Chakra.

Energetic Properties:

- **Alignment and Balance:** Kyanite is known for its ability to align and balance all the chakras without the need for conscious direction. It creates energetic pathways and restores balance to the physical and energetic bodies.

- **Communication:** This stone enhances communication and self-expression. It helps to articulate thoughts and feelings clearly, making it an excellent stone for public speakers and writers.

- **Protection:** Kyanite provides protective energy, particularly against negative influences. It helps to shield the aura and maintain a protective barrier.

Uses and Applications:

- **Chakra Alignment:** Use kyanite to align and balance the chakras. Place it on the body or hold it during meditation to facilitate energetic balance and harmony.

- **Enhancing Communication:** Carry kyanite or wear it as jewellery to benefit from its communication-enhancing properties. It is particularly useful for those who need to express themselves clearly and confidently.

- **Protection:** Use kyanite for protection against negative energies. Place it in your home or workspace to create a protective environment.

Chakra Association:

- **Throat Chakra:** Blue kyanite is strongly associated with the Throat Chakra, located at the throat. It promotes clear communication, self-expression, and truth.

- **Third Eye Chakra:** Kyanite also enhances intuition and psychic abilities, aligning with the Third Eye Chakra.

- **Other Chakras:** Different colours of kyanite can be associated with various chakras. For example, green kyanite aligns with the Heart Chakra, while black kyanite is associated with grounding and the Root Chakra.

Historical and Cultural Significance:

- **Modern Uses**: Kyanite has been valued for its unique properties and beautiful appearance. It is popular in contemporary crystal healing practices for its balancing, communication-enhancing, and protective properties. Kyanite is widely used in holistic health and wellness communities for promoting energetic balance and clear communication.

Scientific Properties:

- **Chemical Composition**: Kyanite is an aluminium silicate mineral with the chemical formula Al_2SiO_5. Its distinctive bladed crystals and colour variations are due to the presence of trace elements and the conditions under which it formed.

- **Hardness**: Kyanite has a variable Mohs hardness rating of 4.5-5 along the length of the crystal and 6.5-7 across the width, making it relatively brittle and requiring careful handling.

- **Formation**: Kyanite forms in metamorphic rocks under high-pressure conditions, typically in association with other aluminium-rich minerals such as quartz, garnet, and staurolite.

Care and Cleansing:

- **Cleansing Methods**: Kyanite should be cleansed regularly to maintain its energetic purity. Effective methods include smudging with sage or palo santo, using sound vibrations, and placing in moonlight. Avoid using water, as kyanite can be brittle and may fracture if exposed to moisture.

- **Recharging**: To recharge kyanite, place it in moonlight or on a selenite charging plate. Avoid prolonged exposure to direct sunlight to prevent colour fading.

Practical Tips:

- **Daily Use**: Carry a small kyanite crystal in your pocket or wear it as jewellery to benefit from its alignment and communication properties throughout the day. It is particularly useful during periods of stress or when clear communication is needed.

- **Home and Workspace**: Place kyanite in strategic locations around your home or workspace to create a balanced and protective environment. Near your meditation area, it can help to enhance spiritual practices and insights.

- **Meditation Space**: Keep kyanite in your meditation space to enhance chakra alignment, communication, and protection during your practice. It can help to open the Throat and Third Eye Chakras, promoting deeper meditation and greater spiritual connection.

Alexandrite: The Stone of Transformation and Intuition

Description and Appearance Appearance: Alexandrite is a rare and highly valued variety of chrysoberyl known for its remarkable colour-changing properties. Under natural daylight, alexandrite appears green to bluish-green, but under incandescent light, it shifts to red, purplish-red, or pink. This colour change is due to the stone's unique ability to absorb light differently depending on the light source. Alexandrite has a vitreous lustre and is typically transparent, often found in faceted gemstones.

Varieties: Alexandrite's colour change can vary in intensity, with the most prized specimens showing a dramatic and vivid shift from green to red. The quality of the colour change and the clarity of the stone significantly affect its value.

Energetic Properties Transformation and Change: Alexandrite is known for its ability to help with transformation and adaptability. It supports navigating change with grace and resilience, making it an excellent stone for periods of significant transition.

Joy and Compassion: This stone promotes feelings of joy, love, and compassion. It helps to open the heart to receive and give love, fostering emotional healing and connection.

Intuition and Psychic Abilities: Alexandrite enhances intuition and psychic abilities, aiding in spiritual growth and the development of inner wisdom.

Uses and Applications Emotional Healing: Carry alexandrite or wear it as jewellery to benefit from its transformative and emotionally healing properties throughout the day. It is particularly useful during times of emotional stress or change.

Enhancing Intuition: Use alexandrite to enhance intuition and psychic abilities. Place it in areas where you practise meditation or spiritual work to deepen your connection to higher consciousness.

Personal Transformation: Incorporate alexandrite into your daily routine to support personal transformation and adaptability. It can be used in energy healing sessions or placed on the body during meditation.

Chakra Association Heart Chakra: Alexandrite is strongly associated with the Heart Chakra, promoting love, compassion, and emotional balance.

Third Eye Chakra: Also associated with the Third Eye Chakra, alexandrite enhances intuition, psychic abilities, and spiritual insight.

Historical and Cultural Significance Discovery and Origins: Alexandrite was first discovered in the Ural Mountains of Russia in the 1830s and was named in honour of the Russian tsar Alexander II. Its unique colour-changing property and rarity made it a highly prized gemstone among the Russian aristocracy.

Modern Uses: Today, alexandrite is widely used in contemporary crystal healing practices for its transformative, intuitive, and emotionally healing properties. It is popular in holistic health and wellness communities for promoting adaptability, emotional balance, and spiritual growth.

Scientific Properties Chemical Composition: Alexandrite is a variety of chrysoberyl with the chemical formula $BeAl_2O_4$. Its colour-changing property is due to the presence of chromium.

Hardness: It has a Mohs hardness rating of 8.5, making it one of the harder gemstones and suitable for various uses.

Formation: Alexandrite forms in pegmatites and mica schists, typically in association with other minerals such as quartz, feldspar, and mica. It is found in Russia, Sri Lanka, Brazil, and East Africa.

Care and Cleansing Cleansing Methods: Alexandrite should be cleansed regularly to maintain its energetic purity. Effective methods include rinsing with water, smudging with sage or palo santo, and using sound vibrations. Avoid using harsh chemicals or prolonged exposure to water, as it can damage the stone.

Recharging: To recharge alexandrite, place it in moonlight or on a selenite charging plate. Avoid prolonged exposure to direct sunlight to prevent colour fading.

Practical Tips Daily Use: Carry a small alexandrite crystal in your pocket or wear it as jewellery to benefit from its transformative and intuitive properties throughout the day. It is particularly useful during stressful situations or when seeking spiritual connection.

Home and Workspace: Place alexandrite in strategic locations around your home or workspace to create a balanced and emotionally uplifting environment. Near your meditation area, it can help to enhance spiritual practices and insights.

Meditation Space: Keep alexandrite in your meditation space to enhance personal transformation, emotional healing, and intuition during your practice. It can help to open the Heart and Third Eye Chakras, promoting deeper meditation and greater spiritual connection.

Charoite: The Stone of Transformation and Spiritual Growth

Description and Appearance Appearance: Charoite is a rare, strikingly beautiful mineral that ranges in colour from lavender to deep violet with swirling patterns of white, black, and purple. It has a pearly to vitreous lustre and is typically opaque to translucent. Charoite often exhibits a unique fibrous or silky texture and is found in cabochons, tumbled stones, and carved shapes.

Varieties: The quality of charoite can vary based on colour intensity, pattern, and overall appearance. High-quality charoite displays vibrant purple hues with intricate swirling patterns.

Energetic Properties Transformation and Change: Charoite is known for its ability to facilitate transformation and change. It supports personal growth and helps to overcome fear and resistance to change.

Healing and Protection: This stone promotes emotional and physical healing. It helps to release negative emotions and provides protection against negative energies.

Spiritual Growth: Charoite enhances spiritual awareness and connection. It aids in accessing higher realms of consciousness and facilitates deep meditation and spiritual practices.

Uses and Applications Emotional Healing: Carry charoite or wear it as jewellery to benefit from its transformative and healing properties throughout the day. It is particularly useful during times of emotional stress or change.

Enhancing Spirituality: Use charoite to enhance spiritual growth and awareness. Place it in areas where you practise meditation or spiritual work to deepen your connection to higher consciousness.

Personal Transformation: Incorporate charoite into your daily routine to support personal transformation and adaptability. It can be used in energy healing sessions or placed on the body during meditation.

Chakra Association Third Eye Chakra: Charoite is strongly associated with the Third Eye Chakra, located between the eyebrows. It enhances intuition, psychic abilities, and spiritual insight.

Crown Chakra: Also associated with the Crown Chakra, charoite promotes spiritual awakening, enlightenment, and a deep connection to higher realms.

Historical and Cultural Significance Discovery and Origins: Charoite was discovered in the Chara River area of Siberia, Russia, in the 1940s and was named after the river. It has gained popularity for its unique appearance and powerful energetic properties.

Modern Uses: Today, charoite is widely used in contemporary crystal healing practices for its transformative, healing, and spiritual properties. It is popular in holistic health and wellness communities for promoting emotional balance, spiritual growth, and protection.

Scientific Properties Chemical Composition: Charoite is a complex silicate mineral with the chemical formula $(K,Na)_5Ca_8Si_{18}O_{46}(OH) \cdot 3(H_2O)$. Its distinctive colour and patterns are due to the presence of various trace elements.

Hardness: It has a Mohs hardness rating of 5-6, making it relatively durable but susceptible to scratches and damage if not handled carefully.

Formation: Charoite forms in hydrothermal environments through the alteration of limestone deposits. It is primarily found in the Chara River area of Siberia, Russia.

Care and Cleansing Cleansing Methods: Charoite should be cleansed regularly to maintain its energetic purity. Effective methods include rinsing with water, smudging with sage or palo santo, and using sound vibrations. Avoid using harsh chemicals or prolonged exposure to water, as it can damage the stone.

Recharging: To recharge charoite, place it in moonlight or on a selenite charging plate. Avoid prolonged exposure to direct sunlight to prevent colour fading.

Practical Tips Daily Use: Carry a small charoite crystal in your pocket or wear it as jewellery to benefit from its transformative and spiritual properties throughout the day. It is particularly useful during periods of stress or when seeking spiritual connection.

Home and Workspace: Place charoite in strategic locations around your home or workspace to create a balanced and spiritually uplifting environment. Near your meditation area, it can help to enhance spiritual practices and insights.

Meditation Space: Keep charoite in your meditation space to enhance personal transformation, emotional healing, and spiritual growth during your practice. It can help to open the Third Eye and Crown Chakras, promoting deeper meditation and greater spiritual connection.

Seraphinite: The Angelic Stone of Healing and Enlightenment

Description and Appearance Appearance: Seraphinite is a striking green stone with silvery-white feathery patterns that resemble angel wings. It has a silky, chatoyant lustre and is typically opaque. The green colour of seraphinite ranges from dark to light green, often with shimmering patterns that create a beautiful, angelic appearance. Seraphinite is commonly found in cabochons, tumbled stones, and beads.

Varieties: Seraphinite does not have distinct varieties, but the quality and intensity of its feathery patterns and green colour can vary.

Energetic Properties Spiritual Enlightenment: Seraphinite is known for its strong connection to the angelic realm and higher consciousness. It promotes spiritual enlightenment and helps to access higher states of consciousness.

Healing and Regeneration: This stone supports physical and emotional healing, promoting regeneration and self-healing. It helps to cleanse and purify the body, mind, and spirit.

Heart Activation: Seraphinite opens and activates the Heart Chakra, fostering love, compassion, and emotional healing. It helps to release old emotional wounds and promotes inner peace.

Uses and Applications Spiritual Practices: Use seraphinite during meditation to enhance spiritual enlightenment and connection to the angelic realm. Hold the stone or place it on the Heart or Crown Chakra to deepen your meditative state.

Healing Sessions: Carry seraphinite or wear it as jewellery to benefit from its healing and regenerative properties throughout the day. It is particularly useful during times of physical or emotional healing.

Emotional Balance: Incorporate seraphinite into your daily routine to support emotional balance and heart activation. It can be used in energy healing sessions or placed on the body during meditation.

Chakra Association Heart Chakra: Seraphinite is strongly associated with the Heart Chakra, promoting love, compassion, and emotional healing. It helps to open the heart to higher vibrations and deeper emotional connections.

Crown Chakra: Also associated with the Crown Chakra, seraphinite enhances spiritual enlightenment, higher consciousness, and connection to the angelic realm.

Historical and Cultural Significance Modern Discovery: Seraphinite was discovered in the Lake Baikal region of Siberia, Russia. It is named after the seraphim, the highest order of angels, due to its feathery patterns that resemble angel wings. Despite being a relatively modern discovery, it has quickly gained popularity for its spiritual and healing properties.

Modern Uses: Today, seraphinite is widely used in contemporary crystal healing practices for its spiritual, healing, and heart-activating properties. It is popular in holistic health and wellness communities for promoting spiritual growth, emotional healing, and connection to the angelic realm.

Scientific Properties Chemical Composition: Seraphinite is a variety of clinochlore, a chlorite mineral with the chemical formula $(Mg,Fe)_5Al(Si_3Al)O_{10}(OH)_8$. Its distinctive green colour and feathery patterns are due to the presence of chlorite minerals.

Hardness: It has a Mohs hardness rating of 2-4, making it relatively soft and susceptible to scratches and damage if not handled carefully.

Formation: Seraphinite forms in metamorphic rocks through the alteration of magnesium-rich minerals. It is primarily found in the Lake Baikal region of Siberia, Russia.

Care and Cleansing Cleansing Methods: Seraphinite should be cleansed regularly to maintain its energetic purity. Effective methods include smudging with sage or palo santo, using sound vibrations, and placing in moonlight. Avoid using water, as seraphinite is relatively soft and can be damaged by moisture.

Recharging: To recharge seraphinite, place it in moonlight or on a selenite charging plate. Avoid prolonged exposure to direct sunlight to prevent colour fading.

Practical Tips Daily Use: Carry a small seraphinite crystal in your pocket or wear it as jewellery to benefit from its spiritual and healing properties throughout the day. It is particularly useful during periods of stress or when seeking spiritual connection.

Home and Workspace: Place seraphinite in strategic locations around your home or workspace to create a balanced and spiritually uplifting environment. Near your meditation area, it can help to enhance spiritual practices and insights.

Meditation Space: Keep seraphinite in your meditation space to enhance personal transformation, emotional healing, and spiritual growth during your practice. It can help to open the Heart and Crown Chakras, promoting deeper meditation and greater spiritual connection.

Bloodstone: The Stone of Vitality and Protection

Description and Appearance Appearance: Bloodstone, also known as heliotrope, is a dark green variety of chalcedony with distinctive red or brownish spots, resembling drops of blood, hence its name. The red inclusions are due to the presence of iron oxide. Bloodstone has a vitreous to waxy lustre and is typically opaque. It is often found in cabochons, tumbled stones, and beads.

Varieties: Bloodstone can vary in the intensity of its green colour and the amount of red spots. The most prized bloodstones have a deep green colour with vibrant red inclusions.

Energetic Properties Healing and Purification: Bloodstone is known for its powerful healing and purifying properties. It supports overall health and well-being, helps detoxify the body, and promotes vitality and strength.

Courage and Strength: This stone enhances courage, strength, and resilience. It helps to overcome challenges and supports perseverance and determination.

Protection and Grounding: Bloodstone provides strong protective and grounding energies. It shields against negative influences and helps to ground and stabilise the user's energy.

Uses and Applications Healing Practices: Use bloodstone in energy healing sessions to support physical and emotional healing. Place it on the body or hold it during healing practices to enhance vitality and well-being.

Enhancing Courage: Carry bloodstone or wear it as jewellery to benefit from its courage-boosting and strength-enhancing properties throughout the day. It is particularly useful during challenging situations or when facing difficult decisions.

Protection and Grounding: Place bloodstone in your home or workspace to create a protective and grounding environment. It can help to shield against negative energies and promote stability and balance.

Chakra Association Root Chakra: Bloodstone is strongly associated with the Root Chakra, located at the base of the spine. It promotes grounding, stability, and physical vitality.

Heart Chakra: Also associated with the Heart Chakra, bloodstone supports emotional healing, love, and compassion.

Historical and Cultural Significance Ancient Cultures: Bloodstone has been valued for thousands of years for its healing and protective properties. In ancient Greece and Rome, it was believed to have the ability to stop bleeding and was used by warriors for protection in battle. In the Middle Ages, bloodstone was believed to have mystical powers and was often used in amulets and talismans.

Modern Uses: Today, bloodstone is widely used in contemporary crystal healing practices for its healing, protective, and grounding properties. It is popular in holistic health and wellness communities for promoting physical and emotional well-being.

Scientific Properties Chemical Composition: Bloodstone is a variety of chalcedony, composed of silicon dioxide (SiO_2) with iron oxide inclusions that give it its distinctive red spots.

Hardness: It has a Mohs hardness rating of 6.5-7, making it relatively durable and suitable for various uses.

Formation: Bloodstone forms in sedimentary and volcanic rocks through the deposition of silica-rich solutions. The presence of iron oxide inclusions gives bloodstone its characteristic red spots.

Care and Cleansing Cleansing Methods: Bloodstone should be cleansed regularly to maintain its energetic purity. Effective methods include rinsing with water, smudging with sage or palo santo, and using sound vibrations. Bloodstone can also be cleansed using mild soap and water.

Recharging: To recharge bloodstone, place it in sunlight or moonlight, or on a selenite charging plate. Avoid prolonged exposure to direct sunlight to prevent colour fading.

Practical Tips Daily Use: Carry a small bloodstone crystal in your pocket or wear it as jewellery to benefit from its healing, protective, and grounding properties throughout the day. It is particularly useful during stressful situations or when needing to enhance physical vitality.

Home and Workspace: Place bloodstone in strategic locations around your home or workspace to create a balanced and protective environment. Near communication areas, it can help to enhance clarity and understanding.

Meditation Space: Keep bloodstone in your meditation space to enhance grounding, protection, and healing during your practice. It can help to open the Root and Heart Chakras, promoting deeper meditation and greater emotional balance.

CHAPTER
THIRTEEN

Using Gemstones for Healing

Techniques and Practices

Across the annals of time, from ancient civilizations to modern-day seekers, the art of gemstone healing has been a revered practice. This ancient alchemy involves the channelling of the unique energetic properties of gemstones to enhance physical, emotional, and spiritual health. Each stone is believed to emanate specific vibrations and frequencies that interact with the energy fields of the human body, weaving a tapestry of healing and harmony.

Overview of Gemstone Healing Principles

Vibrational Energy:

At the heart of gemstone healing lies the principle of vibrational energy. Gemstones, each with their own distinct vibrational frequencies, resonate with different facets of the human energy field. These vibrations possess the power to balance, align, and purify the body's energy centres, known as chakras, restoring equilibrium and vitality.

Colour Therapy:

The hues of gemstones are not mere aesthetics; they correspond to the chakras and emotional states. Green gemstones, like Aventurine, are linked to the heart chakra and are believed to cultivate love and compassion. In contrast, blue gemstones, such as Lapis Lazuli, resonate with the throat chakra, enhancing communication and expression.

Intention Setting:

The potency of gemstones is magnified when paired with clear intentions. This sacred practice involves channelling one's focus and energy towards a desired outcome, be it physical healing, emotional balance, or spiritual enlightenment. The gemstone becomes a conduit, amplifying and directing this intention into the ether.

Absorption and Amplification:

Gemstones have the mystical ability to absorb, store, release, and amplify energy. Clear Quartz, known as the master healer, is a powerful amplifier that can enhance the energy of other stones and magnify intentions, making it a versatile tool in any healing repertoire.

Healing Properties:

Each gemstone harbours unique attributes, making it suitable for diverse healing applications. For instance, Amethyst is renowned for its serene qualities, aiding in restful sleep and alleviating stress, while Carnelian invigorates with a burst of energy and creativity.

How Gemstone Healing Works on an Energetic Level

Gemstone healing is predicated on the understanding that all entities in the cosmos, including the human form, are composed of energy. The human energy field, or aura, is malleable and can be influenced by the vibrational frequencies of gemstones.

Energetic Mechanisms:

Chakra Alignment:

Chakras, the energy vortices within the body, govern various aspects of physical and emotional well-being. Placing gemstones on these chakras can balance and harmonise their energy. For instance, Rose Quartz, when placed on the heart chakra, can heal and open emotional wounds.

Energy Clearing:

Gemstones are adept at dispelling negative energy and blockages within the energy field. Black Tourmaline is particularly potent, absorbing negativity and offering protection against adverse energies.

Aura Cleansing:

The aura, the luminous energy field that envelops the body, can be purified with gemstones like Selenite. This ethereal stone sweeps away negative attachments and stagnant energies, restoring the aura's radiant glow.

Vibration Matching:

Introducing gemstones with specific frequencies into our energy field can induce a harmonious resonance. This alignment process restores balance and promotes holistic healing, allowing the body to resonate with the gemstone's healing frequency.

Resonance and Sympathetic Vibration:

The principle of resonance, where energy fields of similar frequencies amplify each other, underpins gemstone healing. When a gemstone's frequency aligns with that of the body, it induces a sympathetic vibration in the corresponding energy centres, fostering healing and balance.

Practical Applications:

Daily Use:

Gemstones can be seamlessly integrated into daily life. Carrying them, wearing them as adornments, or placing them in living and working spaces provides a continuous flow of supportive energy.

Meditation:

Gemstones can deepen meditative practices, enhancing the connection to their energy. Holding a gemstone or placing it on a chakra during meditation focuses and amplifies intentions, guiding the practitioner towards inner peace and clarity.

Healing Sessions:

In formal healing sessions, gemstones are strategically positioned on or around the body to address specific needs. These sessions, often guided by a skilled crystal healer, combine intention setting with the potent energies of gemstones to facilitate profound healing.

Choosing the Right Gemstones

Selecting the appropriate gemstones for your healing journey involves a blend of knowledge and intuition. Each gemstone carries unique characteristics and energies, capable of supporting diverse aspects of physical, emotional, and spiritual well-being. Herein lies the ancient wisdom of gemstone selection.

Steps to Select Gemstones:

Identify Your Needs:

The first step in this sacred process is to discern what you seek to achieve with gemstone healing. Is it stress reduction, an energy boost, enhanced creativity, or emotional healing that you desire? Clarifying your intentions will illuminate the path to choosing the stones that resonate with your specific needs.

Research Gemstone Properties:

Immerse yourself in the arcane knowledge of gemstone properties. Here are but a few examples to guide your exploration:

- **Amethyst:** Known for its calming aura, it aids in stress relief and sleep.

- **Citrine:** Radiates energy, promoting positivity and abundance.

- **Rose Quartz:** A gentle healer, fostering love and emotional balance.

- **Black Tourmaline:** A stalwart protector, absorbing negative energy and grounding.

- **Clear Quartz:** The amplifier, enhancing the energy of other stones and intentions.

Match Properties to Needs:

Select gemstones that align with your identified needs. For instance:

- If you seek emotional healing, Rose Quartz or Rhodonite may be your allies.

- To enhance focus and mental clarity, look to Fluorite or Clear Quartz.

- For an infusion of energy and motivation, turn to Carnelian or Citrine.

Consider Physical Characteristics:

The colour, shape, and size of a gemstone can influence its energy and interaction with your aura. Choose stones that visually resonate with you, for their appearance can be a sign of their compatibility with your energy field.

Intuitive Selection vs. Systematic Approach

Intuitive Selection:

Trust in your inner guidance as you navigate the selection of gemstones.

- **Trusting Your Intuition:** The stones that call to you most powerfully are often the ones you need. Allow your instincts to guide your choices.

- **Personal Connection:** Hold various gemstones in your hand and attune to the sensations they evoke. A strong personal connection with a gemstone can amplify its effectiveness.

Systematic Approach:

Employ a methodical approach grounded in research and logic.

- **Research-Based Choice:** Delve into the documented properties of gemstones and align them with your healing goals.

- **Structured Process:** Follow a step-by-step method, perhaps making lists or consulting experts, to ensure you select the most suitable stones.

Combining Both Approaches:

Balance intuition with research for a comprehensive selection process.

- **Balanced Selection:** Begin with research to identify gemstones that meet your needs, then use intuition to finalise your choices.

- **Flexibility:** Remain open to adjusting your selection based on your interactions with the gemstones, for sometimes the most effective choice may come as a surprise.

Example Scenario: Selecting Gemstones for Stress Relief

Identify Needs: Your goal is to reduce stress and promote relaxation. **Research Properties:** Discover that Amethyst, Lepidolite, and Blue Lace Agate are renowned for their calming and stress-relieving properties. **Match Properties:** Choose Amethyst for its ability to calm the mind and enhance restful sleep. **Intuitive Check:** Hold Amethyst and other calming stones to determine which resonates most with you. **Final Selection:** Feeling a profound connection with Amethyst, you decide it is the stone to aid your stress relief practice.

Gemstone Placement and Layouts

The arrangement of gemstones on and around the body is a pivotal aspect of maximising their healing effects. Various layouts can be employed to achieve different purposes, such as chakra alignment, pain relief, or overall energy balancing.

Methods for Placing Gemstones on and Around the Body

- **Direct Placement:** Place gemstones directly on the skin at specific points. This method is effective for addressing targeted issues or energy centres.

- **Clothing and Pockets:** Carry gemstones in your pockets or wear them within your clothing to keep them close to your body.

- **Jewellery:** Adorning yourself with gemstone jewellery, such as necklaces, bracelets, and rings, maintains a constant connection with their energy.

Advanced Placement Techniques:

- **Crystal Grids:** Arrange gemstones in geometric patterns around the body to create a focused energy field. Crystal grids can amplify the healing properties of individual stones.

- **Aura Layouts:** Strategically place gemstones around the body to influence the aura and overall energy field, often used in meditation or healing sessions.

Specific Layouts for Different Purposes

Chakra Alignment:

Balancing the chakras with gemstones can harmonise the body's energy centres, fostering holistic well-being.

Steps:

1. **Root Chakra (Muladhara):** Place Red Jasper or Hematite at the base of the spine.

2. **Sacral Chakra (Svadhisthana):** Position Carnelian or Orange Calcite just below the navel.

3. **Solar Plexus Chakra (Manipura):** Place Citrine or Tiger's Eye on the solar

plexus area.

4. **Heart Chakra (Anahata):** Rest Rose Quartz or Green Aventurine over the heart.

5. **Throat Chakra (Vishuddha):** Place Blue Lace Agate or Lapis Lazuli on the throat.

6. **Third Eye Chakra (Ajna):** Position Amethyst or Fluorite on the forehead between the eyebrows.

7. **Crown Chakra (Sahasrara):** Place Clear Quartz or Selenite at the top of the head.

Pain Relief:

Utilise gemstones to alleviate physical pain by placing them directly on the affected area or integrating them with other healing methods.

Steps:

- **Headaches:** Position Amethyst on the forehead or temples.

- **Back Pain:** Align Black Tourmaline or Hematite along the spine.

- **Joint Pain:** Place Amber or Malachite on the affected joint.

- **Stomach Pain:** Position Moonstone or Carnelian on the abdomen.

Emotional Healing:

Layouts focusing on emotional healing target specific areas of the body linked to particular emotions and energy centres.

Steps:

- **Grief:** Place Rose Quartz over the heart and Lepidolite on the forehead.

- **Anxiety:** Position Blue Lace Agate on the throat and Amethyst on the solar plexus.

- **Anger:** Place Rhodonite on the heart and Hematite on the root chakra.

Sample Layout for Chakra Alignment:

Preparation:

Find a tranquil, comfortable space where you can lie down undisturbed. Gather your chosen gemstones and cleanse them.

Placement:

1. Lie down comfortably on your back.

2. Place each gemstone on its corresponding chakra point, starting from the Root Chakra and moving upwards to the Crown Chakra.

Meditation:

1. Close your eyes and breathe deeply, calming your mind.

2. Visualise each chakra opening and balancing, focusing on the energy of the gemstones.

3. Spend 5-10 minutes on each chakra, allowing the energy to flow and align.

Completion

After the session, remove the gemstones and sit quietly for a few moments to integrate the healing energy.

Laying on of Stones: Detailed Steps

The ancient practice of laying on of stones is a cornerstone in the realm of gemstone healing. This venerable technique involves placing stones directly on the body to facilitate healing, targeting specific physical ailments, balancing chakras, and promoting overall well-being. Here, we delve into the detailed steps and best practices to master this mystical art.

Steps for Laying on of Stones:

Preparation:

1. **Cleanse the Stones:** Ensure your gemstones are purified to remove any residual negative energy. This can be achieved through various methods, such as:

   o **Smudging:** Use sacred herbs like sage or palo santo to smudge the stones.

   o **Running Water:** If the stones are water-safe, cleanse them under running water.

- o **Moonlight:** Place the stones under the moonlight, particularly during a full moon, to recharge and purify them.

2. **Set the Space:** Create a serene and comfortable environment, conducive to healing.

- o Use soft, ambient lighting.

- o Play soothing, tranquil music.

- o Ensure the space is free from distractions and clutter.

Set an Intention:

Clearly define your purpose for the session. Whether it is for pain relief, emotional balance, or chakra alignment, hold this intention in your mind and heart throughout the session, imbuing it into the stones.

Placement of Stones:

1. **Lie Down:** Find a comfortable position lying on your back.

2. **Place the Stones:** Methodically place each gemstone on its corresponding area based on your healing goal.

- o **Chakra Alignment:** Position stones on the chakra points as outlined previously.

- o **Pain Relief:** Directly place stones on the areas experiencing discomfort (e.g., Amethyst on the forehead for headaches).

- o **Emotional Healing:** Place stones on the relevant chakras (e.g., Rose Quartz on the heart for emotional healing).

Relax and Meditate:

1. **Close Your Eyes:** Gently close your eyes and take deep, slow breaths, centering your mind.

2. **Focus on the Energy:** Visualise the healing energy of the stones entering and permeating your body.

3. **Duration:** Remain in this relaxed state for about 20-30 minutes, allowing the stones to perform their work.

Completion:

1. **Remove the Stones:** Slowly and gently remove the stones, starting from

the Root Chakra and moving upwards.

2. **Sit Quietly:** Spend a few moments sitting quietly, integrating the healing energy before rising.

Best Practices:

1. **Consistency:** Regular sessions enhance the cumulative effect of the laying on of stones.

2. **Intuition:** Trust your intuitive guidance when placing stones. If a stone feels more beneficial in a different location, follow that instinct.

3. **Combination with Other Techniques:** Amplify the healing effects by combining the laying on of stones with other practices such as meditation, Reiki, or breathwork.

By mastering these steps and practices, you can harness the profound energies of gemstones, guiding them to promote healing, balance, and a harmonious state of being.

Gemstone Massage: Tools, Techniques, and Benefits

Gemstone massage is an ancient and revered technique that melds the physical benefits of traditional massage with the potent energetic properties of gemstones. This practice not only promotes relaxation and alleviates muscle tension but also enhances the flow of energy throughout the body, harmonising both the physical and the ethereal.

Tools and Equipment:

- **Gemstone Wands:** These long, cylindrical stones are ideal for targeted massage, allowing for precision in addressing specific areas.

- **Gemstone Spheres:** Smooth, round stones that glide effortlessly over the skin, perfect for broad, gentle pressure.

- **Palm Stones:** Flat and polished, these stones fit comfortably in the hand, making them excellent for applying steady pressure to specific points.

Techniques for Gemstone Massage:

Preparation:

1. **Cleanse the Stones:** Purify and charge your gemstones before use to ensure they are free of negative energy.

2. **Set the Space:** Create a tranquil environment with soft lighting and soothing music. Ensure a comfortable surface, such as a massage table or yoga mat, is available for the session.

Apply Massage Oil:

Utilise a natural massage oil, such as almond or coconut oil, to reduce friction and allow the gemstones to move smoothly over the skin.

Basic Techniques

- **Rolling:** Use gemstone spheres to roll over large muscle groups with gentle pressure.

- **Stroking:** Employ gemstone wands to stroke along muscles and energy lines, following the body's natural contours.

- **Pressing:** Use palm stones to apply steady pressure to specific points, such as acupressure points or areas of tension.

- **Circular Movements:** Utilise gemstone spheres or wands in circular motions to stimulate energy flow and relax muscles.

Targeted Massage

- **Head and Neck:** Gently roll Amethyst spheres over the temples, forehead, and back of the neck to relieve tension and promote relaxation.

- **Shoulders and Back:** Use Black Tourmaline wands to stroke along the shoulders and spine, easing muscle tension and grounding the body.

- **Arms and Hands:** Press and stroke Citrine palm stones along the arms and hands to boost energy and relieve stress.

- **Legs and Feet:** Roll Hematite spheres along the legs and feet to ground energy and alleviate muscle fatigue.

Completion

Conclude the massage with gentle, soothing strokes using a calming stone like Rose Quartz to promote peace and relaxation. Allow a few moments of quiet reflection to let the energy settle before rising.

Benefits of Gemstone Massage

- **Physical:** Alleviates muscle tension, improves circulation, and fosters relaxation.

- **Emotional:** Reduces stress, calms the mind, and encourages emotional balance.

- **Energetic:** Enhances the flow of energy, balances chakras, and grounds the body.

In embracing the practice of gemstone massage, one taps into a profound method of holistic healing that nurtures the body, mind, and spirit, aligning them in a harmonious dance of tranquillity and vitality.

Elixirs and Essences: Preparation, Usage, and Benefits

Gemstone elixirs and essences are waters imbued with the potent energy of gemstones, serving as versatile tools for promoting healing and balance. Whether for drinking, bathing, or as sprays, these elixirs can profoundly enhance one's well-being.

Preparation of Gemstone Elixirs

Selecting Gemstones

Choose gemstones that are safe to immerse in water. Examples include Clear Quartz and Amethyst. For stones that may release toxins, such as Malachite, use the indirect method to ensure safety.

Cleansing and Charging

1. **Cleanse the Gemstones:** Thoroughly cleanse the gemstones using traditional methods such as smudging with sacred herbs or rinsing them under running water.

2. **Charge the Gemstones:** Amplify the stones' energy by charging them under sunlight or moonlight, allowing them to absorb the celestial energies.

Infusing Water

1. **Direct Method:** Place the cleansed gemstones directly into a glass container filled with purified or spring water. Allow the stones to infuse

the water for several hours, ideally under sunlight or moonlight, to maximise their energetic transfer.

2. **Indirect Method:** Place the gemstones in a smaller glass container or vial. Then, immerse this container into a larger glass jar filled with water. This method ensures that the gemstones do not come into direct contact with the water, yet their energy permeates the elixir.

Storing the Elixir

Store the gemstone elixir in a glass bottle. Keep it in a cool, dark place to preserve its potency, and use it within a few days to a week for optimal benefits.

Usage of Gemstone Elixirs

Drinking

Consume the elixir throughout the day to harness its healing properties. Begin with small amounts to gauge your body's response to the infused energy.

Bathing

Add the elixir to your bathwater, allowing the gemstone's energy to merge with the water, promoting relaxation and holistic healing.

Sprays

Transfer the elixir into a spray bottle and use it to cleanse your environment or aura. This is particularly effective for dispelling negative energy and fostering a positive, harmonious atmosphere.

Benefits of Gemstone Elixirs

Physical

- Supports overall health and well-being.
- Boosts energy levels.
- Promotes physical healing and vitality.

Emotional

- Reduces stress and anxiety.
- Enhances mood and emotional stability.

- Fosters emotional balance and harmony.

Spiritual

- Heightens spiritual awareness and intuition.

- Supports and deepens meditation practices.

- Balances and aligns the energetic field.

Meditation with Gemstones

Incorporating gemstones into your meditation practice can significantly enhance focus, deepen relaxation, and amplify the healing benefits. Each gemstone possesses unique properties that support various aspects of your meditation experience, creating a profound synergy between the physical and the spiritual.

Guided Meditations for Various Intentions

Healing

1. **Select a Gemstone:** Choose a healing stone such as Amethyst or Rose Quartz.

2. **Find a Quiet Space:** Sit comfortably in a serene environment, holding the gemstone in your hand or placing it on a relevant chakra.

3. **Set an Intention:** Focus on your intention for healing, whether it be physical, emotional, or spiritual.

4. **Breathing:** Take deep, slow breaths. Inhale healing energy, exhale any tension or negativity.

5. **Visualisation:** Visualise the gemstone's energy enveloping your body and mind, promoting healing and balance.

6. **Duration:** Meditate for 10-20 minutes, concentrating on the gemstone's energy.

Grounding

1. **Select a Gemstone:** Opt for a grounding stone such as Hematite or Black Tourmaline.

2. **Find a Quiet Space:** Sit comfortably in a tranquil space, holding the

gemstone in your hand or placing it at the base of your spine.

3. **Set an Intention:** Focus on your intention for grounding and stability.

4. **Breathing:** Take deep, slow breaths. Inhale stability and strength, exhale any anxiety or scattered energy.

5. **Visualisation:** Visualise roots growing from your body into the earth, anchoring you firmly to the ground.

6. **Duration:** Meditate for 10-20 minutes, feeling the grounding energy of the gemstone.

Energising

1. **Select a Gemstone:** Choose an energising stone such as Citrine or Carnelian.

2. **Find a Quiet Space:** Sit comfortably in a peaceful space, holding the gemstone in your hand or placing it on your solar plexus.

3. **Set an Intention:** Focus on your intention to boost your energy and motivation.

4. **Breathing:** Take deep, slow breaths. Inhale vibrant energy, exhale any fatigue or lethargy.

5. **Visualisation:** Visualise the gemstone's energy filling your body with light and vitality.

6. **Duration:** Meditate for 10-20 minutes, absorbing the energising properties of the gemstone.

Incorporating Gemstones into Daily Meditation Practices

Daily Practices - Morning Meditation

- **Gemstone:** Choose an energising stone like Citrine to start your day with energy and positivity.

- **Practice:** Hold the gemstone while setting your intentions for the day. Meditate for 5-10 minutes to boost your morning energy.

Afternoon Check-In:

- **Gemstone:** Use a grounding stone like Hematite to re-center yourself during a midday break.

- **Practice:** Hold the gemstone and take a few deep breaths. Meditate for 5 minutes to regain focus and calm.

Evening Relaxation:

- **Gemstone:** Select a calming stone like Amethyst to wind down and prepare for sleep.

- **Practice:** Hold the gemstone or place it under your pillow. Meditate for 10-15 minutes to release the day's stress and promote restful sleep.

Tips for Effective Gemstone Meditation

1. **Consistency:** Regular practice enhances the benefits of gemstone meditation.

2. **Intuition:** Trust your intuition when choosing gemstones and setting intentions.

3. **Environment:** Create a peaceful environment with soft lighting, soothing music, and a comfortable seating arrangement.

4. **Combination:** Combine gemstone meditation with other practices like breathwork, yoga, or affirmations for enhanced results.

Crystal Grids for Healing

Crystal grids are potent tools that synergize the energies of multiple gemstones, magnifying healing intentions through their combined vibrational frequencies. By arranging stones in specific geometric patterns, you create concentrated energy fields that significantly enhance the healing process.

Steps to Design a Crystal Grid

Set Your Intention

Begin by clearly defining your healing goal. This intention could range from physical healing and emotional balance to protection or any other specific objective. Clarity of purpose is essential for the grid's effectiveness.

Choose Your Gemstones

Select gemstones that align with your intention. Here are some examples:

- **Physical Healing:** Amethyst, Clear Quartz, Green Aventurine.

- **Emotional Balance:** Rose Quartz, Lepidolite, Rhodonite.

- **Protection:** Black Tourmaline, Hematite, Smoky Quartz.

Select a Center Stone:

The centre stone serves as the focal point of the grid and should resonate strongly with your intention. Clear Quartz is a popular choice for its amplifying properties.

Choose a Sacred Geometry Pattern:

Select a pattern that enhances the flow of energy within the grid. Common patterns include the Flower of Life, the Seed of Life, and the Star of David.

Arrange the Stones:

1. **Place the Center Stone:** Position the centre stone in the middle of your chosen pattern.

2. **Arrange Supporting Stones:** Place the other gemstones around the centre stone in accordance with the pattern. Ensure a symmetrical and balanced arrangement to promote even energy distribution.

Activate the Grid:

1. **Trace the Pattern:** Use a crystal wand or your finger to trace the pattern, visually connecting the stones and activating the energy flow.

2. **State Your Intention:** Verbally or silently state your intention to further charge the grid with focused energy.

Example of an Effective Grid and Its Purpose

Healing and Balance Grid

- **Intention:** Promote overall healing and balance in the body and mind.

- **Center Stone:** Clear Quartz.

- **Supporting Stones:**

  o **Amethyst:** Calms the mind and aids in emotional healing.

  o **Rose Quartz:** Promotes love and emotional balance.

  o **Green Aventurine:** Supports physical healing and vitality.

- **Pattern:** Seed of Life.

Steps to Create the Healing and Balance Grid:

1. **Center Stone:** Place the Clear Quartz in the centre of the Seed of Life pattern.

2. **Amethyst Stones:** Arrange the Amethyst stones around the centre stone symmetrically.

3. **Rose Quartz Stones:** Add the Rose Quartz stones next, ensuring a balanced layout around the Amethyst.

4. **Green Aventurine Stones:** Finally, place the Green Aventurine stones evenly.

Activate the Grid:

1. **Trace the Pattern:** Use a crystal wand or your finger to trace the pattern, visualising the energy connecting all the stones and amplifying your intention for healing and balance.

2. **State Intention:** Verbally or silently affirm your intention to infuse the grid with focused energy.

Maintenance and Recharging

Cleanse the Stones

Regularly cleanse the gemstones to remove any accumulated negative energy. Use methods such as smudging, running water (if the stones are water-safe), or moonlight.

Reaffirm Your Intention

Periodically revisit the grid and reaffirm your intention to keep the energy strong and focused.

Recharge the Grid

Use sunlight or moonlight to recharge the entire grid and maintain its vibrational energy.

By designing and activating crystal grids with intention and care, you can create powerful energy fields that support your healing goals and enhance your overall well-being. These grids become a sanctum of healing energy, amplifying your intentions and guiding you towards holistic harmony.

Using Gemstone Wands

Gemstone wands are specialised tools in energy healing, designed to direct and amplify energy. They come in various shapes and sizes, each tailored for specific uses. Whether clearing energy blockages, activating energy centres, or enhancing overall healing, gemstone wands can significantly amplify the healing process.

Types of Gemstone Wands and Their Specific Uses

Single-Terminated Wands:

- **Description:** These wands feature a pointed end and a flat or rounded base.

- **Uses:** Directing energy into specific areas, focusing energy on a particular point, or clearing blockages.

- **Examples:**

    - **Clear Quartz:** Amplification.

    - **Black Tourmaline:** Protection.

    - **Amethyst:** Calming.

Double-Terminated Wands:

- **Description:** These wands have points at both ends.

- **Uses:** Facilitating energy flow in both directions, balancing energy, and connecting different energy points.

- **Examples:**

    - **Clear Quartz:** Energy flow.

    - **Labradorite:** Transformation.

    - **Citrine:** Positivity.

Massage Wands:

- **Description:** Rounded or slightly pointed at one end, designed for physical contact.

- **Uses:** Massage therapy, releasing muscle tension, and stimulating acupressure points.

- **Examples:**

  - **Rose Quartz:** Emotional healing.

  - **Sodalite:** Mental clarity.

  - **Hematite:** Grounding.

Chakra Wands:

- **Description:** These wands often feature multiple stones aligned along the wand, each corresponding to a different chakra.

- **Uses:** Balancing and aligning chakras, comprehensive energy work.

- **Examples:** Multi-stone wands with crystals like Amethyst, Lapis Lazuli, Green Aventurine, and Carnelian.

Techniques for Directing Energy with Gemstone Wands

Clearing Energy Blockages

1. **Hold the Wand:** Use your dominant hand.

2. **Set Your Intention:** Focus on clearing blockages and promoting healing.

3. **Sweeping Motion:** Move the wand over the blockage area in a sweeping motion, visualising the blockage being removed.

4. **Continue:** Until the energy flow feels improved.

Activating Chakras

1. **Select a Wand:** Use a chakra wand or a single-terminated wand suitable for the chakra you wish to activate.

2. **Placement:** Point the wand on or near the chakra.

3. **Circular Motion:** Rotate the wand in a circular motion (clockwise or counterclockwise as per intuition).

4. **Visualise:** The chakra opening and energy flowing freely.

5. **Repeat:** For each chakra you wish to activate.

Healing Sessions

1. **Create a Space:** Ensure a calm, quiet environment.

2. **Cleanse and Charge:** Prepare your wand.

3. **Ground Yourself:** Set a clear intention for the session.

4. **Scan the Body:** Use the wand, pausing over heavy or blocked areas.

5. **Direct Energy:** Focus your intention and visualise energy flowing from the wand into the body.

6. **Close the Session:** Ground the energy, ensuring balance and centeredness.

Enhancing Meditation:

1. **Select a Wand:** Align it with your meditation goals (e.g., Amethyst for relaxation, Clear Quartz for focus).

2. **Hold or Place the Wand:** During meditation.

3. **Focus on Energy:** Visualise the wand amplifying your meditation.

4. **Direct Energy:** Use the wand during deep breathing exercises to enhance the meditative experience.

Benefits of Using Gemstone Wands

- **Focused Energy:** Wands help direct and concentrate energy, making healing more effective.

- **Versatility:** Suitable for various healing practices, from chakra work to physical massage.

- **Amplification:** Enhance the energy of other gemstones and healing practices.

By incorporating gemstone wands into your healing practices, you can harness their focused energy to clear blockages, activate chakras, and promote overall well-being, tapping into a powerful tool for holistic healing.

Healing Physical Ailments - Use of Gemstones for Physical Healing

Using Amethyst for Headache Relief

Theory: Amethyst is renowned for its calming and soothing properties, which are believed to alleviate stress-related headaches and migraines.

Application:

1. **Meditation:** Lie down and hold an Amethyst stone to your forehead. Close your eyes, take deep breaths, and visualise the soothing energy of the stone relieving your pain.

2. **Direct Placement:** Place Amethyst on your temples or the back of your neck, where tension often accumulates during headaches.

3. **Crystal Grid:** Create a small grid with Amethyst stones around your head while you rest, enhancing the calming energy.

Using Hematite for Reducing Inflammation:

Theory: Hematite is known for its grounding and detoxifying properties, which can help reduce inflammation in the body.

Application:

1. **Direct Placement:** Place Hematite stones directly on inflamed areas to draw out toxins and reduce swelling.

2. **Massage:** Use a Hematite wand to gently massage the affected area, promoting blood circulation and healing.

3. **Elixir:** Prepare a Hematite elixir (using the indirect method) and apply it as a compress to the inflamed area.

Using Rose Quartz for Heart-Related Issues

Theory: Rose Quartz is associated with the heart chakra and is believed to promote healing of heart-related conditions, both physical and emotional.

Application:

1. **Meditation:** Meditate with Rose Quartz placed on the heart chakra to promote emotional healing and reduce stress, benefiting heart health.

2. **Daily Carry:** Wear a Rose Quartz pendant close to the heart to keep its healing energy near this vital organ.

3. **Elixir:** Drink a Rose Quartz elixir (prepared using the indirect method) to promote overall heart health and emotional balance.

Emotional and Mental Healing

Using Citrine for Combating Depression

Theory: Citrine is known for its uplifting and energising properties, which can help alleviate symptoms of depression.

Application:

1. **Meditation:** Hold Citrine during meditation to absorb its positive energy and visualise light and warmth filling your body.

2. **Crystal Grid:** Create a grid with Citrine stones in your living space to maintain a positive and uplifting environment.

3. **Daily Carry:** Keep a piece of Citrine in your pocket or wear it as jewellery to stay connected to its energising properties throughout the day.

Using Blue Lace Agate for Anxiety Reduction:

Theory: Blue Lace Agate is known for its calming and soothing properties, making it ideal for reducing anxiety and promoting peace.

Application:

1. **Meditation:** Meditate with Blue Lace Agate placed on the throat chakra to promote communication and release tension.

2. **Breathing Exercises:** Hold Blue Lace Agate while performing deep breathing exercises to enhance relaxation and reduce anxiety.

3. **Daily Carry:** Carry Blue Lace Agate in your pocket or wear it as a necklace to stay calm and centred throughout the day.

Using Malachite for Overcoming Emotional Trauma

Theory: Malachite is believed to have powerful transformative properties that can help release emotional trauma and promote deep healing.

Application:

1. **Meditation:** Meditate with Malachite placed on the heart chakra to release old emotional wounds and promote healing.

2. **Crystal Grid:** Create a grid with Malachite stones in your personal space to facilitate ongoing emotional healing.

3. **Therapeutic Baths:** Add Malachite (using the indirect method) to your bath to create a healing and transformative experience.

Spiritual and Energetic Healing

Using Clear Quartz for Enhancing Spiritual Growth

Theory: Clear Quartz is known for its ability to amplify energy and intentions, making it ideal for spiritual growth and enlightenment.

Application:

1. **Meditation:** Meditate with Clear Quartz placed on the crown chakra to enhance spiritual awareness and connect with higher consciousness.

2. **Crystal Grids:** Create grids with Clear Quartz to amplify the energy of other stones and promote spiritual growth.

3. **Daily Carry:** Wear Clear Quartz jewellery to keep its amplifying properties close to your energy field.

Using Labradorite for Protection and Grounding

Theory: Labradorite is known for its protective and grounding properties, shielding the aura and balancing the energy.

Application:

1. **Meditation:** Meditate with Labradorite to protect your energy field and enhance grounding.

2. **Daily Carry:** Carry Labradorite in your pocket or wear it as jewellery to maintain a protective shield throughout the day.

3. **Elixir:** Prepare a Labradorite elixir (using the indirect method) and spray it around your environment to create a protective barrier.

Using Selenite for Cleansing and Purifying Energy

Theory: Selenite is known for its high vibrational energy that can cleanse and purify the aura and environment.

Application

1. **Meditation:** Meditate with Selenite placed on the crown chakra to cleanse your energy field and connect with higher realms.

2. **Crystal Grids:** Create grids with Selenite to purify and cleanse your space.

3. **Aura Cleansing:** Use a Selenite wand to sweep through your aura, removing any negative or stagnant energy.

Precautions and Ethical Considerations

While gemstones offer numerous benefits for healing, it is essential to understand and mitigate potential risks. Being aware of these risks ensures the safe and effective use of gemstones.

Understanding Potential Risks - Allergies and Skin Reactions

Identifying and Avoiding Problematic Stones

- **Awareness of Allergies:** Some individuals may have allergies to certain minerals or metals found in gemstones. For example, people with nickel allergies should avoid stones like Hematite, which can contain trace amounts of nickel.

- **Test for Sensitivity:** Before prolonged use, test a small area of skin with the gemstone to check for any adverse reactions. If redness, itching, or irritation occurs, discontinue use immediately.

- **Protective Measures:** Use indirect methods, such as placing the gemstone in a cloth pouch or using a barrier (e.g., fabric between the stone and skin) to reduce direct contact.

- **Alternative Options:** If a particular stone causes a reaction, consider using another gemstone with similar properties that is less likely to cause irritation.

Overuse and Energy Imbalance - Recognizing Signs and Symptoms:

- **Understanding Energy Overload:** Overuse of powerful gemstones can lead to energy imbalances, such as feeling overly energised, anxious, or ungrounded. Stones like Clear Quartz and Citrine, known for their amplifying properties, should be used with caution.

- **Monitoring Your Response:** Pay attention to how you feel after using gemstones. Signs of overuse may include restlessness, headaches, or irritability. If these symptoms occur, reduce the frequency or duration of use.

- **Balancing Energies:** Balance the use of high-energy stones with grounding stones like Hematite or Black Tourmaline to maintain equilibrium. Alternate between different gemstones to avoid overstimulation.

- **Personal Limits:** Understand and respect your personal limits. Start with short sessions and gradually increase usage as your body adjusts to the energy of the gemstones.

Safe Practices - Proper Cleansing and Charging of Gemstones

Maintaining the Energy of Gemstones:

- **Regular Cleansing:** Cleanse gemstones regularly to remove accumulated negative energy. Methods include smudging with sage, placing the stones in sunlight or moonlight, and using running water (if the stones are water-safe).

- **Effective Charging:** Charge gemstones to restore their energy. Use sunlight, moonlight, or place them on a selenite charging plate. Ensure the charging method is appropriate for the specific gemstone (e.g., some stones may fade in direct sunlight).

- **Intentional Practices:** Set clear intentions when cleansing and charging gemstones. Visualise the negative energy being cleared and positive energy being restored.

Guidelines for Creating Safe Gemstone Elixirs

Preparation and Usage

- **Direct vs. Indirect Method:**

  - **Direct Method:** Use the direct method for water-safe stones like Clear Quartz, Amethyst, and Rose Quartz. Place the stones directly in water.

  - **Indirect Method:** Use the indirect method for stones that may release toxins or are not water-safe, such as Malachite or Selenite. Place the stones in a smaller container within the water or use a glass barrier.

- **Purification:** Ensure the gemstones are thoroughly cleansed before making elixirs. Use purified or spring water to prevent contamination.

- **Storage:** Store elixirs in glass containers in a cool, dark place. Use within a few days to ensure freshness and potency.

Integrating Gemstones with Conventional Medical Treatments

Complementary Practices

Reiki

- **Enhanced Energy Flow:** Use gemstones during Reiki sessions to enhance energy flow and healing. Place stones on or around the body to complement the Reiki energy.

Acupuncture

- **Amplifying Effects:** Incorporate gemstones into acupuncture treatments by placing them on the body's energy points. This can amplify the effects of the acupuncture needles.

Yoga

- **Enhanced Focus:** Use gemstones during yoga practice to enhance focus and intention. Place stones on the mat or wear gemstone jewellery to benefit from their energy.

Being Mindful of Personal Limitations and Experiences

Self-Awareness

Understanding Your Needs

- **Personal Alignment:** Be aware of your personal limitations and experiences. Choose gemstones and practices that align with your current state and healing goals.

Responsibility

- **Proactive Healing:** Take responsibility for your healing journey. Be proactive in seeking information, practising self-care, and integrating gemstones mindfully into your life.

Ethical Considerations in Using Gemstones for Healing Others

Respect and Integrity

Informed Consent

- **Transparency:** Always obtain informed consent before using gemstones for healing others. Ensure they understand the process and potential effects.

Professional Boundaries

- **Respect Autonomy:** Maintain professional boundaries and respect the autonomy of those you are helping. Provide guidance and support without imposing your beliefs or practices.

Ethical Practice

- **Prioritising Well-being:** Follow ethical practices in gemstone healing. Prioritise the well-being of others, respect their cultural contexts, and promote sustainable and responsible use of gemstones.

By understanding and implementing these precautions and ethical considerations, you can ensure the safe and responsible use of gemstones in your healing practices, promoting well-being for yourself and others.

CHAPTER
FOURTEEN

Meditation and Gemstones

Gemstone meditation is a profound practice that melds the calming and centering effects of meditation with the unique energies of gemstones. By weaving these natural elements into your meditation routine, you can enhance your focus, deepen your relaxation, and amplify the healing benefits.

Benefits of Integrating Gemstones into Meditation Practices

Enhanced Focus

Gemstones can clear mental clutter and sharpen your focus during meditation. Stones like Fluorite and Clear Quartz are particularly effective in promoting mental clarity and concentration.

Deepened Relaxation

Certain gemstones, such as Amethyst and Lepidolite, possess calming properties that reduce stress and anxiety, leading to a deeper state of relaxation.

Energy Amplification

Gemstones can amplify your intentions and the overall energy of your meditation practice. Clear Quartz is renowned for its ability to enhance and amplify energy, making it a versatile tool for any meditation session.

Emotional Healing

Integrating gemstones like Rose Quartz and Rhodonite into your meditation can promote emotional healing and balance, helping to release negative emotions and foster a sense of inner peace.

Spiritual Connection

Gemstones can enhance your connection to higher realms and facilitate spiritual growth. Selenite and Amethyst are commonly used to promote spiritual awareness and connection.

How Gemstone Energy Enhances Meditation

Vibrational Alignment

Each gemstone emits a specific vibrational frequency that can align with and influence your personal energy field. By holding or placing gemstones on your body during meditation, you can harmonise your energy with the stone's vibrations, promoting balance and healing.

Chakra Activation

Gemstones can be used to activate and balance the chakras, the energy centres in your body. For example, placing Amethyst on the Third Eye chakra can enhance intuition and spiritual insight, while placing Citrine on the Solar Plexus chakra can boost confidence and personal power.

Intentional Focus

Meditating with gemstones allows you to set clear intentions for your practice. Holding a gemstone that corresponds to your intention (e.g., Rose Quartz for love, Black Tourmaline for protection) can help to focus your mind and amplify your desired outcome.

Grounding and Protection

Gemstones like Hematite and Black Tourmaline can provide grounding and protection during meditation, helping you to stay centred and shielded from negative energies.

Energy Clearing and Purification

Gemstones such as Selenite and Clear Quartz can help to clear and purify your energy field, removing any stagnant or negative energy and promoting a sense of clarity and lightness.

Preparing for Meditation

Creating a Sacred Space: Setting Up Your Meditation Area

A sacred space is essential for a focused and uninterrupted meditation practice. This space should be conducive to relaxation and filled with elements that support your intentions.

Steps to Create a Sacred Space:

Choose a Quiet Location:

Select a place in your home where you can meditate without disturbances. This could be a dedicated room, a corner of a room, or even a peaceful outdoor area.

Cleanse the Space:

Cleanse the area to remove any negative or stagnant energy. Use sage, palo santo, or incense to smudge the space, or use sound cleansing with a singing bowl or bell.

Comfortable Seating:

Ensure you have comfortable seating, such as a meditation cushion, chair, or yoga mat. Comfort is crucial to maintaining focus during meditation.

Incorporate Elements of Nature:

Add natural elements like plants, flowers, and water features to enhance the calming atmosphere. These elements can help you feel more grounded and connected to the earth.

Use Soft Lighting:

Soft, ambient lighting can create a relaxing environment. Consider using candles, salt lamps, or dimmable lights to set the mood.

Add Personal Touches:

Include items that hold personal significance, such as spiritual symbols, photographs, or objects that bring you peace and joy.

Selecting the Right Gemstones for Your Meditation Goals

Choosing the right gemstones is key to aligning your meditation practice with your intentions. Each gemstone has unique properties that can support different aspects of your meditation.

Common Meditation Goals and Recommended Gemstones:

Calm and Relaxation:

- **Amethyst:** Calms the mind and reduces stress.

- **Blue Lace Agate:** Promotes tranquillity and relaxation.

Focus and Clarity:

- **Clear Quartz:** Enhances focus and amplifies energy.

- **Fluorite:** Improves concentration and mental clarity.

Emotional Healing:

- **Rose Quartz:** Promotes love and emotional balance.

- **Rhodonite:** Heals emotional wounds and promotes forgiveness.

Spiritual Connection:

- **Selenite:** Facilitates connection with higher realms and spiritual growth.

- **Labradorite:** Enhances intuition and spiritual awareness.

Grounding and Protection:

- **Black Tourmaline:** Provides grounding and protection.

- **Hematite:** Grounds energy and balances the body.

Cleansing and Charging Your Gemstones Before Use

It is essential to cleanse and charge your gemstones regularly to maintain their effectiveness. Cleansing removes any negative energy they may have absorbed, while charging restores their natural vibrational energy.

Cleansing Methods:

Water:

Hold the gemstone under running water for a few minutes. Ensure the stone is water-safe (e.g., avoid cleansing Selenite with water).

Smudging:

Use sage, palo santo, or incense to smudge the gemstones. Pass the stones through the smoke for a few moments.

Sound:

Use a singing bowl, bell, or tuning fork to cleanse the gemstones with sound. The vibrations will clear away any negative energy.

Earth:

Bury the gemstones in the earth for 24 hours to cleanse and recharge them. This method is especially effective for grounding stones.

Charging Methods:

Sunlight:

Place the gemstones in direct sunlight for a few hours. Be cautious with stones that may fade in sunlight (e.g., Amethyst).

Moonlight:

Leave the gemstones under the light of the full moon overnight to charge them with lunar energy.

Crystal Clusters:

Place the gemstones on a cluster of Clear Quartz or Amethyst to charge them. These crystals naturally amplify and restore energy.

Intentions:

Hold the gemstone in your hands and set your intention. Visualise the stone being filled with vibrant, positive energy.

Incorporating Gemstones into Meditation Practices

Holding Gemstones: Best Practices for Holding Stones During Meditation

Holding gemstones during meditation can help you connect more deeply with their energy. Proper technique ensures that you fully benefit from the stone's properties.

Steps for Holding Gemstones:

1. **Select Your Gemstone:** Choose a gemstone that aligns with your meditation goals. For example, use Amethyst for calming, Clear Quartz for clarity, or Rose Quartz for emotional healing.

2. **Cleansing and Charging:** Before meditating, cleanse and charge your gemstone to ensure it is free of negative energy and fully energised.

3. **Comfortable Position:** Sit or lie down in a comfortable position. Ensure your back is straight, and you are relaxed.

4. **Holding Technique:**

   o Hold the gemstone in your dominant hand. This hand is typically more energetically active and can better channel the stone's energy.

   o You can also hold the gemstone in both hands, cupping it gently to form a connection with its energy.

5. **Focus and Intention:**

   o Close your eyes and take a few deep breaths to centre yourself.

   o Focus on the sensation of the gemstone in your hand. Visualise its energy flowing into your body, aligning with your intention for the meditation.

6. **Breathing:** Maintain slow, deep breaths throughout your meditation. Inhale through your nose, allowing the gemstone's energy to fill you, and

exhale any stress or negativity.

7. **Duration:** Hold the gemstone for the entire duration of your meditation session, typically between 10 to 30 minutes, depending on your practice.

Placing Gemstones: Positioning Stones on or Around the Body

Placing gemstones on or around your body can target specific energy centres (chakras) or areas of need. This technique can enhance the flow of energy and promote healing.

Steps for Placing Gemstones:

1. **Select Your Gemstones:** Choose gemstones based on the areas you want to target. For example:

   - Root Chakra: Red Jasper, Hematite.

   - Heart Chakra: Rose Quartz, Green Aventurine.

   - Third Eye Chakra: Amethyst, Lapis Lazuli.

2. **Preparation:** Cleanse and charge your gemstones before placing them on your body.

3. **Lie Down Comfortably:** Lie down on your back in a comfortable, quiet space. Ensure you have enough room to place the stones around you.

4. **Placement:** Place the gemstones on the corresponding chakras or areas of the body. For example:

   - Place a Rose Quartz on your heart chakra (centre of the chest).

   - Place an Amethyst on your third eye chakra (forehead between the eyebrows).

   - Place a Citrine on your solar plexus chakra (upper abdomen).

5. **Relax and Focus:**

   - Close your eyes and take deep breaths. Focus on the energy of the gemstones and visualise it flowing into your body.

   - Imagine the energy aligning your chakras and promoting healing.

6. **Meditation:** Meditate for 10-30 minutes, allowing the gemstones to work on your energy field. Maintain a state of relaxation and openness to the gemstones' healing properties.

Visualising Gemstone Energy: Techniques for Visualizing and Feeling Gemstone Vibrations

Visualisation can enhance the connection between you and the gemstones, amplifying their effects during meditation.

Steps for Visualizing Gemstone Energy:

1. **Select Your Gemstone:** Choose a gemstone that aligns with your meditation intention.

2. **Cleansing and Charging:** Cleanse and charge your gemstone to ensure it is energetically clear and vibrant.

3. **Comfortable Position:** Sit or lie down in a comfortable position. Hold the gemstone or place it on your body.

4. **Deep Breathing:** Close your eyes and take several deep breaths to centre yourself.

5. **Visualisation:**

   - Focus on the gemstone and visualise its energy. Imagine a light emanating from the stone, filling your body with its unique vibrational frequency.

   - For example, if you are using a Clear Quartz, visualise a bright white light radiating from the stone, purifying and energising your entire being.

6. **Feeling Vibrations:**

   - As you visualise the gemstone's energy, try to feel its vibrations in your body. Notice any sensations, such as warmth, tingling, or a sense of calm.

   - Allow these sensations to deepen your meditation and enhance the connection with the gemstone.

7. **Maintaining Focus:** If your mind starts to wander, gently bring your focus back to the gemstone and its energy. Continue to visualise and feel its vibrations throughout your meditation session.

Crystal Grids: Designing and Using Crystal Grids for Meditation

Introduction to Crystal Grids

Crystal grids are powerful tools that use the geometric arrangement of gemstones to amplify and direct energy. Utilising crystal grids in meditation can enhance the focus and effectiveness of your practice.

Steps to Design a Crystal Grid for Meditation:

Set Your Intention:

Clearly define your meditation goal. Whether it's for healing, protection, love, or spiritual growth, having a clear intention is crucial.

Choose Your Gemstones:

Select stones that align with your intention. For example:

- **Healing:** Amethyst, Clear Quartz, Green Aventurine.

- **Protection:** Black Tourmaline, Hematite, Smoky Quartz.

- **Love:** Rose Quartz, Rhodonite, Pink Tourmaline.

Select a Geometric Pattern:

Choose a sacred geometry pattern, such as the Flower of Life, Seed of Life, or a simple circle. These patterns enhance the flow of energy within the grid.

Arrange the Stones:

1. **Place a Central Stone:** This stone should resonate strongly with your intention. Clear Quartz is often used for its amplifying properties.

2. **Arrange Supporting Stones:** Position the supporting stones around the central stone according to the chosen geometric pattern.

Activate the Grid:

1. **Connect the Stones:** Use a crystal wand or your finger to connect the stones. Visualise energy flowing through the grid, linking the stones, and amplifying your intention.

2. **State Your Intention:** Aloud or silently, affirm your intention as you activate the grid.

Using the Crystal Grid in Meditation:

1. **Sit or Lie Near the Grid:** Position yourself comfortably near the grid, ensuring you can see and connect with it.

2. **Focus on the Grid:** Begin your meditation by focusing on the grid. Visualise the energy of the stones and the pattern flowing into you.

3. **Deep Breathing:** Take deep, slow breaths, drawing in the energy from the grid with each inhale.

4. **Visualisation:** Visualise your intention being fulfilled. See the energy of the grid working to achieve your goal.

5. **Duration:** Meditate for 15-30 minutes, or as long as you feel comfortable.

Gemstone Wands: Directing Energy Flow with Gemstone Wands

Introduction to Gemstone Wands

Gemstone wands are used to direct and amplify energy during meditation and healing practices. They can focus energy on specific points in the body, clear blockages, and enhance the overall flow of energy.

Using Gemstone Wands in Meditation:

Select a Wand:

Choose a gemstone wand that aligns with your meditation goals. For example:

- **Clear Quartz:** Amplifies energy and intention.
- **Amethyst:** Calms and balances the mind.
- **Black Tourmaline:** Grounds and protects.

Prepare the Wand:

Cleanse and charge the wand to ensure it is energetically clear and vibrant.

Directing Energy:

1. **Hold the Wand:** Hold the wand in your dominant hand. Visualise energy flowing from the wand into the area you wish to focus on.

2. **Trace Patterns:** Use the wand to trace patterns in the air or on your body to direct the flow of energy.

Clearing Blockages:

1. **Move the Wand:** Gently move the wand over areas where you feel energy blockages. Visualise the wand dissolving the blockages and restoring the flow of energy.

Enhancing Focus:

1. **Draw Symbols:** Use the wand to draw symbols or shapes that enhance your focus and intention. This can be done in the air or on a surface near you.

Combining Multiple Gemstones: Harmonising Different Energies for a Deeper Experience

Introduction to Combining Gemstones

Combining multiple gemstones can create a synergistic effect, enhancing and balancing the energies of each stone. This technique can deepen your meditation experience and address multiple aspects of healing and growth.

Steps to Combine Gemstones in Meditation:

Select Complementary Stones:

Choose gemstones that work well together. For example:

- **Calming and Grounding:** Amethyst and Black Tourmaline.

- **Love and Healing:** Rose Quartz and Green Aventurine.

- **Clarity and Focus:** Clear Quartz and Fluorite.

Prepare the Stones:

Cleanse and charge all the gemstones you plan to use.

Arrange the Stones:

Place the stones around you in a pattern that feels intuitively right. You can hold one stone in each hand, place them on your chakras, or create a small grid around you.

Focus and Intention:

Set a clear intention for your meditation. Visualise how each gemstone will contribute to achieving this goal.

Meditate with the Stones:

1. **Begin Your Meditation:** Focus on the energy of each stone. Visualise their energies blending and harmonising, creating a powerful field of healing and growth.

2. **Duration:** Meditate for 15-30 minutes, allowing the combined energies to work together.

Daily Meditation Practices

Integrating Gemstone Meditation into Your Daily Routine

Making gemstone meditation a part of your daily routine can provide ongoing benefits for your physical, emotional, and spiritual well-being. Consistent practice helps maintain balance, reduce stress, and enhance your overall energy.

Steps to Integrate Gemstone Meditation into Your Daily Routine:

Set a Regular Time:

Choose a specific time each day for your meditation practice. Morning and evening are ideal times to meditate, as they can set the tone for the day or help you unwind before bed.

Create a Ritual:

Establish a simple ritual to begin your meditation practice. This could include lighting a candle, burning incense, or playing soft music to signal the start of your meditation time.

Select Your Gemstones:

Choose gemstones that align with your daily needs and intentions. For example:

- **Morning:** Citrine for energy and positivity, Clear Quartz for focus.

- **Evening:** Amethyst for relaxation, Rose Quartz for emotional healing.

Short, Focused Sessions:

Morning Practice:

Spend 5-10 minutes in the morning holding a gemstone or placing it nearby. Focus on your breathing and set positive intentions for the day.

Evening Practice:

In the evening, spend 10-15 minutes meditating with a calming gemstone. Focus on releasing the day's stress and promoting relaxation.

Longer, In-Depth Practices:

Set aside time once or twice a week for a longer meditation session, lasting 20-30 minutes. Use this time to delve deeper into your meditation practice, incorporating more advanced techniques like crystal grids or gemstone wands.

Journaling:

Keep a meditation journal to track your experiences and progress. Note any changes in how you feel, insights gained during meditation, and the effects of different gemstones.

Tips for Maintaining Consistency:

Start Small:

If you're new to meditation, start with short sessions and gradually increase the duration as you become more comfortable.

Stay Flexible:

While consistency is important, be flexible and kind to yourself. If you miss a session, simply resume your practice the next day without judgement.

Set Reminders:

Use reminders or alarms to help you remember your meditation time. Consistency is easier to maintain when it's part of your daily schedule.

Create a Supportive Environment:

Make your meditation space inviting and comfortable. Having a dedicated space can make it easier to establish and maintain your practice.

Incorporate Guided Meditations:

Use guided meditations that incorporate gemstones to help you stay focused and enhance your practice. Many apps and online resources offer guided meditations specifically designed for use with gemstones.

Guided Meditations for Different Gemstones

Guided meditations are structured sessions where a facilitator, either live or recorded, leads you through a meditation practice. These meditations often include visualisation, breathing exercises, and affirmations to help you focus and achieve your desired outcomes. Integrating gemstones into guided meditations can amplify the benefits and provide a deeper, more enriching experience.

Benefits of Guided Meditations

Structured Focus

Guided meditations provide a clear structure, making it easier to stay focused and present during your practice. This structure can be especially helpful for beginners or those who struggle with maintaining concentration.

Enhanced Visualisation

Many guided meditations incorporate visualisation techniques, which can help you connect more deeply with the energy of the gemstones. Visualising the stone's energy flowing into and around your body can enhance its healing effects.

Support for Specific Goals

Guided meditations can be tailored to address specific intentions, such as emotional healing, stress relief, or spiritual growth. Using the appropriate gemstones can further support these goals.

Emotional and Mental Support

Listening to a calming and reassuring voice during a guided meditation can provide emotional and mental support, helping to reduce anxiety and promote a sense of peace and well-being.

Accessibility:

Guided meditations are widely available through various apps, websites, and recordings, making it easy to find a practice that suits your needs and preferences.

How to Use Guided Meditations with Gemstones

Select the Appropriate Gemstone

Choose a gemstone that aligns with the specific guided meditation you are using. For example, use Clear Quartz for clarity and amplification, Rose Quartz for love and emotional healing, or Amethyst for spiritual awareness and calm.

Prepare Your Space

Set up a comfortable and quiet meditation area free from distractions. Ensure you have any additional items you need, such as a cushion, blanket, or incense.

Cleansing and Charging

Cleanse and charge your gemstone before beginning the meditation to ensure it is energetically clear and vibrant. Use your preferred method, such as smudging, moonlight, or sound cleansing.

Hold or Place the Gemstone

Hold the gemstone in your hand, place it on a relevant chakra, or position it nearby where you can easily focus on its energy. For example, hold Clear Quartz in your hand or place Rose Quartz on your heart chakra.

Follow the Guided Meditation

Listen to the guided meditation, following the instructions closely. Focus on the gemstone's energy and how it aligns with the meditation's focus. Allow yourself to fully engage with the process, visualising the gemstone's energy flowing into and around your body.

Reflect

After the meditation, take a few moments to reflect on your experience. Note any insights, sensations, or changes you felt during the practice. Consider keeping a meditation journal to track your progress and any effects of the gemstones.

By incorporating guided meditations into your practice, you can harness the structured guidance and focused intentions to deepen your connection with gemstones and enhance their healing properties.

Meditation for Clear Quartz

Purpose: Clarity and Amplification

Clear Quartz is known for its powerful amplifying properties and its ability to enhance mental clarity and focus. This guided meditation uses Clear Quartz to help you achieve greater mental clarity and amplify your intentions.

Guided Meditation Script for Enhancing Mental Clarity and Spiritual Growth

Introduction:

Find a quiet and comfortable place to sit or lie down. Ensure you will not be disturbed for the duration of the meditation.

Hold a piece of Clear Quartz in your hand or place it in front of you.

Centering Yourself:

Close your eyes and take a few deep breaths. Inhale slowly through your nose, allowing your abdomen to expand, and exhale gently through your mouth, releasing any tension.

Setting Your Intention:

Focus on your intention for this meditation. It could be to gain mental clarity, amplify your intentions, or connect more deeply with your spiritual self.

Silently or aloud, state your intention: "I seek mental clarity and amplification of my highest intentions."

Visualising the Energy:

Imagine a bright, white light emanating from the Clear Quartz. See this light surrounding the stone, growing stronger and more vibrant with each breath.

Visualise the light from the Clear Quartz forming a connection with your energy field. See it flowing into your body, starting from the area where you hold or place the stone.

Deepening the Connection:

As you continue to breathe deeply, imagine the white light filling your entire being. See it moving through every cell, clearing away any mental fog, distractions, or negative thoughts.

Focus on the sensation of clarity and lightness as the Clear Quartz energy purifies your mind and amplifies your intentions.

Affirmations:

Silently or aloud, repeat the affirmation: "My mind is clear, my intentions are amplified, and I am aligned with my highest purpose."

Feel the truth of these words resonating within you, supported by the energy of the Clear Quartz.

Maintaining Focus:

If your mind starts to wander, gently bring your focus back to the Clear Quartz and the white light. Continue to visualise the energy flowing into and around you, reinforcing your clarity and intention.

Closing the Meditation:

Gradually bring your awareness back to the present moment. Take a few more deep breaths, grounding yourself in the here and now.

When you are ready, open your eyes. Take a moment to reflect on your experience, noting any insights or sensations.

Expressing Gratitude:

Thank the Clear Quartz for its energy and support. You may choose to hold it close to your heart for a moment, feeling a sense of gratitude and connection.

Integration:

Consider keeping the Clear Quartz with you throughout the day or placing it in a spot where you can easily see and connect with it. This will help to maintain the clarity and amplified energy achieved during your meditation.

Meditation for Rose Quartz

Purpose: Love and Emotional Healing

Rose Quartz is renowned for its gentle, loving energy that promotes emotional healing, compassion, and self-love. This guided meditation uses Rose Quartz to help open your heart, heal emotional wounds, and foster a deep sense of love and compassion.

Guided Meditation Script for Opening the Heart and Promoting Self-Love

Introduction

Find a quiet and comfortable place to sit or lie down. Ensure you will not be disturbed for the duration of the meditation.

Hold a piece of Rose Quartz in your hand or place it on your heart chakra (centre of the chest).

Centering Yourself

Close your eyes and take a few deep breaths. Inhale slowly through your nose, allowing your abdomen to expand, and exhale gently through your mouth, releasing any tension.

Setting Your Intention

Focus on your intention for this meditation. It could be to open your heart, heal emotional wounds, or cultivate self-love.

Silently or aloud, state your intention: "I open my heart to love and healing."

Visualising the Energy

Imagine a soft, pink light emanating from the Rose Quartz. See this light surrounding the stone, growing stronger and more vibrant with each breath.

Visualise the pink light forming a connection with your energy field. See it flowing into your heart chakra, filling your heart with its gentle, loving energy.

Deepening the Connection

As you continue to breathe deeply, imagine the pink light expanding from your heart chakra, radiating throughout your entire body. Feel the warmth and comfort of this loving energy as it heals and soothes your emotional wounds.

Focus on the sensation of love and compassion, allowing the Rose Quartz energy to dissolve any feelings of pain, sadness, or resentment.

Affirmations:

Silently or aloud, repeat the affirmation: "I am worthy of love and compassion. My heart is open and healing."

Feel the truth of these words resonating within you, supported by the energy of the Rose Quartz.

Maintaining Focus:

If your mind starts to wander, gently bring your focus back to the Rose Quartz and the pink light. Continue to visualise the energy flowing into and around you, reinforcing your sense of love and healing.

Closing the Meditation:

Gradually bring your awareness back to the present moment. Take a few more deep breaths, grounding yourself in the here and now.

When you are ready, open your eyes. Take a moment to reflect on your experience, noting any insights or sensations.

Expressing Gratitude:

Thank the Rose Quartz for its energy and support. You may choose to hold it close to your heart for a moment, feeling a sense of gratitude and connection.

Integration:

Consider keeping the Rose Quartz with you throughout the day or placing it in a spot where you can easily see and connect with it. This will help to maintain the love and healing energy achieved during your meditation.

Meditation for Amethyst

Purpose: Spiritual Awareness and Calm

Amethyst is known for its calming and spiritually enhancing properties. It is often used to promote relaxation, reduce stress, and enhance spiritual awareness. This guided meditation uses Amethyst to help calm the mind and deepen your spiritual connection.

Guided Meditation Script for Calming the Mind and Enhancing Intuition

Introduction:

Find a quiet and comfortable place to sit or lie down. Ensure you will not be disturbed for the duration of the meditation.

Hold a piece of Amethyst in your hand or place it on your third eye chakra (forehead between the eyebrows).

Centering Yourself:

Close your eyes and take a few deep breaths. Inhale slowly through your nose, allowing your abdomen to expand, and exhale gently through your mouth, releasing any tension.

Setting Your Intention:

Focus on your intention for this meditation. It could be to calm your mind, reduce stress, or enhance your spiritual awareness and intuition.

Silently or aloud, state your intention: "I seek calm, peace, and spiritual insight."

Visualising the Energy:

Imagine a soft, purple light emanating from the Amethyst. See this light surrounding the stone, growing stronger and more vibrant with each breath.

Visualise the purple light forming a connection with your energy field. See it flowing into your third eye chakra, enhancing your intuition and spiritual awareness.

Deepening the Connection:

As you continue to breathe deeply, imagine the purple light expanding from your third eye chakra, radiating throughout your entire body. Feel the calming and peaceful energy of the Amethyst as it soothes your mind and spirit.

Focus on the sensation of relaxation and spiritual connection, allowing the Amethyst energy to dissolve any stress, anxiety, or mental clutter.

Affirmations:

Silently or aloud, repeat the affirmation: "I am calm, centred, and spiritually connected. My intuition is clear and strong."

Feel the truth of these words resonating within you, supported by the energy of the Amethyst.

Maintaining Focus:

If your mind starts to wander, gently bring your focus back to the Amethyst and the purple light. Continue to visualise the energy flowing into and around you, reinforcing your sense of calm and spiritual awareness.

Closing the Meditation:

Gradually bring your awareness back to the present moment. Take a few more deep breaths, grounding yourself in the here and now.

When you are ready, open your eyes. Take a moment to reflect on your experience, noting any insights or sensations.

Expressing Gratitude:

Thank the Amethyst for its energy and support. You may choose to hold it close to your third eye or heart for a moment, feeling a sense of gratitude and connection.

Integration:

Consider keeping the Amethyst with you throughout the day or placing it in a spot where you can easily see and connect with it. This will help to maintain the calm and spiritual awareness achieved during your meditation.

Meditation for Citrine

Purpose: Abundance and Joy

Citrine is known for its bright, uplifting energy that promotes positivity, joy, and abundance. This guided meditation uses Citrine to help attract positivity, manifest goals, and enhance overall well-being.

Guided Meditation Script for Attracting Positivity and Manifesting Goals

Introduction:

Find a quiet and comfortable place to sit or lie down. Ensure you will not be disturbed for the duration of the meditation.

Hold a piece of Citrine in your hand or place it on your solar plexus chakra (upper abdomen).

Centering Yourself:

Close your eyes and take a few deep breaths. Inhale slowly through your nose, allowing your abdomen to expand, and exhale gently through your mouth, releasing any tension.

Setting Your Intention:

Focus on your intention for this meditation. It could be to attract positivity, manifest a specific goal, or enhance your sense of joy and abundance.

Silently or aloud, state your intention: "I attract positivity and abundance into my life. I manifest my goals with joy."

Visualising the Energy:

Imagine a bright, golden light emanating from the Citrine. See this light surrounding the stone, growing stronger and more vibrant with each breath.

Visualise the golden light forming a connection with your energy field. See it flowing into your solar plexus chakra, filling your entire being with its radiant energy.

Deepening the Connection:

As you continue to breathe deeply, imagine the golden light expanding from your solar plexus chakra, radiating throughout your entire body. Feel the uplifting and joyful energy of the Citrine as it enhances your positivity and sense of abundance.

Focus on the sensation of joy and abundance, allowing the Citrine energy to dissolve any feelings of lack or negativity.

Affirmations:

Silently or aloud, repeat the affirmation: "I am filled with joy and abundance. I attract positive energy and manifest my goals with ease."

Feel the truth of these words resonating within you, supported by the energy of the Citrine.

Maintaining Focus:

If your mind starts to wander, gently bring your focus back to the Citrine and the golden light. Continue to visualise the energy flowing into and around you, reinforcing your sense of positivity and abundance.

Closing the Meditation:

Gradually bring your awareness back to the present moment. Take a few more deep breaths, grounding yourself in the here and now.

When you are ready, open your eyes. Take a moment to reflect on your experience, noting any insights or sensations.

Expressing Gratitude:

Thank the Citrine for its energy and support. You may choose to hold it close to your heart or solar plexus for a moment, feeling a sense of gratitude and connection.

Integration:

Consider keeping the Citrine with you throughout the day or placing it in a spot where you can easily see and connect with it. This will help to maintain the positivity and abundance achieved during your meditation.

Meditation for Black Tourmaline

Purpose: Protection and Grounding

Black Tourmaline is known for its powerful protective and grounding properties. It helps to shield against negative energy, provides a sense of security, and grounds your energy into the earth. This guided meditation uses Black Tourmaline to create a protective shield and enhance grounding.

Guided Meditation Script for Creating a Protective Shield and Grounding Energy

Introduction:

Find a quiet and comfortable place to sit or lie down. Ensure you will not be disturbed for the duration of the meditation.

Hold a piece of Black Tourmaline in your hand or place it at the base of your spine (root chakra).

Centering Yourself:

Close your eyes and take a few deep breaths. Inhale slowly through your nose, allowing your abdomen to expand, and exhale gently through your mouth, releasing any tension.

Setting Your Intention:

Focus on your intention for this meditation. It could be to protect yourself from negative energy, feel more secure, or ground your energy.

Silently or aloud, state your intention: "I am protected and grounded. I release all negative energy and feel secure."

Visualising the Energy:

Imagine a deep, black light emanating from the Black Tourmaline. See this light surrounding the stone, growing stronger and more vibrant with each breath.

Visualise the black light forming a connection with your energy field. See it flowing into your root chakra, grounding your energy and creating a protective shield around you.

Deepening the Connection:

As you continue to breathe deeply, imagine the black light expanding from your root chakra, radiating throughout your entire body and into the earth below. Feel the grounding and protective energy of the Black Tourmaline anchoring you securely to the earth.

Focus on the sensation of being protected and grounded, allowing the Black Tourmaline energy to dissolve any feelings of fear, insecurity, or negativity.

Affirmations:

Silently or aloud, repeat the affirmation: "I am grounded and protected. I release all negative energy and feel secure."

Feel the truth of these words resonating within you, supported by the energy of the Black Tourmaline.

Maintaining Focus:

If your mind starts to wander, gently bring your focus back to the Black Tourmaline and the black light. Continue to visualise the energy flowing into and around you, reinforcing your sense of protection and grounding.

Closing the Meditation:

Gradually bring your awareness back to the present moment. Take a few more deep breaths, grounding yourself in the here and now.

When you are ready, open your eyes. Take a moment to reflect on your experience, noting any insights or sensations.

Expressing Gratitude:

Thank the Black Tourmaline for its energy and support. You may choose to hold it close to your root chakra or place it at your feet for a moment, feeling a sense of gratitude and connection.

Integration:

Consider keeping the Black Tourmaline with you throughout the day or placing it in a spot where you can easily see and connect with it. This will help to maintain the protection and grounding achieved during your meditation.

Meditation for Selenite

Purpose: Cleansing and Purification

Selenite is known for its high vibrational energy that can cleanse and purify the aura, remove negative energy, and enhance clarity. This guided meditation uses Selenite to help clear negative energy and purify your aura.

Guided Meditation Script for Clearing Negative Energy and Purifying the Aura

Introduction:

Find a quiet and comfortable place to sit or lie down. Ensure you will not be disturbed for the duration of the meditation.

Hold a piece of Selenite in your hand or place it above your head (crown chakra).

Centering Yourself:

Close your eyes and take a few deep breaths. Inhale slowly through your nose, allowing your abdomen to expand, and exhale gently through your mouth, releasing any tension.

Setting Your Intention:

Focus on your intention for this meditation. It could be to cleanse your energy, purify your aura, or enhance your clarity.

Silently or aloud, state your intention: "I am cleansed and purified. I release all negative energy and embrace clarity."

Visualising the Energy:

Imagine a bright, white light emanating from the Selenite. See this light surrounding the stone, growing stronger and more vibrant with each breath.

Visualise the white light forming a connection with your energy field. See it flowing into your crown chakra, cleansing and purifying your entire being.

Deepening the Connection:

As you continue to breathe deeply, imagine the white light expanding from your crown chakra, radiating throughout your entire body and aura. Feel the cleansing and purifying energy of the Selenite as it removes any negative or stagnant energy.

Focus on the sensation of being purified and light, allowing the Selenite energy to dissolve any negativity or impurities.

Affirmations:

Silently or aloud, repeat the affirmation: "I am cleansed and purified. My energy is clear and vibrant."

Feel the truth of these words resonating within you, supported by the energy of the Selenite.

Maintaining Focus:

If your mind starts to wander, gently bring your focus back to the Selenite and the white light. Continue to visualise the energy flowing into and around you, reinforcing your sense of purification and clarity.

Closing the Meditation:

Gradually bring your awareness back to the present moment. Take a few more deep breaths, grounding yourself in the here and now.

When you are ready, open your eyes. Take a moment to reflect on your experience, noting any insights or sensations.

Expressing Gratitude:

Thank the Selenite for its energy and support. You may choose to hold it close to your crown chakra or place it near your heart for a moment, feeling a sense of gratitude and connection.

Integration:

Consider keeping the Selenite with you throughout the day or placing it in a spot where you can easily see and connect with it. This will help to maintain the cleansing and purification achieved during your meditation.

By incorporating these guided meditations into your daily practice, you can deepen your connection with gemstones and harness their unique energies to enhance your meditation experience.

Tips for Personalizing Meditation Scripts

Define Your Intention

Clearly define what you want to achieve with your meditation. Whether it's emotional healing, stress relief, or spiritual growth, having a clear intention will guide the structure of your meditation.

Choose the Appropriate Gemstones

Select gemstones that resonate with your intention. For example:

- **Emotional Healing:** Rose Quartz, Rhodonite.

- **Stress Relief:** Amethyst, Blue Lace Agate.

- **Spiritual Growth:** Selenite, Clear Quartz.

Create a Comfortable Environment

Set up a peaceful space for your meditation. Use elements like soft lighting, soothing music, and calming scents to enhance the atmosphere.

Incorporate Visualisation:

Visualisation is a powerful tool in guided meditations. Visualise the energy of the gemstone flowing into your body, aligning with your intention.

Use Affirmations:

Include positive affirmations that reinforce your intention. Repeat these affirmations throughout the meditation to deepen your connection with the energy of the gemstones.

Structure the Meditation:

- **Begin with Deep Breathing:** Relax and centre yourself.

- **Visualisation and Affirmation Phase:** Focus on the gemstone's energy.

- **Conclude with Gratitude and Reflection:** Integrate the experience.

Example Script for Creating Your Own Guided Meditation

Purpose: Emotional Healing with Rose Quartz

Introduction:

Find a quiet and comfortable place to sit or lie down. Hold a piece of Rose Quartz in your hand or place it on your heart chakra.

Centering Yourself:

Close your eyes and take a few deep breaths. Inhale slowly through your nose, allowing your abdomen to expand, and exhale gently through your mouth, releasing any tension.

Setting Your Intention:

Focus on your intention for this meditation: emotional healing. Silently or aloud, state your intention: "I am open to healing my heart and embracing love."

Visualising the Energy:

Imagine a soft, pink light emanating from the Rose Quartz. See this light surrounding the stone, growing stronger and more vibrant with each breath.

Visualise the pink light forming a connection with your energy field. See it flowing into your heart chakra, filling your heart with its gentle, loving energy.

Deepening the Connection:

As you continue to breathe deeply, imagine the pink light expanding from your heart chakra, radiating throughout your entire body. Feel the warmth and comfort of this loving energy as it heals and soothes your emotional wounds.

Focus on the sensation of love and compassion, allowing the Rose Quartz energy to dissolve any feelings of pain, sadness, or resentment.

Affirmations:

Silently or aloud, repeat the affirmation: "I am worthy of love and compassion. My heart is open and healing."

Feel the truth of these words resonating within you, supported by the energy of the Rose Quartz.

Maintaining Focus:

If your mind starts to wander, gently bring your focus back to the Rose Quartz and the pink light. Continue to visualise the energy flowing into and around you, reinforcing your sense of love and healing.

Closing the Meditation:

Gradually bring your awareness back to the present moment. Take a few more deep breaths, grounding yourself in the here and now.

When you are ready, open your eyes. Take a moment to reflect on your experience, noting any insights or sensations.

Expressing Gratitude:

Thank the Rose Quartz for its energy and support. You may choose to hold it close to your heart for a moment, feeling a sense of gratitude and connection.

Integration:

Consider keeping the Rose Quartz with you throughout the day or placing it in a spot where you can easily see and connect with it. This will help to maintain the love and healing energy achieved during your meditation.

Incorporating Specific Intentions and Goals

Identify Your Goals:

Determine what you hope to achieve with your meditation. This could be related to physical health, emotional well-being, spiritual growth, or other personal goals.

Select Supporting Gemstones:

Choose gemstones that support your specific goals. For example:

- **Physical Health:** Green Aventurine, Bloodstone.

- **Emotional Well-Being:** Lepidolite, Rhodochrosite.

- **Spiritual Growth:** Labradorite, Selenite.

Customise Affirmations:

Create affirmations that align with your goals. Repeat these affirmations during the meditation to reinforce your intentions.

Tailor the Visualization:

Visualise the gemstone's energy working towards your specific goals. For example, if your goal is to improve physical health, visualise the gemstone's energy healing and strengthening your body.

Track Your Progress:

Keep a journal to track your meditation experiences and progress towards your goals. Note any changes, insights, or shifts in your well-being.

By creating personalised guided meditations, you can harness the unique energies of gemstones to support your specific intentions and goals, enhancing your meditation practice and overall well-being.

Enhancing Focus and Intuition

Gemstones can be powerful tools to enhance mental focus and concentration. Their unique energies can help to clear mental fog, sharpen cognitive abilities, and maintain sustained attention during tasks. Incorporating these stones into your daily routine or meditation practices can provide a natural way to boost your mental clarity and productivity.

How Gemstones Can Improve Mental Focus and Concentration

Mechanisms of Action - Vibrational Energy

Gemstones emit specific vibrational frequencies that can interact with the body's energy field. These frequencies can help to balance and align the mind, promoting a state of focused attention.

Chakra Alignment

Certain gemstones resonate with chakras that are associated with mental functions. For example, stones that resonate with the third eye chakra (Ajna) can enhance cognitive abilities and mental clarity.

Calming Effects

Some gemstones have calming properties that can reduce stress and anxiety, which often interfere with concentration. By promoting a calm and relaxed state, these stones can help maintain focus.

Energy Amplification:

Gemstones like Clear Quartz can amplify your intentions and mental energy, making it easier to stay focused on tasks and goals.

Recommended Gemstones for Focus and Concentration

Fluorite

- **Properties:** Known as the "Genius Stone," Fluorite is highly effective for mental clarity, focus, and organisation. It helps to clear mental fog and enhance cognitive functions.

- **Usage:** Hold a piece of Fluorite during study sessions or place it on your desk to enhance mental performance. Meditate with Fluorite placed on your third eye chakra to boost concentration.

Tiger's Eye

- **Properties:** Tiger's Eye is a grounding stone that promotes mental clarity and focus. It helps to balance emotions and reduces anxiety, allowing for sustained concentration.

- **Usage:** Wear Tiger's Eye jewellery or carry a stone in your pocket to maintain focus throughout the day. Use it during meditation to align your mind and body, enhancing overall concentration.

Hematite

- **Properties:** Hematite is known for its strong grounding and balancing properties. It helps to organise thoughts, improve focus, and provide mental clarity.

- **Usage:** Place Hematite on your desk or hold it during stressful tasks to enhance focus and reduce mental distractions. Meditate with Hematite to ground your energy and improve concentration.

Single-Point Focus Meditation with Gemstones

Single-point focus meditation, also known as Trataka, is a powerful technique for improving concentration and mental clarity. When combined with the energy of gemstones, this practice can be even more effective.

Steps for Single-Point Focus Meditation

Choose Your Gemstone

Select a gemstone that promotes focus and clarity, such as Fluorite, Tiger's Eye, or Hematite. Cleanse and charge the gemstone to ensure it is energetically clear.

Set Up Your Space

Find a quiet, comfortable place to sit. Ensure the space is free from distractions. Place the gemstone at eye level on a small stand or table in front of you.

Begin the Meditation

Sit in a comfortable position with your back straight. Close your eyes and take a few deep breaths to centre yourself.

Focus on the Gemstone

Open your eyes and fix your gaze on the gemstone. Keep your focus on the stone, trying not to blink or look away. As you concentrate on the gemstone, notice its colour, shape, and any reflections or patterns it creates.

Deep Breathing

Continue to breathe deeply and evenly. Inhale slowly through your nose, allowing your abdomen to expand, and exhale gently through your mouth.

Maintaining Focus

If your mind starts to wander, gently bring your focus back to the gemstone. Use the stone's energy to help anchor your attention. Visualise the gemstone's energy merging with your mind, enhancing your focus and mental clarity.

Duration

Practise this meditation for 5-10 minutes initially, gradually increasing the duration as your ability to maintain focus improves.

Closing the Meditation

Gently close your eyes and take a few deep breaths. Reflect on the experience and any changes in your mental clarity. When you are ready, open your eyes and bring your awareness back to the present moment.

Breathing Exercises with Gemstone Support

Breathing exercises, or pranayama, can be enhanced by incorporating gemstones that promote focus and concentration.

Steps for Breathing Exercises with Gemstones:

Choose Your Gemstone:

Select a focus-enhancing gemstone such as Fluorite, Tiger's Eye, or Hematite. Cleanse and charge the gemstone.

Set Up Your Space:

Find a quiet, comfortable place to sit. Ensure the space is free from distractions.

Begin the Breathing Exercise:

Sit in a comfortable position with your back straight. Hold the gemstone in your hand or place it on your lap.

Deep Breathing:

Inhale slowly through your nose, allowing your abdomen to expand, and exhale gently through your mouth. Focus on your breath and the gemstone's energy.

Visualise the gemstone's energy flowing into your body with each inhale, enhancing your focus and mental clarity.

Rhythmic Breathing:

Practise rhythmic breathing by inhaling for a count of four, holding for a count of four, exhaling for a count of four, and holding for a count of four. Repeat this cycle for several minutes, maintaining your focus on the gemstone's energy.

Visualisation:

As you breathe, visualise the gemstone's energy merging with your breath, clearing any mental fog and sharpening your focus. See the energy filling your mind, promoting clarity and concentration.

Duration:

Practise this exercise for 5-10 minutes, gradually increasing the duration as your ability to maintain focus improves.

Closing the Exercise:

Take a few deep breaths and reflect on the experience. Notice any changes in your mental clarity and focus. When you are ready, bring your awareness back to the present moment.

Visualisation Techniques to Sharpen Focus

Visualisation techniques can help to sharpen your focus by engaging your imagination and aligning your mind with the gemstone's energy.

Steps for Visualisation Techniques:

Choose Your Gemstone:

Select a focus-enhancing gemstone such as Fluorite, Tiger's Eye, or Hematite. Cleanse and charge the gemstone.

Set Up Your Space:

Find a quiet, comfortable place to sit. Ensure the space is free from distractions.

Begin the Visualisation:

Sit in a comfortable position with your back straight. Hold the gemstone in your hand or place it in front of you.

Deep Breathing:

Close your eyes and take a few deep breaths. Inhale slowly through your nose, allowing your abdomen to expand, and exhale gently through your mouth.

Visualise the Gemstone's Energy:

Imagine the gemstone's energy as a bright light. Visualise this light flowing into your mind, clearing away any mental fog and enhancing your focus. See the light spreading throughout your brain, sharpening your cognitive abilities and promoting clarity.

Focus on the Visualization:

Maintain your focus on the visualisation, allowing the gemstone's energy to merge with your mind. If your mind starts to wander, gently bring your focus back to the visualisation and the gemstone's energy.

Affirmations:

Silently or aloud, repeat affirmations such as: "My mind is clear and focused. I am fully present and concentrated on my tasks."

Duration

Practise this visualisation for 5-10 minutes, gradually increasing the duration as your ability to maintain focus improves.

Closing the Visualization

Gently open your eyes and take a few more deep breaths. Reflect on the experience and any changes in your mental clarity. When you are ready, bring your awareness back to the present moment.

Intuition and Psychic Abilities

Gemstones can play a significant role in enhancing intuition and developing psychic abilities. Their unique energies can help open and activate the third eye chakra, heighten sensitivity to subtle energies, and strengthen the connection to higher consciousness.

Mechanisms of Action

Energy Amplification

Certain gemstones, such as Clear Quartz, can amplify your intentions and psychic abilities, making it easier to connect with higher realms and receive intuitive insights.

Chakra Activation

Gemstones that resonate with the third eye chakra (Ajna) and crown chakra (Sahasrara) can enhance psychic abilities and spiritual awareness. These stones help to open and balance these energy centres, allowing for clearer intuition and deeper spiritual connection.

Vibrational Frequency

Gemstones emit specific vibrational frequencies that can align with and enhance your own energy field. This alignment can facilitate the reception of intuitive information and psychic insights.

Recommended Gemstones for Enhancing Intuition and Psychic Abilities

Labradorite

- **Properties:** Known as the "Stone of Magic," Labradorite enhances intuition, psychic abilities, and spiritual awareness. It helps to reveal hidden truths and protect against negative energies.

- **Usage:** Meditate with Labradorite placed on your third eye chakra to enhance intuition. Carry it with you to stay attuned to subtle energies throughout the day.

Lapis Lazuli

- **Properties:** Lapis Lazuli is a powerful stone for enhancing intuition, spiritual insight, and inner wisdom. It helps to open the third eye chakra and facilitate connection with higher realms.

- **Usage:** Wear Lapis Lazuli jewellery or place the stone on your third eye chakra during meditation to enhance intuitive abilities and spiritual awareness.

Moonstone

- **Properties:** Moonstone is known for its ability to enhance intuition, psychic abilities, and emotional balance. It is particularly effective for developing feminine energy and connecting with the cycles of the moon.

- **Usage:** Use Moonstone during meditation to enhance intuition and psychic abilities. Place it under your pillow to receive intuitive insights through dreams.

Exercises for Developing Intuition

Third Eye Activation Meditation with Gemstones

Activating the third eye chakra can enhance your intuition and psychic abilities. Using gemstones that resonate with this chakra can amplify the effects of your meditation practice.

Steps for Third Eye Activation Meditation:

Choose Your Gemstone:

Select a gemstone that enhances intuition, such as Labradorite, Lapis Lazuli, or Amethyst. Cleanse and charge the gemstone.

Set Up Your Space:

Find a quiet, comfortable place to sit. Ensure the space is free from distractions.

Begin the Meditation:

Sit in a comfortable position with your back straight. Hold the gemstone in your hand or place it on your third eye chakra (forehead between the eyebrows).

Deep Breathing:

Close your eyes and take a few deep breaths. Inhale slowly through your nose, allowing your abdomen to expand, and exhale gently through your mouth.

Focus on the Gemstone's Energy:

Visualise the gemstone's energy as a bright, indigo or purple light. See this light surrounding the stone, growing stronger and more vibrant with each breath.

Visualise the light forming a connection with your third eye chakra, opening and activating it.

Affirmations:

Silently or aloud, repeat affirmations such as: "My intuition is strong and clear. I am open to receiving intuitive insights."

Feel the truth of these words resonating within you, supported by the energy of the gemstone.

Maintaining Focus:

If your mind starts to wander, gently bring your focus back to the gemstone and the indigo or purple light. Continue to visualise the energy flowing into your third eye chakra, enhancing your intuition.

Duration:

Practise this meditation for 10-15 minutes, gradually increasing the duration as your intuition develops.

Closing the Meditation:

Gently open your eyes and take a few more deep breaths. Reflect on the experience and any intuitive insights you received. When you are ready, bring your awareness back to the present moment.

Journaling and Reflecting with Gemstone Guidance

Journaling is a powerful tool for developing intuition. Reflecting on your experiences and insights can help you understand and trust your intuitive abilities.

Steps for Journaling with Gemstones:

Choose Your Gemstone:

Select a gemstone that enhances intuition, such as Moonstone, Lapis Lazuli, or Clear Quartz. Cleanse and charge the gemstone.

Set Up Your Space:

Find a quiet, comfortable place to sit. Ensure the space is free from distractions.

Begin Journaling:

Hold the gemstone in your hand or place it nearby. Close your eyes and take a few deep breaths to centre yourself.

Set an Intention:

Focus on your intention for journaling. It could be to receive intuitive insights, understand a situation better, or reflect on your experiences.

Silently or aloud, state your intention: "I am open to receiving intuitive guidance and insights."

Start Writing:

Begin writing whatever comes to mind. Don't censor yourself or worry about grammar or structure. Allow your thoughts to flow freely onto the paper.

If you feel stuck, hold the gemstone and focus on its energy to help clear your mind and enhance your intuition.

Reflect on Your Writing:

After journaling, take a few moments to read over what you've written. Reflect on any insights or intuitive guidance that emerged. Note any patterns, symbols, or recurring themes that may provide deeper understanding.

Closing the Exercise:

Thank the gemstone for its guidance and support. Place it in a spot where you can easily see and connect with it throughout the day.

Dream Work and Gemstone Placement Under the Pillow

Using gemstones during sleep can enhance intuition and provide intuitive insights through dreams.

Steps for Dream Work with Gemstones:

Choose Your Gemstone:

Select a gemstone that enhances intuition and dream recall, such as Moonstone, Amethyst, or Lapis Lazuli. Cleanse and charge the gemstone.

Prepare for Sleep:

Place the gemstone under your pillow or on your bedside table. Ensure your sleeping area is comfortable and free from distractions.

Set an Intention:

Focus on your intention for dream work. It could be to receive intuitive insights, remember your dreams, or gain clarity on a specific issue.

Silently or aloud, state your intention: "I am open to receiving intuitive guidance through my dreams."

Keep a Dream Journal:

Place a journal and pen next to your bed. When you wake up, immediately write down any dreams, impressions, or intuitive insights you received during the night.

Reflect on Your Dreams:

Reflect on your dreams and any intuitive guidance you received. Note any patterns, symbols, or recurring themes that may provide deeper understanding.

Balancing Focus and Intuition in Meditation

Combining focus and intuition in meditation can create a powerful synergy, enhancing your mental clarity while deepening your spiritual awareness. This balanced approach allows you to stay grounded and centred while being open to intuitive insights.

Techniques for Harmonizing Mental Clarity with Intuitive Insights

Integrative Meditation with Gemstones

Select Your Gemstones

- Choose a gemstone that promotes focus, such as Fluorite or Tiger's Eye, and a gemstone that enhances intuition, such as Labradorite or Lapis Lazuli.

- Cleanse and charge both gemstones.

Set Up Your Space

- Find a quiet, comfortable place to sit. Ensure the space is free from distractions.

Begin the Meditation

- Sit in a comfortable position with your back straight. Hold the focus-enhancing gemstone in one hand and the intuition-enhancing gemstone in the other.

Deep Breathing

- Close your eyes and take a few deep breaths. Inhale slowly through your nose, allowing your abdomen to expand, and exhale gently through your mouth.

Focus on the Gemstones' Energies

- Visualise the energy of the focus-enhancing gemstone as a bright, clear light. See this light surrounding the stone, growing stronger and more vibrant with each breath.

- Visualise the energy of the intuition-enhancing gemstone as a soft, indigo or purple light. See this light surrounding the stone, growing stronger and more vibrant with each breath.

Balancing the Energies

- Imagine the clear light of the focus-enhancing gemstone merging with the indigo or purple light of the intuition-enhancing gemstone. See these energies blending and harmonising within you, creating a balanced flow of mental clarity and intuitive insight.

- Feel the combined energy aligning your mind and spirit, enhancing both your focus and intuition.

Affirmations

- Silently or aloud, repeat affirmations such as: "I am clear and focused. My intuition is strong and clear. I am open to receiving intuitive insights."

- Feel the truth of these words resonating within you, supported by the balanced energies of the gemstones.

Maintaining Focus

- If your mind starts to wander, gently bring your focus back to the gemstones and the harmonised light. Continue to visualise the energy flowing into and around you, reinforcing your sense of balance.

Duration

- Practise this meditation for 10-15 minutes, gradually increasing the duration as your ability to maintain focus and intuition improves.

Closing the Meditation

- Gently open your eyes and take a few more deep breaths. Reflect on the experience and any insights you received.

- When you are ready, bring your awareness back to the present moment.

Visualisation Techniques for Combined Focus and Intuition

Choose Your Gemstones:

- Select a gemstone that promotes focus, such as Fluorite, and a gemstone that enhances intuition, such as Moonstone.

- Cleanse and charge both gemstones.

Set Up Your Space:

- Find a quiet, comfortable place to sit. Ensure the space is free from distractions.

Begin the Visualisation

- Sit in a comfortable position with your back straight. Hold both gemstones in your hands.

Deep Breathing

- Close your eyes and take a few deep breaths. Inhale slowly through your nose, allowing your abdomen to expand, and exhale gently through your mouth.

Visualise the Gemstones' Energies

- Visualise the energy of the focus-enhancing gemstone as a bright, clear light. See this light flowing into your mind, enhancing your mental clarity and concentration.

- Visualise the energy of the intuition-enhancing gemstone as a soft, indigo or purple light. See this light flowing into your third eye chakra, enhancing your intuitive abilities and spiritual awareness.

Combining the Energies

- Imagine the clear light of the focus-enhancing gemstone merging with the indigo or purple light of the intuition-enhancing gemstone. See these energies blending and harmonising within you, creating a balanced flow of mental clarity and intuitive insight.

- Focus on the combined energy, allowing it to align your mind and spirit, enhancing both your focus and intuition.

Affirmations

- Silently or aloud, repeat affirmations such as: "I am clear and focused. My intuition is strong and clear. I am open to receiving intuitive insights."

- Feel the truth of these words resonating within you, supported by the balanced energies of the gemstones.

Maintaining Focus

- If your mind starts to wander, gently bring your focus back to the gemstones and the harmonised light. Continue to visualise the energy flowing into and around you, reinforcing your sense of balance.

Duration

- Practise this visualisation for 10-15 minutes, gradually increasing the duration as your ability to maintain focus and intuition improves.

Closing the Visualization

- Gently open your eyes and take a few more deep breaths. Reflect on the experience and any insights you received.

- When you are ready, bring your awareness back to the present moment.

CHAPTER FIFTEEN

Creating Gemstone Elixirs

What are Gemstone Elixirs?

Gemstone elixirs are infused waters that capture the energetic properties of gemstones. By immersing gemstones in water, either directly or indirectly, the water absorbs the unique vibrations and healing energies of the stones. These elixirs can be consumed or used topically to promote physical, emotional, and spiritual well-being.

Historical Background and Traditional Uses

The use of gemstone elixirs dates back to ancient civilizations, where they were considered powerful tools for healing and transformation. Various cultures have harnessed the energies of gemstones through elixirs:

Ancient Egypt

The Egyptians believed in the powerful healing properties of gemstones. They used gemstone elixirs for protection, health, and spiritual rituals. Cleopatra was known to have used gemstone elixirs to maintain her beauty and health.

Traditional Chinese Medicine

In Chinese culture, gemstone elixirs have been used for centuries in traditional medicine practices. They were believed to balance the body's energy (Qi) and support overall health and longevity.

Ayurveda

In India, Ayurveda has long incorporated gemstones in healing practices. Gemstone elixirs are used to balance the doshas (body energies) and support physical and emotional health.

Native American Traditions

Native American tribes have utilised the energies of gemstones in their healing rituals. Gemstone elixirs were used to enhance spiritual connection, protect against negative energies, and support healing.

Modern Uses

Today, gemstone elixirs are widely used in holistic and alternative medicine practices. They are valued for their ability to support emotional balance, enhance meditation, and promote overall well-being.

By understanding the historical and cultural significance of gemstone elixirs, we can appreciate their timeless appeal and effectiveness in promoting health and harmony.

Methods and Recipes

How Gemstone Elixirs Work on an Energetic Level

Gemstone elixirs work by transferring the vibrational frequencies and energetic properties of gemstones into water. Water is an excellent conductor of energy and can easily absorb and store the subtle vibrations emitted by gemstones. When consumed or applied, the elixir can influence the body's energy field, promoting balance, healing, and transformation.

Key Principles of Gemstone Elixirs

Vibrational Frequency

Every gemstone emits a specific vibrational frequency that corresponds to its unique properties. These frequencies interact with the body's energy field, promoting healing and balance.

Water Memory

Water has the ability to "remember" and store energetic information. When gemstones are infused in water, the water retains the energetic imprint of the stones, making it a powerful medium for transferring their healing properties.

Intentional Infusion

The process of creating gemstone elixirs involves setting clear intentions. By focusing your intention on the desired outcome, you can enhance the effectiveness of the elixir. This intentional approach aligns the energy of the gemstones with your specific goals.

The Importance of Intention in Creating Elixirs

Setting a clear intention is crucial when creating gemstone elixirs. Your intention guides the energetic process and amplifies the healing properties of the gemstones. Here's how to set and incorporate intention into your elixir-making practice:

Define Your Goal

Clearly define what you want to achieve with your gemstone elixir. Whether it's physical healing, emotional balance, or spiritual growth, having a specific goal in mind will direct the energy of the elixir.

Focus Your Mind

Take a moment to centre yourself and focus your mind on your intention. This can be done through meditation, deep breathing, or visualisation.

State Your Intention

Silently or aloud, state your intention while holding the gemstones you plan to use. For example, if you're creating an elixir for emotional healing, you might say, "I infuse this elixir with the energy of love and healing to bring emotional balance and peace."

Visualise the Process

As you prepare the elixir, visualise the energy of the gemstones being transferred into the water. See the water being filled with light and vibrant energy, aligned with your intention.

Gratitude and Affirmation

Express gratitude for the healing properties of the gemstones and affirm that the elixir will achieve your desired outcome. This positive reinforcement strengthens the energetic connection and enhances the elixir's effectiveness.

Direct Method

Step-by-Step Instructions for Creating Elixirs by Direct Infusion

The direct method involves placing gemstones directly into water to infuse it with their energies. This method is simple and effective, but it requires careful selection of non-toxic gemstones to ensure safety.

Steps for Creating Gemstone Elixirs Using the Direct Method:

Choose Your Gemstones: Select gemstones based on your desired intention. Ensure the gemstones are non-toxic and water-safe. Examples include Clear Quartz, Amethyst, and Rose Quartz.

Cleanse and Charge the Gemstones: Cleanse the gemstones to remove any negative or stagnant energy. This can be done using water, smudging with sage, or placing them in sunlight or moonlight. Charge the gemstones with your intention. Hold each stone and focus on your desired outcome, visualising the energy being absorbed by the gemstone.

Prepare Your Materials: You will need a glass or ceramic container, purified or spring water, and a cover for the container.

Infuse the Water: Place the cleansed and charged gemstones directly into the container of water. Cover the container to protect it from dust and contaminants.

Set Your Intention: Focus on your intention for the elixir. Silently or aloud, state your intention, visualising the gemstones infusing the water with their energies.

Infusion Time: Allow the gemstones to infuse the water for a minimum of 4 hours. For stronger elixirs, let the gemstones sit overnight or for up to 24 hours.

Remove the Gemstones: After the infusion period, remove the gemstones from the water. Your gemstone elixir is now ready for use.

Store the Elixir: Store the elixir in a clean, glass container with a lid. Keep it in a cool, dark place to maintain its potency.

List of Suitable Gemstones for Direct Method

Only certain gemstones are safe for direct infusion due to their chemical composition. Here are some suitable gemstones for the direct method:

- **Clear Quartz:** Amplifies energy and intention, enhances clarity and focus.

- **Amethyst:** Calms the mind, promotes emotional balance and spiritual growth.

- **Rose Quartz:** Encourages love, compassion, and emotional healing.

- **Citrine:** Attracts abundance, joy, and positivity.

- **Smoky Quartz:** Provides grounding and protection, dispels negative energy.

- **Aventurine:** Promotes healing, luck, and prosperity.

Precautions and Tips for Effective Infusion

- **Avoid Toxic Gemstones:** Some gemstones can release harmful substances into water. Avoid gemstones like Malachite, Selenite, and Azurite for direct infusion.

- **Use Clean, Purified Water:** Ensure the water used for infusion is clean and free from contaminants. Purified or spring water is recommended.

- **Maintain Hygiene:** Use clean containers and utensils to avoid contamination. Wash your hands before handling the gemstones and water.

- **Regular Cleansing:** Regularly cleanse and charge your gemstones to maintain their energetic potency.

- **Monitor Your Body's Response:** Pay attention to how your body reacts to the gemstone elixir. Discontinue use if you experience any adverse effects.

By following these steps and precautions, you can create effective and safe gemstone elixirs using the direct method.

Indirect Method

Step-by-Step Instructions for Creating Elixirs by Indirect Infusion

The indirect method involves infusing water with the energy of gemstones without direct contact. This method is ideal for gemstones that are toxic, porous, or fragile.

Steps for Creating Gemstone Elixirs Using the Indirect Method:

Choose Your Gemstones: Select gemstones based on your desired intention. The indirect method is suitable for all gemstones, including those that are toxic or water-sensitive. Examples include Malachite, Selenite, and Lapis Lazuli.

Cleanse and Charge the Gemstones: Cleanse the gemstones to remove any negative or stagnant energy. This can be done using water, smudging with sage, or placing them in sunlight or moonlight. Charge the gemstones with your intention. Hold each stone and focus on your desired outcome, visualising the energy being absorbed by the gemstone.

Prepare Your Materials: You will need two containers: one larger container for the water and one smaller glass container to hold the gemstones. Ensure both containers are clean and preferably made of glass. Use purified or spring water for the infusion.

Infuse the Water: Place the cleansed and charged gemstones in the smaller glass container. Fill the larger container with purified or spring water. Place the smaller container with the gemstones inside the larger container of water, ensuring the two do not touch. The gemstones should not come into direct contact with the water.

Set Your Intention: Focus on your intention for the elixir. Silently or aloud, state your intention, visualising the gemstones infusing the water with their energies through the indirect method.

Infusion Time: Allow the gemstones to infuse the water for a minimum of 4 hours. For stronger elixirs, let the gemstones sit overnight or for up to 24 hours.

Remove the Containers: After the infusion period, remove the smaller container with the gemstones from the water. Your gemstone elixir is now ready for use.

Store the Elixir: Store the elixir in a clean, glass container with a lid. Keep it in a cool, dark place to maintain its potency.

Using a Barrier (e.g., Glass Container) to Separate Gemstones from Water

The barrier method ensures that gemstones do not directly touch the water, making it safe for use with all types of stones. A small glass container or vial is ideal for this purpose, as it allows the gemstone's energy to infuse the water without direct contact.

List of Gemstones Suitable for Indirect Method

The indirect method is suitable for all gemstones, especially those that are toxic or fragile. Here are some examples:

- **Malachite:** Provides deep healing and transformation. Contains copper, which can be toxic if ingested directly.

- **Selenite:** Promotes cleansing and purification. Water-sensitive and can dissolve in water.

- **Azurite:** Enhances intuition and psychic abilities. Contains copper and should not be used in direct contact with water.

- **Pyrite:** Attracts abundance and protects against negative energy. Can release harmful substances if immersed in water.

- **Lapis Lazuli:** Promotes spiritual growth and enhances intuition. Can be porous and fragile in water.

Tips for Effective Indirect Infusion

- **Ensure Separation:** Use a reliable barrier to separate the gemstones from the water. A small glass container or vial is ideal.

- **Use Clean, Purified Water:** Ensure the water used for infusion is clean and free from contaminants. Purified or spring water is recommended.

- **Maintain Hygiene:** Use clean containers and utensils to avoid contamination. Wash your hands before handling the gemstones and water.

- **Regular Cleansing:** Regularly cleanse and charge your gemstones to maintain their energetic potency.

- **Monitor Your Body's Response:** Pay attention to how your body reacts to the gemstone elixir. Discontinue use if you experience any adverse effects.

By following these steps and precautions, you can create effective and safe gemstone elixirs using the indirect method.

Solar and Lunar Infusion

Solar infusion uses the energy of the sun to amplify the properties of gemstone elixirs. Sunlight can energise the elixir, adding a vibrant, dynamic quality to its effects.

Steps for Solar Infusion:

Choose Your Gemstones: Select gemstones suitable for solar infusion. Ensure they are safe for exposure to sunlight. Examples include Clear Quartz, Citrine, and Sunstone.

Cleanse and Charge the Gemstones: Cleanse the gemstones using your preferred method, such as water, smudging, or sound. Charge the gemstones with your intention.

Prepare Your Materials: Use a glass container filled with purified or spring water. Place the gemstones inside the container if using the direct method or in a smaller glass container if using the indirect method.

Set Up the Infusion: Place the container with the gemstones in a sunny spot where it can receive direct sunlight. Morning sunlight is preferred for its gentle, yet potent energy.

Infusion Time: Allow the gemstones to infuse in the sunlight for 2-4 hours. Avoid leaving the elixir in the sun for too long, as prolonged exposure can degrade certain gemstones and the water.

Remove the Gemstones: After the infusion period, remove the gemstones from the water. Your solar-infused gemstone elixir is now ready for use.

Store the Elixir: Store the elixir in a clean, glass container with a lid. Keep it in a cool, dark place to maintain its potency.

Using Lunar Energy to Enhance Gemstone Elixirs

Lunar infusion uses the energy of the moon to enhance gemstone elixirs. Moonlight adds a soothing, intuitive quality to the elixir, making it ideal for emotional healing and spiritual growth.

Steps for Lunar Infusion:

Choose Your Gemstones: Select gemstones suitable for lunar infusion. Examples include Moonstone, Amethyst, and Selenite.

Cleanse and Charge the Gemstones: Cleanse the gemstones using your preferred method. Charge the gemstones with your intention.

Prepare Your Materials: Use a glass container filled with purified or spring water. Place the gemstones inside the container if using the direct method or in a smaller glass container if using the indirect method.

Set Up the Infusion: Place the container with the gemstones in a spot where it can receive direct moonlight. The night of the full moon is ideal for maximum energy infusion.

Infusion Time: Allow the gemstones to infuse in the moonlight overnight. The gentle energy of the moon will enhance the properties of the elixir.

Remove the Gemstones: After the infusion period, remove the gemstones from the water. Your lunar-infused gemstone elixir is now ready for use.

Store the Elixir: Store the elixir in a clean, glass container with a lid. Keep it in a cool, dark place to maintain its potency.

Recommended Gemstones for Solar and Lunar Infusion

Solar Infusion:

- **Clear Quartz:** Amplifies energy and intention, enhances clarity and focus.

- **Citrine:** Attracts abundance, joy, and positivity.

- **Sunstone:** Promotes vitality, personal power, and leadership.

Lunar Infusion:

- **Moonstone:** Enhances intuition, emotional balance, and spiritual growth.

- **Amethyst:** Calms the mind, promotes emotional balance and spiritual growth.

- **Selenite:** Promotes cleansing and purification.

By using solar and lunar energies to enhance gemstone elixirs, you can create powerful, dynamic infusions that harness the natural energies of the sun and moon to support your well-being.

Recipes for Specific Intentions

Healing and Wellness Elixir

This Healing and Wellness Elixir combines the powerful energies of Clear Quartz, Amethyst, and Rose Quartz to promote physical and emotional healing. The direct infusion method with a solar charge amplifies the gemstones' properties, creating a potent elixir for overall well-being.

Gemstones:

- **Clear Quartz:** Known as the "Master Healer," Clear Quartz amplifies energy and intention, enhances clarity, and supports healing on all levels.

- **Amethyst:** Amethyst has calming and balancing properties, promoting emotional stability and spiritual growth. It aids in stress relief and enhances the immune system.

- **Rose Quartz:** Rose Quartz is the stone of unconditional love and emotional healing. It opens the heart chakra, promotes self-love, and encourages deep inner healing.

Method: Direct Infusion, Solar Charge

Steps for Creating the Healing and Wellness Elixir:

1. **Choose Your Gemstones:** Select high-quality pieces of Clear Quartz, Amethyst, and Rose Quartz. Ensure they are cleansed and charged.

2. **Cleanse and Charge the Gemstones:** Cleanse the gemstones using your preferred method, such as running water, smudging, or sound. Charge them by setting a clear intention for healing and wellness. Hold each gemstone and visualise it absorbing this intention.

3. **Prepare Your Materials:** Use a clean glass container filled with purified or spring water. Ensure the container is large enough to hold the gemstones.

4. **Infuse the Water:** Place the cleansed and charged gemstones directly into the glass container of water. Ensure the stones are fully submerged.

5. **Set Your Intention:** Focus on your intention for the elixir. Silently or aloud, state your intention: "I infuse this elixir with the energies of healing, wellness, and balance."

6. **Solar Charge:** Place the container in a sunny spot where it can receive direct sunlight. Morning sunlight is preferred for its gentle, yet potent energy.

7. **Infusion Time:** Allow the gemstones to infuse in the sunlight for 2-4 hours. This period will charge the water with the vibrant energies of the sun and the gemstones.

8. **Remove the Gemstones:** After the infusion period, remove the gemstones from the water. Your Healing and Wellness Elixir is now ready for use.

9. **Store the Elixir:** Store the elixir in a clean, glass container with a lid. Keep it in a cool, dark place to maintain its potency.

Usage:

- **Internal Use:** Drink a small amount (1-2 tablespoons) of the elixir daily to support overall healing and wellness. You can also add it to your drinking water throughout the day.

- **Topical Use:** Apply the elixir to your skin to promote healing and balance. It can be used as a facial mist or added to bathwater for a relaxing and rejuvenating experience.

By following these steps, you can create a powerful Healing and Wellness Elixir that harnesses the energies of Clear Quartz, Amethyst, and Rose Quartz to support your physical and emotional well-being.

Love and Compassion Elixir

This Love and Compassion Elixir combines the soothing and heart-opening energies of Rose Quartz, Rhodonite, and Green Aventurine. Using the indirect infusion method with a lunar charge, this elixir promotes love, compassion, and emotional healing.

Gemstones:

- **Rose Quartz:** Known as the stone of unconditional love, Rose Quartz opens the heart chakra, promotes self-love, and fosters deep emotional healing.

- **Rhodonite:** Rhodonite is a powerful heart healer that promotes forgiveness, compassion, and emotional balance. It helps to release past emotional trauma.

- **Green Aventurine:** Green Aventurine is a stone of comfort and heart healing. It promotes emotional recovery, compassion, and a sense of well-being.

Method: Indirect Infusion, Lunar Charge

Steps for Creating the Love and Compassion Elixir:

1. **Choose Your Gemstones:** Select high-quality pieces of Rose Quartz, Rhodonite, and Green Aventurine. Ensure they are cleansed and charged.

2. **Cleanse and Charge the Gemstones:** Cleanse the gemstones using your preferred method, such as running water, smudging, or sound. Charge them by setting a clear intention for love and compassion. Hold each gemstone and visualise it absorbing this intention.

3. **Prepare Your Materials:** Use two glass containers: one larger container for the water and one smaller container for the gemstones. Ensure both containers are clean and preferably made of glass. Use purified or spring water for the infusion.

4. **Infuse the Water:** Place the cleansed and charged gemstones in the smaller glass container. Fill the larger container with purified or spring water. Place the smaller container with the gemstones inside the larger container of water, ensuring the two do not touch.

5. **Set Your Intention:** Focus on your intention for the elixir. Silently or aloud, state your intention: "I infuse this elixir with the energies of love,

compassion, and emotional healing."

6. **Lunar Charge:** Place the container in a spot where it can receive direct moonlight. The night of the full moon is ideal for maximum energy infusion.

7. **Infusion Time:** Allow the gemstones to infuse in the moonlight overnight. The gentle energy of the moon will enhance the properties of the elixir.

8. **Remove the Gemstones:** After the infusion period, remove the smaller container with the gemstones from the water. Your Love and Compassion Elixir is now ready for use.

9. **Store the Elixir:** Store the elixir in a clean, glass container with a lid. Keep it in a cool, dark place to maintain its potency.

Usage

- **Internal Use:** Drink a small amount (1-2 tablespoons) of the elixir daily to support emotional healing and promote feelings of love and compassion. You can also add it to your drinking water throughout the day.

- **Topical Use:** Apply the elixir to your skin to promote love and emotional healing. It can be used as a facial mist or added to bathwater for a soothing and heart-opening experience.

By following these steps, you can create a powerful Love and Compassion Elixir that harnesses the energies of Rose Quartz, Rhodonite, and Green Aventurine to support emotional healing and foster love and compassion.

Protection and Grounding Elixir

This Protection and Grounding Elixir combines the stabilising and shielding energies of Black Tourmaline, Hematite, and Smoky Quartz. Using the direct infusion method with a solar charge, this elixir provides a strong protective shield and promotes grounding and stability.

Gemstones

- **Black Tourmaline:** Known for its powerful protective properties, Black Tourmaline shields against negative energy and promotes grounding.

- **Hematite:** Hematite is a grounding stone that enhances stability and balance. It helps to absorb negative energy and promotes a sense of security.

- **Smoky Quartz:** Smoky Quartz provides grounding and protection. It helps to transmute negative energy and promote emotional calmness.

Method: Direct Infusion, Solar Charge

Steps for Creating the Protection and Grounding Elixir

1. **Choose Your Gemstones:** Select high-quality pieces of Black Tourmaline, Hematite, and Smoky Quartz. Ensure they are cleansed and charged.

2. **Cleanse and Charge the Gemstones:** Cleanse the gemstones using your preferred method, such as running water, smudging, or sound. Charge them by setting a clear intention for protection and grounding. Hold each gemstone and visualise it absorbing this intention.

3. **Prepare Your Materials:** Use a clean glass container filled with purified or spring water. Ensure the container is large enough to hold the gemstones.

4. **Infuse the Water:** Place the cleansed and charged gemstones directly into the glass container of water. Ensure the stones are fully submerged.

5. **Set Your Intention:** Focus on your intention for the elixir. Silently or aloud, state your intention: "I infuse this elixir with the energies of protection, grounding, and stability."

6. **Solar Charge:** Place the container in a sunny spot where it can receive direct sunlight. Morning sunlight is preferred for its gentle, yet potent energy.

7. **Infusion Time:** Allow the gemstones to infuse in the sunlight for 2-4 hours. This period will charge the water with the vibrant energies of the sun and the gemstones.

8. **Remove the Gemstones:** After the infusion period, remove the gemstones from the water. Your Protection and Grounding Elixir is now ready for use.

9. **Store the Elixir:** Store the elixir in a clean, glass container with a lid. Keep it in a cool, dark place to maintain its potency.

Usage

- **Internal Use:** Drink a small amount (1-2 tablespoons) of the elixir daily to support grounding and protection. You can also add it to your drinking water throughout the day.

- **Topical Use:** Apply the elixir to your skin to promote grounding and stability. It can be used as a body spray or added to bathwater for a grounding and protective experience.

By following these steps, you can create a powerful Protection and Grounding Elixir that harnesses the energies of Black Tourmaline, Hematite, and Smoky Quartz to support your physical and emotional well-being.

Abundance and Prosperity Elixir

This Abundance and Prosperity Elixir combines the energising and wealth-attracting properties of Citrine, Green Aventurine, and Pyrite. Using the direct infusion method with a solar charge, this elixir helps to attract positivity, abundance, and prosperity.

Gemstones

- **Citrine:** Citrine is known as the "Merchant's Stone" for its ability to attract wealth, success, and abundance. It promotes positivity and dispels negative energy.

- **Green Aventurine:** Green Aventurine is considered the "Stone of Opportunity" and is thought to be one of the luckiest crystals, especially in manifesting prosperity and wealth.

- **Pyrite:** Pyrite is a powerful stone for manifesting wealth and abundance. It also provides protection and shields against negative energy.

Method: Direct Infusion, Solar Charge

Steps for Creating the Abundance and Prosperity Elixir:

1. **Choose Your Gemstones:** Select high-quality pieces of Citrine, Green Aventurine, and Pyrite. Ensure they are cleansed and charged.

2. **Cleanse and Charge the Gemstones:** Cleanse the gemstones using your preferred method, such as running water, smudging, or sound. Charge them by setting a clear intention for abundance and prosperity. Hold each gemstone and visualise it absorbing this intention.

3. **Prepare Your Materials:** Use a clean glass container filled with purified or spring water. Ensure the container is large enough to hold the gemstones.

4. **Infuse the Water:** Place the cleansed and charged gemstones directly into the glass container of water. Ensure the stones are fully submerged.

5. **Set Your Intention:** Focus on your intention for the elixir. Silently or aloud, state your intention: "I infuse this elixir with the energies of abundance, prosperity, and positivity."

6. **Solar Charge:** Place the container in a sunny spot where it can receive direct sunlight. Morning sunlight is preferred for its gentle, yet potent energy.

7. **Infusion Time:** Allow the gemstones to infuse in the sunlight for 2-4 hours. This period will charge the water with the vibrant energies of the sun and the gemstones.

8. **Remove the Gemstones:** After the infusion period, remove the gemstones from the water. Your Abundance and Prosperity Elixir is now ready for use.

9. **Store the Elixir:** Store the elixir in a clean, glass container with a lid. Keep it in a cool, dark place to maintain its potency.

Usage:

- **Internal Use:** Drink a small amount (1-2 tablespoons) of the elixir daily to attract abundance and prosperity. You can also add it to your drinking water throughout the day.

- **Topical Use:** Apply the elixir to your skin to promote positivity and attract prosperity. It can be used as a body spray or added to bathwater for a wealth-attracting experience.

By following these steps, you can create a powerful Abundance and Prosperity Elixir that harnesses the energies of Citrine, Green Aventurine, and Pyrite to attract wealth, success, and positivity into your life.

Intuition and Insight Elixir

This Intuition and Insight Elixir combines the spiritual and intuitive energies of Amethyst, Labradorite, and Lapis Lazuli. Using the indirect infusion method with a lunar charge, this elixir enhances intuition, spiritual awareness, and insight.

Gemstones:

- **Amethyst:** Amethyst is known for its calming and spiritually uplifting properties. It enhances intuition, spiritual awareness, and promotes a deep meditative state.

- **Labradorite:** Labradorite is a stone of transformation and magic. It enhances intuition, psychic abilities, and spiritual insights.

- **Lapis Lazuli:** Lapis Lazuli is a powerful stone for activating the higher mind and enhancing intellectual ability. It stimulates the desire for knowledge, truth, and understanding, and enhances intuition.

Method: Indirect Infusion, Lunar Charge

Steps for Creating the Intuition and Insight Elixir:

1. **Choose Your Gemstones:** Select high-quality pieces of Amethyst, Labradorite, and Lapis Lazuli. Ensure they are cleansed and charged.

2. **Cleanse and Charge the Gemstones:** Cleanse the gemstones using your preferred method, such as running water, smudging, or sound. Charge them by setting a clear intention for intuition and insight. Hold each gemstone and visualise it absorbing this intention.

3. **Prepare Your Materials:** Use two glass containers: one larger container for the water and one smaller container for the gemstones. Ensure both containers are clean and preferably made of glass. Use purified or spring water for the infusion.

4. **Infuse the Water:** Place the cleansed and charged gemstones in the smaller glass container. Fill the larger container with purified or spring water. Place the smaller container with the gemstones inside the larger container of water, ensuring the two do not touch.

5. **Set Your Intention:** Focus on your intention for the elixir. Silently or aloud, state your intention: "I infuse this elixir with the energies of intuition, insight, and spiritual awareness."

6. **Lunar Charge:** Place the container in a spot where it can receive direct

moonlight. The night of the full moon is ideal for maximum energy infusion.

7. **Infusion Time:** Allow the gemstones to infuse in the moonlight overnight. The gentle energy of the moon will enhance the properties of the elixir.

8. **Remove the Gemstones:** After the infusion period, remove the smaller container with the gemstones from the water. Your Intuition and Insight Elixir is now ready for use.

9. **Store the Elixir:** Store the elixir in a clean, glass container with a lid. Keep it in a cool, dark place to maintain its potency.

Usage:

- **Internal Use:** Drink a small amount (1-2 tablespoons) of the elixir daily to enhance intuition and spiritual awareness. You can also add it to your drinking water throughout the day.

- **Topical Use:** Apply the elixir to your skin to promote spiritual awareness and insight. It can be used as a facial mist or added to bathwater for a calming and spiritually uplifting experience.

How to Incorporate Gemstone Elixirs into Daily Life

Gemstone elixirs can be seamlessly integrated into your daily routine to harness their energetic benefits. Here are some practical ways to incorporate gemstone elixirs into your everyday life:

Morning Ritual: Start your day with a small amount of gemstone elixir. Drink 1-2 tablespoons of the elixir upon waking to set a positive tone for the day. You can also add it to a glass of water or your morning tea.

Hydration Boost: Add a few drops of gemstone elixir to your water bottle or drinking water throughout the day. This can help to continuously support your energy levels and overall well-being.

Meditation and Mindfulness: Use gemstone elixirs during meditation or mindfulness practices. Drink a small amount before starting your session to enhance your focus and intention. You can also mist your meditation space with the elixir to create a calming environment.

Topical Application: Apply gemstone elixirs directly to your skin for topical benefits. Use a spray bottle to mist your face and body, or add a few drops to your favourite lotion or skincare products. This can help to promote emotional balance and skin health.

Bath Rituals: Add gemstone elixirs to your bathwater for a relaxing and rejuvenating experience. This allows the elixir to interact with your body's largest organ, the skin, enhancing its benefits.

Culinary Use: Incorporate gemstone elixirs into your cooking and beverages. Add a few drops to soups, smoothies, or salad dressings to infuse your meals with the elixir's energetic properties.

Recommended Dosages and Frequency of Use

Internal Use: For internal use, start with 1-2 tablespoons of the elixir per day. You can gradually increase the dosage as you become more accustomed to its effects. Ensure you listen to your body and adjust the dosage based on your individual response.

Topical Use: When using gemstone elixirs topically, mist your face and body 1-2 times daily or as needed. You can also add a few drops to your skincare products for regular use.

Bath Rituals: Add 1-2 ounces of the gemstone elixir to your bathwater. Enjoy the bath for at least 20 minutes to fully absorb the elixir's benefits.

Hydration: Add a few drops of the elixir to your water bottle or drinking water throughout the day. This provides a gentle and continuous infusion of the elixir's energy.

Meditation and Mindfulness: Use the elixir before meditation or mindfulness practices. Drink 1-2 tablespoons or mist your meditation space before starting your session.

By incorporating gemstone elixirs into your daily routine, you can experience their continuous support and benefits. Consistency is key to maximising the elixir's effects, so find a routine that works best for you.

Physical Health Benefits

Common Ailments Addressed by Gemstone Elixirs

Gemstone elixirs can provide supportive benefits for a variety of physical health concerns. By incorporating the healing energies of specific gemstones, elixirs can help to alleviate symptoms and promote overall well-being.

Headaches and Migraines:

- **Gemstones:** Amethyst, Clear Quartz, Lapis Lazuli

- **Usage:** Drink 1-2 tablespoons of the elixir at the onset of symptoms. Apply the elixir to the temples and forehead for additional relief.

Digestive Issues:

- **Gemstones:** Carnelian, Citrine, Green Aventurine

- **Usage:** Drink a small amount of the elixir before meals to support digestion. Add a few drops to a glass of water and sip throughout the day.

Immune Support:

- **Gemstones:** Amethyst, Clear Quartz, Bloodstone

- **Usage:** Drink 1-2 tablespoons of the elixir daily to boost the immune system. Add a few drops to your water bottle for continuous support.

Joint and Muscle Pain:

- **Gemstones:** Hematite, Smoky Quartz, Malachite

- **Usage:** Drink the elixir daily to reduce inflammation. Apply topically to affected areas for targeted relief.

Respiratory Issues:

- **Gemstones:** Aquamarine, Clear Quartz, Blue Lace Agate

- **Usage:** Drink the elixir to support respiratory health. Use as a steam inhalation by adding a few drops to hot water and inhaling the vapour.

Skin Conditions:

- **Gemstones:** Rose Quartz, Amethyst, Green Aventurine

- **Usage:** Apply the elixir directly to the skin to soothe irritation and promote healing. Add to skincare products or use as a facial mist.

Emotional and Mental Well-being

Gemstone elixirs can significantly impact emotional balance and mental clarity. The unique energies of gemstones can help to alleviate stress, reduce anxiety, and promote a sense of calm and well-being. Here are some ways to use elixirs for emotional and mental health:

Stress Relief:

- **Gemstones:** Amethyst, Lepidolite, Blue Lace Agate

- **Usage:** Drink 1-2 tablespoons of the elixir during stressful moments. Apply it to your wrists and temples for immediate calming effects. Add a few drops to a diffuser for a soothing environment.

Anxiety Reduction:

- **Gemstones:** Rose Quartz, Rhodonite, Black Tourmaline

- **Usage:** Incorporate the elixir into your daily routine, drinking a small amount in the morning and evening. Use it as a facial mist or add to bathwater to promote relaxation and reduce anxiety.

Emotional Healing:

- **Gemstones:** Rose Quartz, Rhodochrosite, Green Aventurine

- **Usage:** Drink the elixir daily to support emotional healing and balance. Apply topically to the heart chakra area and use in meditation practices.

Mental Clarity:

- **Gemstones:** Clear Quartz, Fluorite, Sodalite

- **Usage:** Use the elixir before studying or working on tasks that require focus. Drink 1-2 tablespoons and mist your workspace to enhance mental clarity and concentration.

Benefits for Stress Relief, Anxiety Reduction, and Emotional Healing

Calming and Soothing Effects: The energies of gemstones like Amethyst and Lepidolite can calm the mind and soothe emotional turbulence. These stones help to reduce stress and promote a sense of peace.

Emotional Balance: Rose Quartz and Rhodochrosite are powerful for emotional healing. They open the heart chakra, promote self-love, and encourage forgiveness and compassion, helping to heal past emotional wounds.

Anxiety Reduction: Black Tourmaline and Blue Lace Agate are known for their grounding and protective properties. They help to dispel negative energy and reduce feelings of anxiety and fear.

Mental Clarity and Focus: Clear Quartz and Fluorite enhance mental clarity and focus. They help to clear mental fog, improve concentration, and support cognitive functions.

Spiritual Growth and Development

Enhancing Meditation and Spiritual Practices with Gemstone Elixirs

Gemstone elixirs can greatly enhance meditation and other spiritual practices by aligning your energy with higher vibrations and deepening your spiritual connection. Here are some ways to incorporate elixirs into your spiritual routine:

Pre-Meditation Ritual:

- **Gemstones:** Amethyst, Clear Quartz, Selenite

- **Usage:** Drink 1-2 tablespoons of the elixir before starting your meditation session to promote a calm mind and deepen your spiritual connection.

Chakra Balancing:

- **Gemstones:** Rose Quartz, Blue Lace Agate, Carnelian
- **Usage:** Apply the elixir to specific chakra points to balance and align your energy centres before or during meditation.

Sacred Space Cleansing:

- **Gemstones:** Black Tourmaline, Smoky Quartz, Clear Quartz
- **Usage:** Mist your meditation or sacred space with the elixir to cleanse and protect the area, creating a positive and focused environment for spiritual practices.

Spiritual Journaling:

- **Gemstones:** Lapis Lazuli, Amethyst, Labradorite
- **Usage:** Drink a small amount of the elixir before journaling to enhance intuitive insights and spiritual reflections.

Elixirs for Intuition, Psychic Development, and Spiritual Awakening

Intuition Enhancement:

- **Gemstones:** Moonstone, Labradorite, Amethyst
- **Usage:** Drink the elixir or apply it to the third eye chakra to enhance intuition and psychic abilities. Use before practices such as tarot reading or divination.

Psychic Development:

- **Gemstones:** Lapis Lazuli, Sodalite, Fluorite
- **Usage:** Incorporate the elixir into your daily routine to develop psychic skills. Drink it before engaging in psychic exercises or training.

Spiritual Awakening:

- **Gemstones:** Selenite, Clear Quartz, Amethyst
- **Usage:** Use the elixir during meditation or spiritual practices to facilitate spiritual awakening and enlightenment. Drink it or use it as a facial mist.

CHAPTER SIXTEEN

Advanced Techniques and Customizations

Enhancing Elixirs with Essential Oils

Combining the powerful energies of gemstones with the therapeutic properties of essential oils can create a potent elixir that enhances physical, emotional, and spiritual well-being. Essential oils can add additional layers of healing and support to gemstone elixirs.

Combining Essential Oils and Gemstones:

Selecting Essential Oils: Choose essential oils that align with the properties of your gemstones and the intention of your elixir. For example, lavender oil can complement the calming properties of Amethyst, while citrus oils like lemon or orange can enhance the energising effects of Citrine.

Synergistic Combinations:

- **For Relaxation and Stress Relief:**

    ○ Gemstones: Amethyst, Lepidolite, Blue Lace Agate

    ○ Essential Oils: Lavender, Chamomile, Bergamot

- **For Emotional Healing and Love:**

    ○ Gemstones: Rose Quartz, Rhodonite, Green Aventurine

    ○ Essential Oils: Rose, Ylang Ylang, Geranium

- **For Abundance and Prosperity:**

  - Gemstones: Citrine, Green Aventurine, Pyrite

  - Essential Oils: Patchouli, Frankincense, Clary Sage

- **For Protection and Grounding:**

  - Gemstones: Black Tourmaline, Hematite, Smoky Quartz

  - Essential Oils: Vetiver, Cedarwood, Myrrh

Steps to Create a Gemstone and Essential Oil Elixir:

1. **Choose Your Gemstones and Essential Oils:** Select the gemstones and essential oils that align with your intention.

2. **Cleanse and Charge the Gemstones:** Cleanse the gemstones using your preferred method. Charge them by setting a clear intention.

3. **Prepare Your Materials:** Use a clean glass container filled with purified or spring water. Ensure the container is large enough to hold the gemstones (for the direct method) or a smaller glass container (for the indirect method).

4. **Infuse the Water:**

   - **Direct Method:** Place the gemstones directly into the water.

   - **Indirect Method:** Place the gemstones in a smaller container and then into the larger container of water.

5. **Add Essential Oils:** Add 2-3 drops of essential oil to the water. Ensure the oils are well-dispersed in the water.

6. **Set Your Intention:** Focus on your intention for the elixir. Silently or aloud, state your intention while visualising the energies of the gemstones and essential oils infusing the water.

7. **Infusion Time:** Allow the gemstones and essential oils to infuse the water for at least 4 hours. For stronger elixirs, let the infusion sit overnight.

8. **Remove the Gemstones:** After the infusion period, remove the gemstones from the water.

9. **Store the Elixir:** Store the elixir in a clean, glass container with a lid. Keep it in a cool, dark place to maintain its potency.

Creating Elixirs with Sacred Geometry

Incorporating sacred geometry into your gemstone elixirs can amplify their energies and enhance their healing properties. Sacred geometry involves using specific geometric patterns that resonate with the fundamental structures of the universe.

Using Crystal Grids: Crystal grids are arrangements of gemstones in specific geometric patterns. These patterns help to focus and amplify the energy of the gemstones, making them more effective in elixirs.

Steps to Create a Gemstone Elixir with a Crystal Grid:

1. **Choose Your Gemstones:** Select gemstones that align with your intention.

2. **Select a Sacred Geometry Pattern:** Choose a pattern such as the Flower of Life, Seed of Life, or Metatron's Cube. These patterns enhance the flow of energy within the grid.

3. **Create the Crystal Grid:** Arrange the gemstones in the chosen geometric pattern. Place a central stone that resonates strongly with your intention in the middle.

4. **Infuse the Water:** Place a glass container of purified or spring water in the centre of the crystal grid. Ensure the water container is within the energy field of the grid.

5. **Set Your Intention:** Focus on your intention for the elixir. Silently or aloud, state your intention while visualising the energy of the crystal grid infusing the water.

6. **Infusion Time:** Allow the water to infuse within the crystal grid for at least 4 hours. For stronger elixirs, let the infusion sit overnight.

7. **Store the Elixir:** After the infusion period, store the elixir in a clean, glass container with a lid. Keep it in a cool, dark place to maintain its potency.

Examples of Sacred Geometry Patterns:

- **Flower of Life:** A symbol of creation and interconnectedness, enhancing the unity and harmony of the elixir.

- **Seed of Life:** Represents the foundation of life and the interconnectedness of all things, promoting balance and growth.

- **Metatron's Cube:** A complex geometric pattern that contains all the shapes in the universe, enhancing spiritual connection and protection.

Using Intention and Affirmations

The power of intention and affirmations can significantly enhance the effectiveness of gemstone elixirs. By focusing your thoughts and setting clear, positive intentions, you can amplify the energies of the gemstones and align them with your specific goals.

Setting Intention:

- **Before Creating the Elixir:**

  ○ Meditate on your intention. Visualise the desired outcome and infuse this intention into the gemstones and water.

  ○ Hold each gemstone and state your intention clearly, either silently or aloud.

- **During Infusion:**

  ○ Repeat affirmations that align with your intention. For example, "I am calm and at peace" for a stress relief elixir, or "I attract abundance and prosperity" for a wealth-attracting elixir.

  ○ Visualise the gemstones infusing the water with their energies, and see the elixir glowing with vibrant energy.

Using Affirmations:

- **Daily Use:**

  ○ Incorporate affirmations into your daily routine when using the elixir. For example, say, "I am healed and whole" when drinking a healing elixir.

  ○ Write down your affirmations and place them near your elixir container to continuously infuse the water with positive energy.

Examples of Affirmations:

- **For Healing:** "I am healthy, vibrant, and full of energy."

- **For Love:** "I am surrounded by love and compassion."

- **For Abundance:** "I attract prosperity and abundance into my life."

- **For Protection:** "I am safe, grounded, and protected."

By combining the power of gemstones, essential oils, sacred geometry, intention, and affirmations, you can create customised elixirs that are uniquely tailored to your needs and intentions. These advanced techniques enhance the energetic properties of your elixirs, making them powerful tools for healing, transformation, and spiritual growth.

Ancient Rituals and Beliefs

Gemstones have played a significant role in the rituals and spiritual practices of ancient civilizations. Their perceived magical properties and vibrant energies made them valuable tools for healing, protection, and spiritual connection. Different cultures around the world have harnessed the power of gemstones in various ways, integrating them into their religious, healing, and magical practices.

Overview of How Ancient Civilizations Used Gemstones in Rituals

Examples from Egyptian, Greek, Roman, and Native American Cultures

Ancient Egyptian Practices

- **Use of Gemstones:** The ancient Egyptians believed that gemstones possessed powerful protective and healing properties. They used gemstones like Lapis Lazuli, Turquoise, and Carnelian in their amulets, jewellery, and burial rituals.

- **Rituals:** Gemstones were often placed in the tombs of the deceased to provide protection and guidance in the afterlife. Lapis Lazuli was associated with the goddess Isis and was used to promote spiritual enlightenment and protection.

Ancient Greek Practices

- **Use of Gemstones:** The Greeks valued gemstones for their beauty and believed in their metaphysical properties. Amethyst, for example, was thought to prevent intoxication and promote clarity of mind.

- **Rituals:** Gemstones were used in various rituals to honour the gods and goddesses. They were also worn as talismans to attract love, prosperity, and protection. The Oracle of Delphi used gemstones to enhance divination and communication with the divine.

Ancient Roman Practices

- **Use of Gemstones:** Romans believed that gemstones could bring good fortune, health, and protection. They used a wide variety of gemstones, including Emerald, Garnet, and Amber.

- **Rituals:** Gemstones were used in daily rituals and ceremonies. Soldiers wore Amethyst and Carnelian for protection in battle. Emeralds were associated with Venus and used in love spells and rituals.

Native American Practices

- **Use of Gemstones:** Native American tribes utilised gemstones in their spiritual and healing practices. Turquoise, considered sacred, was often used in ceremonies and as a protective amulet.

- **Rituals:** Gemstones were integrated into healing rituals and spiritual ceremonies. Turquoise was used in rain ceremonies and for protection during travel. Quartz crystals were used by shamans to communicate with the spirit world and perform healing rituals.

Detailed Examples of Rituals and Their Significance

Egyptian Amulets

- **Lapis Lazuli Amulet:** Used to invoke the protection of the goddess Isis, Lapis Lazuli amulets were believed to provide spiritual guidance and protection. They were often buried with the deceased to aid in their journey through the afterlife.

Greek Amethyst Rituals

- **Amethyst Drinking Vessels:** The Greeks crafted drinking vessels from Amethyst to prevent intoxication and ensure clarity of mind. During religious ceremonies, these vessels were used to promote spiritual awareness and divine connection.

Roman Protective Jewelry

- **Carnelian Rings:** Roman soldiers wore Carnelian rings engraved with protective symbols to shield themselves in battle. These rings were believed to provide courage and protection from harm.

Native American Turquoise Ceremonies

- **Turquoise Healing Rituals:** Turquoise was used in healing rituals to restore health and balance. Shamans placed Turquoise stones on the body to draw out negative energy and promote physical and spiritual healing.

By understanding how ancient civilizations used gemstones in their rituals, we can appreciate the deep-rooted significance and powerful energies that these stones have carried through history.

Modern Rituals and Practices

Gemstones continue to play an essential role in modern rituals and spiritual practices. Their use has evolved, integrating ancient wisdom with contemporary spiritual practices.

Integrating Gemstones into Modern Rituals

Personal Protection Ritual

- **Gemstones:** Black Tourmaline, Obsidian, Hematite

- **Ritual:** Create a protective barrier around yourself by placing these stones at the four cardinal points. Visualise a protective shield forming, infused with the grounding and shielding energies of the gemstones.

Love and Attraction Spell

- **Gemstones:** Rose Quartz, Rhodochrosite, Garnet

- **Ritual:** Create a small altar with these stones. Light a pink candle and place it in the centre. Meditate on your intention to attract love, visualising the energy of the gemstones amplifying your desire.

Abundance and Prosperity Ritual

- **Gemstones:** Citrine, Pyrite, Green Aventurine

- **Ritual:** Arrange these gemstones in a grid pattern on a piece of green cloth. Place a gold candle in the centre. Light the candle and focus on your intention to attract wealth and prosperity, visualising the stones' energies drawing abundance to you.

Healing Meditation

- **Gemstones:** Amethyst, Clear Quartz, Selenite

- **Ritual:** Hold the gemstones in your hands or place them around you in a circle. Meditate on your intention for healing, visualising the light of the stones filling your body with healing energy.

Creating a Sacred Space:

- **Gemstones:** Amethyst, Smoky Quartz, Selenite

- **Ritual:** Place these gemstones at the corners of your space to create a protective and purifying energy field. Regularly cleanse the stones and set intentions for your sacred space.

Crystal Grids: Crystal grids are powerful tools for focusing and amplifying the energy of gemstones. By arranging stones in geometric patterns, you can create grids for various intentions such as healing, protection, or manifestation.

Steps to Create a Crystal Grid:

1. **Choose Your Intention:** Clearly define the purpose of your grid.

2. **Select Gemstones:** Choose stones that align with your intention.

3. **Set Up the Grid:** Arrange the stones in a geometric pattern, placing a central stone that resonates with your intention.

4. **Activate the Grid:** Use a crystal wand or your hand to draw lines connecting the stones, visualising the energy flow.

5. **Maintain the Grid:** Regularly cleanse and recharge the stones, revisiting and reinforcing your intention.

Medieval and Renaissance Uses

Gemstones in Alchemy and European Magical Practices

During the Medieval and Renaissance periods, gemstones continued to hold a significant place in alchemy and European magical practices. Alchemists and magicians believed that gemstones possessed intrinsic powers that could be harnessed for various purposes, including healing, protection, and transformation.

Alchemy

- **Philosopher's Stone:** In alchemy, the Philosopher's Stone was a legendary substance believed to have the ability to turn base metals into gold and grant immortality. While not a gemstone itself, the quest for the Philosopher's Stone often involved the use of various gemstones believed to contain transformative properties.

- **Gemstone Elixirs:** Alchemists created gemstone elixirs, similar to those used today, by infusing water or other liquids with the energy of gemstones. These elixirs were believed to possess healing properties and could be used to treat various ailments.

European Magical Practices

- **Talismanic Magic:** During the Medieval and Renaissance periods, talismans made with gemstones were commonly used for protection, luck, and love. Specific gemstones were selected based on their associated properties and were often inscribed with magical symbols or words of power.

- **Astrological Correspondences:** Gemstones were also linked to astrological signs and planetary influences. For example, Sapphire was associated with Saturn and was believed to bring wisdom and protection, while Ruby was linked to the Sun and was thought to enhance vitality and courage.

Symbolism and Magical Properties Assigned to Gemstones

Gemstones were assigned various symbolic meanings and magical properties during the Medieval and Renaissance periods. Here are a few examples:

- **Amethyst**

  - **Symbolism:** Associated with sobriety and clarity of mind.

  - **Magical Properties:** Used to prevent drunkenness, enhance mental clarity, and protect against psychic attacks.

- **Ruby**

  - **Symbolism:** Linked to passion, vitality, and courage.

  - **Magical Properties:** Believed to bring protection in battle, attract love, and ensure good health.

- **Sapphire**

  - **Symbolism:** Represented wisdom, purity, and divine favour.

  - **Magical Properties:** Used for protection against envy and harm, to enhance spiritual insight, and to attract divine blessings.

- **Emerald**

  - **Symbolism:** Symbolised fertility, rebirth, and eternal life.

  - **Magical Properties:** Believed to enhance memory, attract wealth, and promote physical and emotional healing.

- **Garnet**

  - **Symbolism:** Associated with protection, strength, and regeneration.

  - **Magical Properties:** Used to protect travellers, ensure safe passage, and promote physical health and vitality.

Detailed Examples of Practices and Their Significance

Amethyst Drinking Vessels

- **Practice:** Similar to the Greeks, Medieval practitioners used Amethyst drinking vessels to prevent intoxication and enhance clarity of mind.

- **Significance:** These vessels were believed to imbue the drink with the protective properties of Amethyst, ensuring mental clarity and spiritual purity.

Ruby Amulets for Protection

- **Practice:** Warriors and knights wore Ruby amulets for protection in battle, believing that the stone's fiery energy would keep them safe and imbue them with courage.

- **Significance:** Rubies were seen as powerful protectors, capable of warding off harm and providing the wearer with additional strength and bravery.

Sapphire Rings for Divine Favour

- **Practice:** Sapphire rings were worn by clergy and royalty to attract divine favour and protection. These rings were often inscribed with religious symbols or prayers.

- **Significance:** Sapphires were believed to connect the wearer with divine energies, offering spiritual insight and protection from negative influences.

Emeralds in Healing Rituals

- **Practice:** Healers used Emeralds in their rituals to promote physical and emotional healing. Emeralds were often placed on the body or used in elixirs.

- **Significance:** Emeralds were valued for their regenerative properties, symbolising rebirth and renewal, and were believed to restore health and balance.

By examining the uses and symbolic meanings of gemstones during the Medieval and Renaissance periods, we can gain a deeper understanding of their enduring significance and the magical properties attributed to them throughout history.

Modern Adaptations of Medieval and Renaissance Practices

Reviving Ancient Techniques

- **Talisman Creation**

  - Modern practitioners create talismans using gemstones, often inscribing them with symbols and words of power, drawing from Medieval and Renaissance traditions.

  - **Example:** Crafting a protective amulet with Black Tourmaline and inscribing it with a sigil of protection.

Astrological Gemstone Uses

- **Gemstone Astrology**

  - Incorporating gemstones into astrological practices, aligning stones with planetary influences for enhanced spiritual work.

  - **Example:** Using a Moonstone during the full moon for heightened intuition and emotional balance.

Alchemy-Inspired Elixirs

- **Gemstone Elixirs**

  - Creating elixirs that draw on alchemical principles, using gemstones for physical and spiritual healing.

  - **Example:** An elixir made with Clear Quartz for energy amplification and spiritual clarity.

Healing Rituals

- **Integrating Gemstones**

  - Using gemstones in healing rituals inspired by Medieval and Renaissance practices.

  - **Example:** Placing an Emerald on the heart chakra during a healing session to promote emotional healing and balance.

By adapting these historical practices to modern spiritual and magical work, we continue to honour the rich traditions of the past while enhancing our contemporary rituals and practices.

Cultural and Religious Significance

Gemstones in Hindu, Buddhist, and Other Religious Rituals

Hinduism

- **Navaratna (Nine Gems):** In Hindu culture, the Navaratna is a sacred combination of nine gemstones, each representing a different planet and deity. These gemstones are worn to balance planetary influences and bring harmony.

  - **Gemstones:** Ruby, Pearl, Red Coral, Emerald, Yellow Sapphire, Diamond, Blue Sapphire, Hessonite, and Cat's Eye.

  - **Usage:** The Navaratna is often worn as jewellery to protect the wearer from negative planetary influences and to enhance health, prosperity, and spiritual growth.

- **Gemstones in Ayurveda:** In Ayurvedic medicine, gemstones are used to balance the doshas (body energies) and promote physical and spiritual well-being.

  - **Example:** Blue Sapphire is associated with Saturn and used to calm the mind and enhance focus.

Buddhism

- **Mala Beads:** In Buddhist practice, mala beads are used for counting mantras during meditation. These beads often incorporate gemstones such as Jade, Amethyst, and Turquoise, each chosen for their spiritual properties.

- **Usage:** Mala beads are used to focus the mind during meditation, with each gemstone adding its specific energy to the practice.

- **Gemstone Offerings:** Gemstones are often used as offerings in Buddhist rituals to honour the Buddha and bodhisattvas.

  - **Usage:** Gemstones such as Jade and Lapis Lazuli are offered to purify negative karma and bring spiritual merit.

Other Religious Traditions

- **Christianity**

  - **Biblical References:** Gemstones are mentioned in the Bible and are often used in church decorations, religious artefacts, and clerical vestments.

  - **Example:** The Twelve Stones of the High Priest's Breastplate, each representing a tribe of Israel.

- **Islam**

  - **Prayer Rings and Amulets:** Gemstones such as Agate and Carnelian are used in prayer rings and amulets.

  - **Usage:** These gemstones are believed to offer protection and blessings.

- **Judaism**

  - **High Priest's Breastplate:** The High Priest's Breastplate contained twelve gemstones, each representing one of the twelve tribes of Israel.

  - **Usage:** These stones were believed to have divine significance and were used in religious rituals.

The Role of Gemstones in Indigenous and Tribal Ceremonies

Native American Cultures

- **Turquoise**

  - **Usage:** Considered a sacred stone, Turquoise is used in various ceremonies for protection, healing, and communication with the spirit world. It is often incorporated into jewellery and ceremonial objects.

- **Quartz Crystals**

  - **Usage:** Used by shamans for healing and divination, Quartz crystals are believed to connect the physical and spiritual realms.

African Traditions

- **Carnelian**

  - **Usage:** In some African cultures, Carnelian is used in rituals to bring strength, protection, and vitality. It is often worn as a talisman to safeguard against negative energies.

- **Malachite**

  - **Usage:** Known for its transformative properties, Malachite is used in healing ceremonies to draw out negative energies and promote physical and emotional balance.

Australian Aboriginal Cultures

- **Opal**

  - **Usage:** Opal holds significant cultural and spiritual importance among Australian Aboriginal tribes. It is considered a stone of dreams and visions and is used in rituals to enhance spiritual journeys and connection to the Dreamtime.

Detailed Examples of Cultural and Religious Practices

Hindu Navaratna Jewelry

- **Practice:** The Navaratna, or Nine Gems, is a traditional Hindu jewellery piece that includes Ruby, Pearl, Red Coral, Emerald, Yellow Sapphire, Diamond, Blue Sapphire, Hessonite, and Cat's Eye. Each gemstone represents a planet and its corresponding deity.

- **Significance:** Wearing the Navaratna is believed to balance planetary influences, protect against negative energies, and bring health, prosperity, and spiritual growth.

Buddhist Mala Beads

- **Practice:** Buddhist practitioners use mala beads made with gemstones such as Jade and Amethyst during meditation to count mantras and focus the mind.

- **Significance:** The gemstones in mala beads enhance the spiritual practice by providing specific energies that support meditation, clarity, and spiritual connection.

Native American Turquoise Ceremonies

- **Practice:** Turquoise is used in Native American healing and protection rituals. It is often worn by shamans and incorporated into ceremonial tools and jewellery.

- **Significance:** Turquoise is believed to provide protection, enhance communication with the spirit world, and promote physical and spiritual healing.

Christian Clerical Vestments with Gemstones

- **Practice:** Gemstones are used in the decoration of clerical vestments and religious artefacts in Christian traditions. The Twelve Stones of the High Priest's Breastplate, representing the twelve tribes of Israel, are an example.

- **Significance:** These gemstones are believed to symbolise divine connection, spiritual authority, and protection.

By understanding the cultural and religious significance of gemstones, we can appreciate their profound impact on various spiritual practices and their enduring legacy in rituals and ceremonies across the world.

Modern Uses in Rituals and Magic

Incorporating Ancient Practices into Modern Rituals

- **Talisman Creation**

  - **Practice:** Modern practitioners create talismans using gemstones, often inscribing them with symbols and words of power, drawing from historical traditions.

  - **Example:** Crafting a protective amulet with Black Tourmaline and inscribing it with a sigil of protection.

Astrological Gemstone Uses

- **Practice:** Incorporating gemstones into astrological practices, aligning stones with planetary influences for enhanced spiritual work.

  - **Example:** Using a Moonstone during the full moon for heightened intuition and emotional balance.

Alchemy-Inspired Elixirs

- **Practice:** Creating elixirs that draw on alchemical principles, using gemstones for physical and spiritual healing.

  - **Example:** An elixir made with Clear Quartz for energy amplification and spiritual clarity.

Healing Rituals

- **Practice:** Using gemstones in healing rituals inspired by ancient practices.

  - **Example:** Placing an Emerald on the heart chakra during a healing session to promote emotional healing and balance.

Modern Practices

Revival of Gemstone Magic in Contemporary Spirituality

In recent decades, there has been a revival of interest in gemstone magic within contemporary spirituality. This resurgence is often associated with the New Age movement, which blends ancient wisdom with modern practices to explore the metaphysical properties of gemstones.

How New Age and Wiccan Traditions Incorporate Gemstones

New Age Movement

- **Holistic Healing**

  - **Practice:** Gemstones are used in various holistic healing practices, such as crystal therapy and Reiki. Practitioners place gemstones on or around the body to balance the chakras, enhance energy flow, and promote physical and emotional healing.

  - **Popular Gemstones:** Amethyst for calming and spiritual awareness, Clear Quartz for energy amplification and clarity, and Selenite for purification and connection to higher realms.

- **Meditation and Mindfulness**

  - **Practice:** Many individuals use gemstones during meditation and mindfulness practices to deepen their connection to the spiritual realm and enhance inner peace.

- **Popular Gemstones:** Amethyst for spiritual growth, Clear Quartz for focus and clarity, and Selenite for tranquillity and connection to higher energies.

- **Energy Grids**

  - **Practice:** Creating crystal grids is a common practice in the New Age community. These grids involve arranging gemstones in specific patterns to amplify their energies and manifest intentions.

  - **Popular Patterns:** Flower of Life for universal harmony, Star of David for protection, and Spiral for growth and evolution.

Wiccan Traditions

- **Rituals and Spells**

  - **Practice:** Wiccans use gemstones in rituals and spells to harness their magical properties. Each gemstone corresponds to different elements, deities, and magical intentions.

  - **Examples:** Rose Quartz in love spells, Black Tourmaline for protection, and Citrine for abundance.

- **Altar Tools**

  - **Practice:** Gemstones are often placed on altars as offerings or as part of ritual tools. They are used to represent the elements, enhance the power of ritual work, and create sacred space.

  - **Common Gemstones:** Amethyst for spiritual work, Obsidian for grounding, and Moonstone for lunar rituals.

- **Sabbats and Esbats**

  - **Practice:** Gemstones are incorporated into celebrations of Sabbats (seasonal festivals) and Esbats (full moon rituals). They are used to honour deities, align with natural cycles, and perform magical workings.

  - **Examples:** Garnet for Yule (Winter Solstice), Sunstone for Litha (Summer Solstice), and Moonstone for Esbats.

Integration with Other Practices

Combining Gemstone Magic with Herbal Magic

- **Synergy of Energies**

  - **Practice:** Gemstones and herbs are often used together to create powerful magical tools.

  - **Examples:** Combining Rose Quartz with rose petals in a love spell to amplify love and compassion, or using Amethyst with lavender in a calming ritual.

- **Ritual Baths**

  - **Practice:** Herbal and gemstone infusions are used in ritual baths to cleanse and empower the practitioner.

  - **Examples:** Using lavender and chamomile with Amethyst and Clear Quartz for a calming and purifying bath.

Combining Gemstone Magic with Tarot

- **Enhancing Intuition**

  - **Practice:** Placing gemstones like Amethyst or Labradorite on a tarot deck or reading area to enhance intuitive insights and protect against negative energies.

  - **Examples:** Using Amethyst for clarity during readings, Labradorite for protection, and Sodalite for enhanced communication.

- **Charging Tarot Decks**

  - **Practice:** Practitioners often place gemstones like Clear Quartz or Selenite on their tarot decks to cleanse and charge them between readings.

  - **Examples:** Clear Quartz to amplify the deck's energy, Selenite to purify and cleanse.

Role of Intention and Energy in Modern Gemstone Rituals

- **Setting Intentions**

  - **Practice:** Modern gemstone magic emphasises the importance of setting clear intentions. By focusing on a specific goal or desire, practitioners align their energy with the gemstone's properties to manifest their intentions.

- ○ **Examples:** Meditating with a piece of Citrine while focusing on financial abundance, or using Rose Quartz to set an intention for self-love and healing.

- **Energy Amplification**

  - ○ **Practice:** Gemstones are believed to amplify the practitioner's energy and intention. This amplification helps to bring about desired changes and outcomes in various aspects of life, from health and love to prosperity and protection.

  - ○ **Examples:** Using Clear Quartz to amplify the energies of other gemstones in a healing grid, or placing Selenite around the home to enhance spiritual practices.

Detailed Examples of Modern Practices

Crystal Healing Sessions

- **Practice:** A crystal healer places specific gemstones on the client's body to balance the chakras and promote healing.

- **Examples:** Amethyst on the third eye chakra to enhance spiritual awareness, Rose Quartz on the heart chakra to promote emotional healing.

- **Significance:** These sessions aim to restore the body's natural energy flow and promote overall well-being.

Wiccan Protection Ritual

- **Practice:** A Wiccan practitioner creates a protection spell using Black Tourmaline, Sage, and a protective chant.

- **Examples:** The gemstone is charged with the intention of protection and placed at the entrance of the home to ward off negative energies.

- **Significance:** This ritual helps to create a safe and sacred space, protecting the practitioner and their home from harm.

Crystal Grids for Manifestation

- **Practice:** A crystal grid is created using Citrine, Clear Quartz, and Aventurine to attract abundance and prosperity.

- **Examples:** The gemstones are arranged in a specific pattern, and the practitioner sets a clear intention for financial success.

- **Significance:** The grid amplifies the energies of the gemstones, helping to manifest the practitioner's financial goals.

Meditation with Gemstones

- **Practice:** A practitioner meditates with a piece of Amethyst to enhance their spiritual connection and intuition.

- **Examples:** The gemstone is held or placed in front of them during the meditation session.

- **Significance:** The Amethyst helps to calm the mind, deepen the meditation, and facilitate spiritual insights.

Protection Rituals

Creating a Protective Shield: Using Black Tourmaline, Obsidian, and Hematite

Gemstones like Black Tourmaline, Obsidian, and Hematite are renowned for their powerful protective properties. By creating a protective shield with these stones, you can safeguard your home and personal space from negative energies and unwanted influences.

Gemstones:

- **Black Tourmaline:**

  - Known for its strong protective and grounding abilities, Black Tourmaline absorbs negative energy and provides a shield against psychic attacks.

- **Obsidian:**

  - Obsidian is a powerful protective stone that shields against negativity and removes emotional blockages. It also helps to ground and stabilise energy.

- **Hematite:**

  - Hematite is a grounding stone that enhances protection and stability. It absorbs negative energy and transforms it into positive vibrations.

Step-by-Step Protection Ritual for the Home and Personal Space

Gather Your Materials:

- Black Tourmaline, Obsidian, and Hematite stones

- A small bowl or dish

- Sage or Palo Santo for smudging

- A white candle

- Salt (optional)

Cleanse the Space:

- Begin by cleansing your home or personal space. Light the Sage or Palo Santo and walk around the area, allowing the smoke to purify the space. Focus on corners, doorways, and windows where negative energy may accumulate.

Set Up Your Altar:

- Place the Black Tourmaline, Obsidian, and Hematite stones in the small bowl or dish. Arrange them in a way that feels harmonious to you.

- Light the white candle and place it near the bowl of gemstones.

Set Your Intention:

- Take a moment to centre yourself and set a clear intention for protection. You can say a prayer or affirmation, such as, "I call upon the protective energies of Black Tourmaline, Obsidian, and Hematite to create a shield of light around my home and personal space."

Activate the Gemstones:

- Hold each gemstone in your hand and visualise it glowing with protective light. Imagine this light expanding and forming a shield around you and your space.

- Place the activated gemstones back in the bowl.

Create the Protective Shield:

- Walk around your home or personal space with the bowl of gemstones. Visualise the protective energy radiating from the stones and forming a barrier around the area.

- As you move through each room, visualise the shield becoming stronger and more impenetrable.

Seal the Ritual:

- Once you have completed the circuit, return to your altar. Thank the gemstones for their protective energy and extinguish the candle.

- If desired, sprinkle salt around the perimeter of your home or personal space to reinforce the protective barrier.

Crafting Protection Charms and Amulets

Materials Needed:

- Small Black Tourmaline, Obsidian, and Hematite stones

- Small fabric pouch or charm bag

- Protective herbs (e.g., rosemary, sage)

- Black thread or ribbon

Cleanse and Charge the Gemstones:

- Cleanse the gemstones using Sage or Palo Santo. Hold each stone and set your intention for protection, visualising the stones absorbing this energy.

Prepare the Pouch:

- Fill the fabric pouch with the protective herbs. Add the cleansed and charged gemstones to the pouch.

Seal the Charm:

- Close the pouch and tie it securely with the black thread or ribbon. As you tie the knot, say an affirmation of protection, such as, "May this charm shield me from harm and negative energies."

Carry or Place the Charm:

- Carry the protection charm with you in your bag or pocket, or place it in a significant location in your home or workspace. The charm will serve as a constant source of protective energy.

Love Rituals

Attracting Love: Using Rose Quartz, Rhodonite, and Pink Tourmaline

Gemstones like Rose Quartz, Rhodonite, and Pink Tourmaline are known for their powerful energies that attract love, promote self-love, and enhance emotional healing. These stones can be used in rituals to bring more love into your life, whether you seek to attract a romantic partner or deepen your self-love.

Gemstones:

- **Rose Quartz:**

  - Known as the stone of unconditional love, Rose Quartz opens the heart chakra, promotes self-love, and attracts romantic love.

- **Rhodonite:**

  - Rhodonite is a powerful heart healer that encourages forgiveness, compassion, and emotional balance, helping to heal past emotional wounds.

- **Pink Tourmaline:**

  - Pink Tourmaline promotes love, joy, and emotional healing. It is particularly effective for attracting romantic love and enhancing relationships.

Step-by-Step Love Ritual to Enhance Self-Love and Attract Romantic Love

Gather Your Materials:

- Rose Quartz, Rhodonite, and Pink Tourmaline stones

- A pink or red candle

- Rose petals

- A small bowl of water

- Essential oils (e.g., rose, lavender)

- A piece of paper and a pen

Cleanse the Space:

- Begin by cleansing your space. Light Sage or Palo Santo and walk around the area, allowing the smoke to purify the space. Focus on the area where you will perform the ritual.

Set Up Your Altar:

- Place the Rose Quartz, Rhodonite, and Pink Tourmaline stones on your altar. Light the pink or red candle and arrange the rose petals around the stones.

- Add a few drops of rose or lavender essential oil to the bowl of water and place it on the altar.

Set Your Intention:

- Take a moment to centre yourself and set a clear intention for the ritual. You can say a prayer or affirmation, such as, "I open my heart to love, attract a loving and harmonious relationship, and deepen my self-love."

Activate the Gemstones:

- Hold each gemstone in your hand and visualise it glowing with loving energy. Imagine this energy filling your heart and radiating outwards, attracting love and compassion.

- Place the activated gemstones back on the altar.

Write Your Intentions:

- Write down your specific intentions on the piece of paper. Be clear and detailed about what you want to attract or enhance in your life regarding love.

Perform the Ritual:

- Sit comfortably in front of your altar. Focus on the candle flame and take a few deep breaths. Visualise your intentions manifesting in your life.

- Place the piece of paper with your intentions under the bowl of water. Dip your fingers into the water and gently sprinkle it over the gemstones and rose petals, symbolising the infusion of love into your intentions.

Close the Ritual:

- Thank the gemstones for their loving energy and extinguish the candle. You can keep the gemstones and rose petals on your altar or carry the stones with you to continue attracting love and enhancing self-love.

Creating Love Talismans and Charm Bags

Materials Needed:

- Small Rose Quartz, Rhodonite, and Pink Tourmaline stones

- A small pink or red fabric pouch or charm bag

- Rose petals or lavender buds

- Pink or red thread or ribbon

Cleanse and Charge the Gemstones:

- Cleanse the gemstones using Sage or Palo Santo. Hold each stone and set your intention for attracting love and enhancing self-love, visualising the stones absorbing this energy.

Prepare the Pouch:

- Fill the fabric pouch with the rose petals or lavender buds. Add the cleansed and charged gemstones to the pouch.

Seal the Charm:

- Close the pouch and tie it securely with the pink or red thread or ribbon. As you tie the knot, say an affirmation of love, such as, "May this charm attract love and deepen my self-love."

Carry or Place the Charm:

- Carry the love charm with you in your bag or pocket, or place it under your pillow or in a significant location in your home. The charm will serve as a constant source of loving energy.

Prosperity Rituals

Manifesting Abundance: Using Citrine, Green Aventurine, and Pyrite

Gemstones like Citrine, Green Aventurine, and Pyrite are known for their powerful energies that attract prosperity, enhance luck, and promote financial success. These stones can be used in rituals to bring more abundance into your life and support your goals for wealth and success.

Gemstones:

- **Citrine:**

    - Citrine is known as the "Merchant's Stone" for its ability to attract wealth, success, and abundance. It promotes positivity and dispels negative energy.

- **Green Aventurine:**

    - Green Aventurine is considered the "Stone of Opportunity" and is thought to be one of the luckiest crystals, especially in manifesting prosperity and wealth.

- **Pyrite:**

    - Pyrite is a powerful stone for manifesting wealth and abundance. It also provides protection and shields against negative energy.

Step-by-Step Prosperity Ritual to Attract Wealth and Success

Gather Your Materials:

- Citrine, Green Aventurine, and Pyrite stones

- A gold or green candle

- Coins or paper money

- A small bowl of water

- Essential oils (e.g., patchouli, bergamot)

- A piece of paper and a pen

Cleanse the Space:

- Begin by cleansing your space. Light Sage or Palo Santo and walk around the area, allowing the smoke to purify the space. Focus on the area where you will perform the ritual.

Set Up Your Altar:

- Place the Citrine, Green Aventurine, and Pyrite stones on your altar.

- Light the gold or green candle and arrange the coins or paper money around the stones.

- Add a few drops of patchouli or bergamot essential oil to the bowl of water and place it on the altar.

Set Your Intention:

- Take a moment to centre yourself and set a clear intention for the ritual. You can say a prayer or affirmation, such as, "I attract abundance, prosperity, and financial success into my life."

Activate the Gemstones:

- Hold each gemstone in your hand and visualise it glowing with abundant energy. Imagine this energy attracting wealth and prosperity into your life.

- Place the activated gemstones back on the altar.

Write Your Intentions:

- Write down your specific intentions on the piece of paper. Be clear and detailed about what you want to attract or enhance in your life regarding wealth and success.

Perform the Ritual:

- Sit comfortably in front of your altar. Focus on the candle flame and take a few deep breaths. Visualise your intentions manifesting in your life.

- Place the piece of paper with your intentions under the bowl of water. Dip your fingers into the water and gently sprinkle it over the gemstones and coins, symbolising the infusion of abundance into your intentions.

Close the Ritual:

- Thank the gemstones for their abundant energy and extinguish the candle. You can keep the gemstones and coins on your altar or carry the stones with you to continue attracting prosperity and success.

Creating Prosperity Talismans and Charm Bags

Materials Needed:

- Small Citrine, Green Aventurine, and Pyrite stones

- A small gold or green fabric pouch or charm bag

- Coins or paper money

- Gold or green thread or ribbon

Cleanse and Charge the Gemstones:

- Cleanse the gemstones using Sage or Palo Santo. Hold each stone and set your intention for attracting wealth and prosperity, visualising the stones absorbing this energy.

Prepare the Pouch:

- Fill the fabric pouch with the coins or paper money. Add the cleansed and charged gemstones to the pouch.

Seal the Charm:

- Close the pouch and tie it securely with the gold or green thread or ribbon. As you tie the knot, say an affirmation of abundance, such as, "May this charm attract wealth and success."

Carry or Place the Charm:

- Carry the prosperity charm with you in your bag or pocket, or place it in a significant location in your home or workspace. The charm will serve as a constant source of abundant energy.

Healing Rituals

Physical and Emotional Healing: Using Amethyst, Clear Quartz, and Malachite

Gemstones like Amethyst, Clear Quartz, and Malachite are known for their powerful healing properties. They can be used in rituals to promote overall wellness and address specific physical and emotional ailments.

Gemstones:

- **Amethyst:**

  - Known for its calming and balancing properties, Amethyst promotes emotional stability, relieves stress, and enhances spiritual growth.

- **Clear Quartz:**

  - Clear Quartz is a versatile healing stone that amplifies energy and intention. It promotes clarity, enhances the immune system, and balances all the chakras.

- **Malachite:**

  - Malachite is a powerful stone for transformation and healing. It absorbs negative energies, promotes physical healing, and supports emotional balance.

Step-by-Step Healing Ritual for Overall Wellness and Specific Ailments

Gather Your Materials:

- Amethyst, Clear Quartz, and Malachite stones

- A white or purple candle

- A small bowl of water

- Essential oils (e.g., lavender, eucalyptus)

- A piece of paper and a pen

Cleanse the Space:

- Begin by cleansing your space. Light Sage or Palo Santo and walk around the area, allowing the smoke to purify the space. Focus on the area where you will perform the ritual.

Set Up Your Altar:

- Place the Amethyst, Clear Quartz, and Malachite stones on your altar. Light the white or purple candle and arrange the stones around the candle.

- Add a few drops of lavender or eucalyptus essential oil to the bowl of water and place it on the altar.

Set Your Intention:

- Take a moment to centre yourself and set a clear intention for healing. You can say a prayer or affirmation, such as, "I call upon the healing energies of Amethyst, Clear Quartz, and Malachite to promote physical and emotional wellness."

Activate the Gemstones:

- Hold each gemstone in your hand and visualise it glowing with healing light. Imagine this light filling your body and promoting healing and balance.

- Place the activated gemstones back on the altar.

Write Your Intentions:

- Write down your specific healing intentions on the piece of paper. Be clear and detailed about what you want to heal or improve.

Perform the Ritual:

- Sit comfortably in front of your altar. Focus on the candle flame and take a few deep breaths. Visualise your intentions manifesting in your life.

- Place the piece of paper with your intentions under the bowl of water. Dip your fingers into the water and gently sprinkle it over the gemstones, symbolising the infusion of healing energy into your intentions.

Close the Ritual:

- Thank the gemstones for their healing energy and extinguish the candle. You can keep the gemstones on your altar or carry them with you to continue promoting healing and wellness.

Creating Healing Charms and Elixirs

Materials Needed:

- Small Amethyst, Clear Quartz, and Malachite stones

- A small white or purple fabric pouch or charm bag

- Healing herbs (e.g., chamomile, peppermint)

- White or purple thread or ribbon

Cleanse and Charge the Gemstones:

- Cleanse the gemstones using Sage or Palo Santo. Hold each stone and set your intention for healing, visualising the stones absorbing this energy.

Prepare the Pouch:

- Fill the fabric pouch with the healing herbs. Add the cleansed and charged gemstones to the pouch.

Seal the Charm:

- Close the pouch and tie it securely with the white or purple thread or ribbon. As you tie the knot, say an affirmation of healing, such as, "May this charm promote healing and wellness in my life."

Carry or Place the Charm:

- Carry the healing charm with you in your bag or pocket, or place it in a significant location in your home or workspace. The charm will serve as a constant source of healing energy.

Creating Healing Elixirs:

Materials Needed:

- Amethyst, Clear Quartz, and Malachite stones

- A glass container filled with purified or spring water

- A small glass container for indirect infusion (if using Malachite)

Cleanse and Charge the Gemstones:

- Cleanse the gemstones using Sage or Palo Santo. Set your intention for healing and visualise the stones absorbing this energy.

Prepare the Elixir:

- For a direct method, place the Amethyst and Clear Quartz directly into the glass container of water.

- For an indirect method (Malachite), place the Malachite in the small glass container and submerge it in the larger container of water without direct contact.

Infuse the Water:

- Allow the gemstones to infuse the water for several hours or overnight, visualising the healing energy being transferred to the water.

Use the Elixir:

- Drink a small amount (1-2 tablespoons) of the elixir daily to promote healing. You can also apply it topically or add it to bathwater for additional benefits.

Spiritual Growth Rituals

Enhancing Spiritual Awareness: Using Selenite, Labradorite, and Lapis Lazuli

Gemstones like Selenite, Labradorite, and Lapis Lazuli are known for their powerful abilities to enhance spiritual awareness, intuition, and enlightenment. By incorporating these stones into your rituals, you can deepen your spiritual practice and connect more profoundly with higher realms.

Gemstones:

- **Selenite:**

  - Selenite is a high-vibration stone that promotes spiritual growth, mental clarity, and connection to higher consciousness. It cleanses the aura and opens the crown chakra.

- **Labradorite:**

  - Labradorite is a stone of transformation and intuition. It enhances psychic abilities, strengthens spiritual awareness, and protects against negative energies.

- **Lapis Lazuli:**

  - Lapis Lazuli is known for its deep connection to wisdom, truth, and spiritual enlightenment. It opens the third eye chakra and enhances intellectual ability and spiritual insight.

Step-by-Step Spiritual Growth Ritual for Intuition and Enlightenment

Gather Your Materials:

- Selenite, Labradorite, and Lapis Lazuli stones

- A white or blue candle

- A small bowl of water

- Essential oils (e.g., frankincense, sandalwood)

- A piece of paper and a pen

Cleanse the Space:

- Begin by cleansing your space. Light Sage or Palo Santo and walk around the area, allowing the smoke to purify the space. Focus on the area where you will perform the ritual.

Set Up Your Altar:

- Place the Selenite, Labradorite, and Lapis Lazuli stones on your altar. Light the white or blue candle and arrange the stones around the candle.

- Add a few drops of frankincense or sandalwood essential oil to the bowl of water and place it on the altar.

Set Your Intention:

- Take a moment to centre yourself and set a clear intention for spiritual growth and enlightenment. You can say a prayer or affirmation, such as, "I call upon the energies of Selenite, Labradorite, and Lapis Lazuli to enhance my spiritual awareness and guide me on my path to enlightenment."

Activate the Gemstones:

- Hold each gemstone in your hand and visualise it glowing with radiant, spiritual light. Imagine this light filling your aura and connecting you to higher realms.

- Place the activated gemstones back on the altar.

Write Your Intentions:

- Write down your specific spiritual intentions on the piece of paper. Be clear and detailed about what you want to enhance in your spiritual practice and awareness.

Perform the Ritual:

- Sit comfortably in front of your altar. Focus on the candle flame and take a few deep breaths. Visualise your intentions manifesting in your spiritual life.

- Place the piece of paper with your intentions under the bowl of water. Dip your fingers into the water and gently sprinkle it over the gemstones, symbolising the infusion of spiritual energy into your intentions.

Meditate:

- Spend some time meditating with the gemstones. Hold each stone or place them around you, focusing on their energy and how it enhances your spiritual connection.

Close the Ritual:

- Thank the gemstones for their spiritual energy and extinguish the candle. You can keep the gemstones on your altar or carry them with you to continue enhancing your spiritual practice.

Crafting Spiritual Talismans and Meditation Aids

Materials Needed:

- Small Selenite, Labradorite, and Lapis Lazuli stones

- A small white or blue fabric pouch or charm bag

- Spiritual herbs (e.g., sage, lavender)

- White or blue thread or ribbon

Cleanse and Charge the Gemstones:

- Cleanse the gemstones using Sage or Palo Santo. Hold each stone and set your intention for spiritual growth and enlightenment, visualising the stones absorbing this energy.

Prepare the Pouch:

- Fill the fabric pouch with the spiritual herbs. Add the cleansed and charged gemstones to the pouch.

Seal the Charm:

- Close the pouch and tie it securely with the white or blue thread or ribbon. As you tie the knot, say an affirmation of spiritual growth, such as, "May this charm enhance my spiritual awareness and guide me on my path to enlightenment."

Use the Talisman:

- Carry the spiritual talisman with you during meditation or place it in your sacred space. The talisman will serve as a constant source of spiritual energy.

By using these spiritual growth rituals and crafting spiritual talismans, you can enhance your intuition, deepen your spiritual practice, and connect more profoundly with higher realms through the powerful energies of Selenite, Labradorite, and Lapis Lazuli.

Crafting Amulets and Talismans

Definitions and Differences Between Amulets and Talismans

Amulets

- **Definition:** An amulet is an object, typically a piece of jewellery or a small charm, believed to provide protection, bring good luck, or ward off evil. Amulets are often worn or carried to benefit from their protective energies.

- **Purpose:** Amulets are primarily used for protection. They safeguard the wearer from negative influences, physical harm, and spiritual attacks. Amulets can also attract positive energies, such as good fortune and health.

Talismans

- **Definition:** A talisman is an object believed to contain magical properties and is used to attract a specific benefit or achieve a particular outcome. Talismans are created with a specific intention and often incorporate symbols, inscriptions, and gemstones.

- **Purpose:** Talismans are used to bring about a desired result or influence. They can be crafted for various purposes, such as attracting love, enhancing prosperity, or boosting personal power.

Key Differences

- **Function:** Amulets are generally protective, while talismans are created to achieve a specific goal or intention.

- **Creation:** Talismans are often more personalised and may involve a more intricate creation process, including the use of symbols, inscriptions, and rituals to empower them.

Historical Significance and Cultural Variations

Historical Significance

Ancient Civilizations

- Both amulets and talismans have been used since ancient times. Civilizations such as the Egyptians, Greeks, and Romans incorporated these objects into their daily lives and spiritual practices. For example, the Egyptian Ankh is a well-known amulet representing life and protection.

Medieval and Renaissance Europe

- During the Medieval and Renaissance periods, amulets and talismans were widely used in European magical practices. They were believed to offer protection against disease, misfortune, and malevolent forces. The use of gemstones, metals, and specific symbols was common in crafting these objects.

Cultural Variations

Hindu and Buddhist Traditions

- In Hindu and Buddhist cultures, amulets and talismans are used to invoke the protection of deities and attract blessings. Yantras (geometric designs) and mantras (sacred chants) are often incorporated into these objects to enhance their power.

African Traditions

- In various African cultures, amulets and talismans are crafted using natural materials such as bones, shells, and stones. They are used in rituals for protection, healing, and attracting prosperity.

Native American Traditions

- Native American tribes use amulets and talismans, such as medicine pouches and dreamcatchers, to protect against negative energies and bring about healing and spiritual growth. These objects often include gemstones, feathers, and herbs.

Islamic Traditions

- In Islamic culture, amulets often contain verses from the Quran and are believed to provide protection and blessings. Talismans, known as taweez, are created for various purposes, including protection from evil and attracting prosperity.

Examples of Historical and Cultural Amulets and Talismans

Egyptian Scarab

- **Description:** A beetle-shaped amulet symbolising regeneration, protection, and transformation.

- **Usage:** Worn as jewellery or placed in tombs to ensure safe passage to the afterlife.

Greek Evil Eye (Mati)

- **Description:** An eye-shaped amulet used to ward off the evil eye and protect against envy and harm.

- **Usage:** Worn as jewellery or hung in homes and vehicles for protection.

Native American Medicine Pouch

- **Description:** A small pouch containing herbs, stones, and other sacred objects used for healing and protection.

- **Usage:** Worn around the neck or carried to benefit from its protective and healing properties.

Islamic Taweez

- **Description:** A small pendant or scroll containing verses from the Quran, used for protection and blessings.

- **Usage:** Worn around the neck or kept in the home or vehicle for continuous protection.

Understanding the definitions, differences, and historical significance of amulets and talismans provides a foundation for crafting your own powerful objects with specific intentions. These objects have been used across cultures and throughout history to harness the protective and transformative energies of gemstones and other materials.

Selecting Gemstones for Specific Intentions

Choosing the right gemstones for your amulets and talismans is crucial to ensuring they effectively serve their intended purposes. Each gemstone has unique properties that can enhance specific outcomes, from protection and love to prosperity and spiritual growth.

Choosing the Right Gemstones Based on Desired Outcomes

Protection

- **Black Tourmaline:** Provides strong protective energies, shields against negative influences, and enhances grounding.

- **Obsidian:** Offers powerful protection against negativity, absorbs harmful energies, and promotes emotional stability.

- **Hematite:** Grounds and protects, absorbs negative energy, and enhances courage and strength.

Love and Emotional Healing

- **Rose Quartz:** Known as the stone of unconditional love, it promotes self-love, emotional healing, and attracts romantic love.

- **Rhodonite:** Encourages forgiveness, compassion, and emotional balance, and helps heal past emotional wounds.

- **Pink Tourmaline:** Enhances love, joy, and emotional healing, particularly effective for attracting romantic relationships.

Prosperity and Abundance

- **Citrine:** Attracts wealth, success, and abundance, promotes positivity, and dispels negative energy.

- **Green Aventurine:** Known as the "Stone of Opportunity," it is one of the luckiest crystals for manifesting prosperity and wealth.

- **Pyrite:** A powerful stone for manifesting wealth and abundance, provides protection, and shields against negative energy.

Healing and Wellness

- **Amethyst:** Calms the mind, balances emotions, and enhances spiritual growth and healing.

- **Clear Quartz:** Amplifies energy and intention, promotes clarity, enhances the immune system, and balances all chakras.

- **Malachite:** Absorbs negative energies, promotes physical healing, and supports emotional balance.

Spiritual Growth and Intuition

- **Selenite:** Promotes spiritual growth, mental clarity, and connection to higher consciousness, cleanses the aura, and opens the crown chakra.

- **Labradorite:** Enhances intuition and psychic abilities, strengthens spiritual awareness, and protects against negative energies.

- **Lapis Lazuli:** Deeply connected to wisdom, truth, and spiritual enlightenment, opens the third eye chakra, and enhances intellectual ability and spiritual insight.

Combinations of Gemstones for Enhanced Effects

Combining different gemstones can amplify their energies and create synergistic effects, enhancing the overall power of your amulet or talisman.

Protection Amulet

- **Gemstones:** Black Tourmaline, Obsidian, Hematite

- **Combined Properties:** Strong protection against negativity, grounding, emotional stability, and courage.

Love Talisman

- **Gemstones:** Rose Quartz, Rhodonite, Pink Tourmaline

- **Combined Properties:** Unconditional love, emotional healing, compassion, forgiveness, joy, and attraction of romantic relationships.

Prosperity Charm

- **Gemstones:** Citrine, Green Aventurine, Pyrite

- **Combined Properties:** Wealth, success, abundance, positivity, opportunity, and protection.

Healing Amulet

- **Gemstones:** Amethyst, Clear Quartz, Malachite

- **Combined Properties:** Emotional balance, spiritual growth, clarity, immune system enhancement, physical healing, and emotional support.

Spiritual Growth Talisman

- **Gemstones:** Selenite, Labradorite, Lapis Lazuli

- **Combined Properties:** Spiritual growth, mental clarity, higher consciousness, intuition, psychic abilities, wisdom, and enlightenment.

Examples of Gemstone Combinations and Their Uses

Protection Amulet

- **Purpose:** To provide strong protection against negative influences and enhance grounding.

- **Gemstones:** Black Tourmaline, Obsidian, Hematite

- **Usage:** Wear as a necklace or carry in a pouch to protect against negativity, enhance grounding, and promote emotional stability.

Love Talisman

- **Purpose:** To attract romantic love and enhance self-love and emotional healing.

- **Gemstones:** Rose Quartz, Rhodonite, Pink Tourmaline

- **Usage:** Place under your pillow or carry in a pouch to attract love, promote self-love, and heal emotional wounds.

Prosperity Charm

- **Purpose:** To attract wealth, success, and abundance.

- **Gemstones:** Citrine, Green Aventurine, Pyrite

- **Usage:** Keep in your wallet or place in your workspace to attract financial success, opportunities, and protection.

Healing Amulet

- **Purpose:** To promote physical and emotional healing and overall wellness.

- **Gemstones:** Amethyst, Clear Quartz, Malachite

- **Usage:** Wear as a bracelet or carry in a pouch to support healing, balance emotions, and enhance spiritual growth.

Spiritual Growth Talisman

- **Purpose:** To enhance spiritual awareness, intuition, and enlightenment.

- **Gemstones:** Selenite, Labradorite, Lapis Lazuli

- **Usage:** Use during meditation or keep in your sacred space to enhance spiritual connection, intuition, and wisdom.

By selecting the right gemstones and combining them for synergistic effects, you can create powerful amulets and talismans that align with your specific intentions and enhance your spiritual and magical practices.

Creating Personal Amulets

Crafting personal amulets involves a thoughtful selection of materials and tools to ensure that the amulet effectively serves its intended purpose. Here's a detailed guide on the necessary materials, tools, and steps to create amulets for protection, love, or prosperity.

Materials and Tools Needed for Crafting Amulets

1. **Gemstones**: Select gemstones based on the specific intention of your amulet (e.g., protection, love, prosperity).

2. **Metal Wire or Chains**: Use for securing the gemstones and creating wearable amulets.

3. **Fabric Pouches or Bags**: Ideal for carrying loose gemstones or small amulets.

4. **Herbs and Essential Oils**: Enhance the energy of your amulet and add additional magical properties.

5. **Candles**: Use in rituals to consecrate and charge the amulet.

6. **Incense or Sage**: For cleansing the gemstones and space.

7. **Thread or Ribbon**: To tie and secure the amulet.

8. **Parchment Paper and Pen**: For writing intentions, sigils, or prayers to include with the amulet.

9. **Mortar and Pestle**: For grinding herbs if necessary.

10. **Small Tools**: Such as pliers, scissors, and tweezers for handling and assembling materials.

Step-by-Step Guide to Creating an Amulet for Protection, Love, or Prosperity

1. Protection Amulet

Materials:

- Black Tourmaline, Obsidian, and Hematite stones
- Black thread or ribbon
- Small black fabric pouch
- Sage for cleansing

Steps:

1. **Cleanse the Gemstones**: Use Sage to cleanse the gemstones, removing any negative energies.

2. **Set Your Intention**: Hold each gemstone and set your intention for protection. Visualise the stones absorbing protective energy.

3. **Prepare the Pouch**: Fill the small fabric pouch with the cleansed gemstones.

4. **Seal the Amulet**: Tie the pouch securely with the black thread or ribbon. As you tie the knot, say an affirmation such as, "May this amulet protect me from harm and negative energies."

5. **Charge the Amulet**: Light a black candle and hold the amulet near the flame. Visualise a protective shield surrounding you and the amulet.

2. Love Amulet

Materials:

- Rose Quartz, Rhodonite, and Pink Tourmaline stones
- Pink thread or ribbon
- Small pink fabric pouch

- Rose petals or lavender buds

- Rose essential oil

Steps:

1. **Cleanse the Gemstones:** Use Sage or rose incense to cleanse the gemstones.

2. **Set Your Intention:** Hold each gemstone and set your intention for love and emotional healing. Visualise the stones absorbing loving energy.

3. **Prepare the Pouch:** Fill the small fabric pouch with the gemstones and rose petals or lavender buds.

4. **Add Essential Oil:** Add a few drops of rose essential oil to the pouch.

5. **Seal the Amulet:** Tie the pouch securely with the pink thread or ribbon. As you tie the knot, say an affirmation such as, "May this amulet attract love and promote emotional healing."

6. **Charge the Amulet:** Light a pink candle and hold the amulet near the flame. Visualise loving energy surrounding you and the amulet.

3. Prosperity Amulet

Materials:

- Citrine, Green Aventurine, and Pyrite stones

- Green or gold thread or ribbon

- Small green or gold fabric pouch

- Cinnamon sticks or bay leaves

- Bergamot essential oil

Steps:

1. **Cleanse the Gemstones:** Use Sage or cinnamon incense to cleanse the gemstones.

2. **Set Your Intention:** Hold each gemstone and set your intention for prosperity and abundance. Visualise the stones absorbing abundant energy.

3. **Prepare the Pouch**: Fill the small fabric pouch with the gemstones and cinnamon sticks or bay leaves.

4. **Add Essential Oil**: Add a few drops of bergamot essential oil to the pouch.

5. **Seal the Amulet**: Tie the pouch securely with the green or gold thread or ribbon. As you tie the knot, say an affirmation such as, "May this amulet attract wealth and prosperity into my life."

6. **Charge the Amulet**: Light a green or gold candle and hold the amulet near the flame. Visualise abundant energy surrounding you and the amulet.

Consecrating and Charging Your Amulet

Cleansing:

- Cleanse the amulet and gemstones using Sage, Palo Santo, or incense to remove any residual energies.

Setting Intention:

- Hold the amulet and set a clear, focused intention for its purpose. Visualise the desired outcome and infuse the amulet with this energy.

Charging: Use the energy of the four elements (Earth, Air, Fire, Water) to charge the amulet:

- **Earth:** Bury the amulet in the soil for a day to ground it.

- **Air:** Pass the amulet through incense smoke to purify it.

- **Fire:** Hold the amulet near a candle flame to empower it.

- **Water:** Sprinkle the amulet with purified water to cleanse it.

Final Blessing

- Hold the amulet in your hands and say a final blessing or prayer to seal its energy. Thank the elements and any deities or spirits you have called upon.

By following these steps, you can create personal amulets that are powerful, effective, and aligned with your specific intentions. These amulets will serve as ongoing sources of protection, love, prosperity, or any other desired outcome.

Crafting Talismans

Creating talismans involves thoughtful selection of symbols and gemstones that resonate with specific intentions. The design and symbolism imbued in a talisman greatly enhance its power and effectiveness.

Design and Symbolism in Talisman Creation

Symbols and Their Meanings:

- **Pentacle**

  - **Meaning:** Represents protection, balance, and the elements of earth, air, fire, water, and spirit.

  - **Usage:** Often inscribed on talismans for protection and balance.

- **Ankh**

  - **Meaning:** Symbol of eternal life and spiritual enlightenment.

  - **Usage:** Used to attract health, longevity, and spiritual growth.

- **Eye of Horus**

  - **Meaning:** Symbolises protection, healing, and restoration.

  - **Usage:** Incorporated into talismans for protection and health.

- **Tree of Life**

  - **Meaning:** Represents growth, strength, and interconnectedness.

  - **Usage:** Used to promote personal growth, wisdom, and spiritual connection.

- **Triskelion**

  - **Meaning:** Symbolises the flow of life and spiritual development.

  - **Usage:** Used in talismans for growth, progress, and personal transformation.

Choosing the Right Symbols

- **Intention:** Select symbols that resonate with your specific intention. For example, if your talisman is for protection, you might choose the Pentacle or the Eye of Horus.

- **Personal Connection:** Choose symbols that have personal significance to you, as this will strengthen your connection to the talisman.

Step-by-Step Guide to Crafting a Talisman for Specific Purposes

Materials Needed

- A base material (e.g., metal disc, wood slice, or stone)
- Gemstones that align with your intention
- Engraving tools or a fine-tipped marker
- Thread or cord for wearing the talisman (if desired)
- Essential oils (optional)
- Small pouch or box for storage

Steps to Create a Talisman

1. Design Your Talisman

- Decide on the symbols and inscriptions you want to include. Sketch your design on paper first.
- If using gemstones, determine where they will be placed on the talisman.

2. Prepare the Base Material

- Cleanse the base material using Sage or another preferred method to remove any residual energies.
- Engrave or draw the chosen symbols onto the base material. If engraving, use appropriate tools; if drawing, use a fine-tipped marker.

3. Attach the Gemstones

- Cleanse the gemstones and set your intention for each stone.
- Attach the gemstones to the base material using a strong adhesive or by embedding them if the base material allows.

4. Set Your Intention

- Hold the talisman in your hands and set a clear intention for its purpose. Visualise the desired outcome and infuse the talisman with this energy.

5. Charge the Talisman

- Use the energy of the four elements (Earth, Air, Fire, Water) to charge the talisman:

  - **Earth:** Bury the talisman in the soil for a day to ground it.

  - **Air:** Pass the talisman through incense smoke to purify it.

  - **Fire:** Hold the talisman near a candle flame to empower it.

  - **Water:** Sprinkle the talisman with purified water to cleanse it.

6. Final Blessing

- Hold the talisman in your hands and say a final blessing or prayer to seal its energy. Thank the elements and any deities or spirits you have called upon.

Examples of Talismans for Specific Purposes

1. Protection Talisman

- **Symbols:** Pentacle and Eye of Horus

- **Gemstones:** Black Tourmaline, Obsidian

- **Purpose:** To protect against negative influences and ensure safety.

2. Love Talisman

- **Symbols:** Heart and Rose

- **Gemstones:** Rose Quartz, Rhodonite

- **Purpose:** To attract love and enhance emotional healing.

3. Prosperity Talisman

- **Symbols:** Coin and Tree of Life

- **Gemstones:** Citrine, Green Aventurine

- **Purpose:** To attract wealth, success, and abundance.

4. Healing Talisman

- **Symbols:** Ankh and Lotus

- **Gemstones:** Amethyst, Malachite

- **Purpose:** To promote physical and emotional healing.

5. Spiritual Growth Talisman

- **Symbols:** Triskelion and Crescent Moon

- **Gemstones:** Selenite, Lapis Lazuli

- **Purpose:** To enhance spiritual awareness and personal transformation.

Rituals for Empowering and Activating Your Talisman

1. Cleansing

- Cleanse the talisman and gemstones using Sage, Palo Santo, or incense to remove any residual energies.

2. Setting Intention

- Hold the talisman and set a clear, focused intention for its purpose. Visualise the desired outcome and infuse the talisman with this energy.

3. Charging

- Use the energy of the four elements (Earth, Air, Fire, Water) to charge the talisman:

  - **Earth:** Bury the talisman in the soil for a day to ground it.

  - **Air:** Pass the talisman through incense smoke to purify it.

  - **Fire:** Hold the talisman near a candle flame to empower it.

  - **Water:** Sprinkle the talisman with purified water to cleanse it.

4. Final Blessing

- Hold the talisman in your hands and say a final blessing or prayer to seal its energy. Thank the elements and any deities or spirits you have called upon.

By following these steps, you can create and empower talismans that are powerful, effective, and aligned with your specific intentions. These talismans will serve as ongoing sources of energy and support for your desired outcomes.

Creating Amulets and Talismans for Others

Crafting amulets and talismans for others is a thoughtful and meaningful way to share the benefits of these powerful objects. When creating these items as gifts, it is important to consider the recipient's specific needs and intentions, ensuring that the amulet or talisman is tailored to their personal goals and desires.

Steps for Creating Amulets and Talismans for Others:

1. Understand the Recipient's Needs

- Take the time to understand the recipient's specific needs, intentions, and preferences. This will help you select the appropriate gemstones, symbols, and materials to create a personalised and effective amulet or talisman.

2. Select Gemstones and Symbols

- Choose gemstones that align with the recipient's intentions. For example, if they seek protection, select stones like Black Tourmaline and Obsidian. If they seek love, choose Rose Quartz and Rhodonite.

- Incorporate symbols that resonate with the recipient and enhance the intended purpose of the amulet or talisman.

3. Cleanse and Charge the Materials

- Cleanse the gemstones and base materials using Sage, Palo Santo, or another preferred method. This removes any residual energies and prepares the materials for charging.

- Set a clear intention for the recipient's specific needs and charge the materials with this focused energy.

4. Craft the Amulet or Talisman

- Follow the steps for creating personal amulets or talismans, incorporating the selected gemstones and symbols.

- Ensure the final product is both aesthetically pleasing and energetically potent, reflecting the care and intention you have put into its creation.

5. Consecrate and Empower the Gift

- Perform a consecration ritual to empower the amulet or talisman. This can involve invoking the four elements, saying a blessing, or using specific rituals that align with the recipient's spiritual beliefs.

6. Package the Gift Thoughtfully

- Present the amulet or talisman in a beautiful pouch, box, or wrapping that reflects its significance. Include a note explaining the purpose and care instructions for the amulet or talisman.

Ethical Considerations in Gifting Magical Items

1. Respect the Recipient's Beliefs

- Ensure that the recipient is open to receiving and using an amulet or talisman. Respect their spiritual beliefs and practices, and avoid imposing your own views.

2. Informed Consent

- Provide the recipient with information about the purpose and intended use of the amulet or talisman. This includes explaining the significance of the gemstones and symbols used.

3. Cultural Sensitivity

- Be mindful of the cultural origins and significance of the materials and symbols used in the amulet or talisman. Avoid cultural appropriation and ensure that the gift honours the traditions it draws from.

4. Transparency

- Be transparent about the creation process and the intentions behind the gift. This fosters trust and ensures that the recipient feels comfortable and informed about the magical item they are receiving.

Examples of Thoughtful Gift Amulets and Talismans

1. Protection Amulet for a Friend

- **Gemstones:** Black Tourmaline, Obsidian

- **Symbols:** Pentacle, Eye of Horus

- **Presentation:** Packaged in a black velvet pouch with a note explaining its protective properties and instructions for use.

2. Love Talisman for a Partner:

- **Gemstones:** Rose Quartz, Rhodonite

- **Symbols:** Heart, Rose

- **Presentation:** Wrapped in a pink silk scarf with a personalised message expressing your love and the talisman's purpose.

3. Prosperity Charm for a Colleague:

- **Gemstones:** Citrine, Green Aventurine

- **Symbols:** Coin, Tree of Life

- **Presentation:** Placed in a green satin bag with a card explaining its use for attracting wealth and success.

4. Healing Amulet for a Family Member:

- **Gemstones:** Amethyst, Malachite

- **Symbols:** Ankh, Lotus

- **Presentation:** Housed in a wooden box with a note detailing its healing properties and instructions for regular cleansing and charging.

By creating and gifting amulets and talismans with care and intention, you can offer meaningful support and positive energy to your loved ones. These magical items serve as personalised tokens of love, protection, prosperity, and healing, enhancing the lives of those who receive them.

CHAPTER
SEVENTEEN

Scrying and Divination

Scrying and Divination

Scrying is an ancient practice used to gain insight, foretell the future, or receive guidance from the spiritual realm by gazing into a reflective surface or an object. This divination technique allows practitioners to see visions, symbols, or images that provide answers to their questions or reveal hidden knowledge. The reflective surface can be a mirror, a bowl of water, a crystal ball, or any other medium that aids in focusing the mind and accessing deeper levels of consciousness.

Historical Background and Cultural Significance of Scrying

Ancient Egypt

- **Practice:** Scrying has been practised since ancient times, with one of the earliest recorded uses in ancient Egypt.

- **Tools:** Egyptian priests and priestesses used bowls of water or highly polished stones.

- **Purpose:** They received divine messages and guidance from the gods.

Ancient Greece

- **Terminology:** In ancient Greece, scrying was known as "hydromancy" (using water) and "crystallomancy" (using crystals).

- **Usage:** Oracles and seers used these techniques for insights and prophecies.

- **Example:** The Oracle of Delphi used reflective surfaces to receive visions from the gods.

Medieval Europe

- **Popularity:** Scrying gained popularity during the mediaeval period.

- **Notable Figures:** Nostradamus used a bowl of water or a black mirror for scrying to predict future events.

- **Tools:** Scrying mirrors made of black obsidian or polished metal were used by alchemists and magicians.

Indigenous Cultures

- **Native American:** Shamans used crystal gazing and water scrying to connect with the spirit world and receive community guidance.

- **African and Aboriginal Traditions:** Scrying was used to communicate with ancestors and spiritual beings.

Modern Practices

- **Popularity:** Scrying remains popular among those interested in spirituality, divination, and personal development.

- **Tools:** Modern practitioners use crystal balls, mirrors, and water bowls to access intuition and receive insights.

- **Incorporation:** Often incorporated into meditation practices to enhance psychic abilities and spiritual awareness.

Tools and Techniques for Scrying

Crystal Balls

- **Material:** Typically made of clear quartz, amethyst, or other clear crystals.

- **Preparation:** Cleanse the crystal ball with saltwater, smudging, or moonlight before use.

- **Method:** Sit in a dimly lit room, relax, and gaze into the crystal ball, allowing your mind to enter a meditative state.

Scrying Mirrors

- **Material:** Usually made of black obsidian, polished metal, or glass painted black on one side.

- **Preparation:** Cleanse the mirror and sit in a dimly lit room with a candle or low light source behind you.

- **Method:** Gaze softly into the mirror, allowing your mind to relax and visions or images to appear.

Water Scrying

- **Tools:** A bowl of water, sometimes with a dark base or ink added to the water.

- **Preparation:** Cleanse the bowl and water, and sit in a dimly lit room.

- **Method:** Gaze into the water, allowing your mind to enter a meditative state and observe any images or symbols that appear.

Techniques for Enhancing Scrying

Preparation and Setting

- **Quiet Space:** Choose a quiet, dimly lit space free from distractions.

- **Meditation:** Begin with a few minutes of meditation to clear your mind and centre yourself.

- **Intention Setting:** Set a clear intention or question you seek guidance on before starting.

Focus and Relaxation

- **Soft Gaze:** Keep a soft, unfocused gaze on the scrying tool, allowing your mind to relax.

- **Breathing:** Practise deep, rhythmic breathing to maintain a relaxed state.

- **Patience:** Allow images, symbols, or visions to come naturally without forcing them.

Recording Insights

- **Journal:** Keep a journal to record any images, symbols, or insights you receive during scrying.

- **Interpretation:** Reflect on the meanings of the images and how they relate to your intention or question.

Enhancing Psychic Abilities with Gemstones

Amethyst

- **Properties:** Enhances intuition, spiritual awareness, and psychic abilities.

- **Usage:** Hold or place an Amethyst near your scrying tool to enhance your connection to the spiritual realm.

Labradorite

- **Properties:** Protects against negative energies and enhances psychic abilities.

- **Usage:** Wear or place Labradorite near you during scrying to protect your energy and enhance your intuitive insights.

Clear Quartz

- **Properties:** Amplifies energy and intentions, enhances clarity and focus.

- **Usage:** Place Clear Quartz near your scrying tool to amplify your focus and the clarity of the visions received.

By using these advanced gemstone techniques and tools for scrying and divination, you can deepen your connection to the spiritual realm, enhance your psychic abilities, and gain valuable insights and guidance. This practice, enriched with historical knowledge and modern adaptations, continues to be a powerful tool for spiritual growth and self-discovery.

Gemstones for Scrying

Choosing the right gemstones for scrying is essential for enhancing your divination practice. Different gemstones have unique properties that can aid in accessing deeper levels of consciousness, amplifying intuition, and providing clarity during scrying sessions. Here are some of the best gemstones for scrying:

Obsidian

- **Properties:** Protection, grounding, clarity.

- **Benefits:** Black Obsidian is a powerful stone for protection and grounding. Its reflective surface makes it ideal for scrying, as it can reveal hidden truths and provide clear insights. Obsidian helps to clear mental fog and enhance psychic abilities, making it easier to interpret scrying visions.

- **Use in Scrying:** Black Obsidian mirrors or spheres are commonly used for scrying. Their dark, reflective surface can help you focus and access deeper levels of consciousness.

Clear Quartz

- **Properties:** Amplification, clarity, healing.

- **Benefits:** Clear Quartz is known as the "Master Healer" for its ability to amplify energy and intentions. It enhances clarity and can be programmed to support specific goals during scrying. Clear Quartz helps to sharpen your focus and increase the accuracy of your divination.

- **Use in Scrying:** Clear Quartz spheres or points can be used for scrying. Their clarity and amplification properties make them excellent tools for enhancing visions and insights.

Amethyst

- **Properties:** Intuition, spiritual awareness, protection.

- **Benefits:** Amethyst is a powerful stone for enhancing intuition and spiritual awareness. It provides protection and supports the development of psychic abilities. Amethyst helps to calm the mind and create a focused environment for scrying.

- **Use in Scrying:** Amethyst spheres or clusters can be used for scrying. Their calming and intuitive properties make them ideal for accessing deeper levels of consciousness and receiving clear insights.

Creating and Preparing a Scrying Stone or Sphere

Choosing the Right Stone

Select a gemstone that resonates with you and your scrying goals. Consider the properties of the stone and how they align with your intentions. For example, if you seek protection and clarity, Black Obsidian might be the best choice. If you want to enhance intuition and spiritual awareness, Amethyst would be suitable.

Cleansing the Stone

Before using your scrying stone, cleanse it to remove any negative or residual energies. You can cleanse the stone by rinsing it under running water, smudging it with sage or palo santo, or placing it in sunlight or moonlight for a few hours.

Charging the Stone

Charge your scrying stone with your intentions by holding it in your hands and focusing on your goals for the scrying session. Visualise white light or energy flowing into the stone, filling it with positive energy and your specific intentions.

Creating a Sacred Space

Prepare a quiet, undisturbed area for your scrying practice. Set up your space with items that help you focus and create a sacred atmosphere, such as candles, incense, and calming music. Place your scrying stone or sphere in a central position where you can comfortably gaze into it.

Scrying Techniques

Different techniques can be used in scrying, each offering unique ways to access deeper levels of consciousness and receive insights. Here are some of the most effective scrying techniques using gemstones:

Mirror Scrying with Black Obsidian

Preparation

- Select a Black Obsidian mirror or a highly polished piece of Black Obsidian.

- Cleanse and charge the mirror as previously described.

- Set up your sacred space with candles, incense, and other items that help you focus.

Technique:

- Sit comfortably in front of the Obsidian mirror with a candle placed behind you so that its light reflects off the mirror without causing glare.

- Gaze into the mirror, focusing your eyes on its surface while allowing your mind to relax.

- Allow your vision to soften and let images, symbols, or scenes appear in the reflection.

- Maintain a state of relaxed concentration, and avoid forcing any images to appear.

Interpretation:

- Pay attention to any images, feelings, or thoughts that arise during the session.

- Note the symbols or patterns you see and consider their possible meanings.

- Keep a journal to record your experiences and insights.

Water Scrying with Gemstone Bowls

Preparation

- Choose a bowl made of a suitable gemstone like Clear Quartz or Amethyst, or use a glass bowl and place gemstones around it.

- Fill the bowl with water and cleanse and charge it as described earlier.

- Set up your sacred space with calming elements like candles and incense.

Technique:

- Sit comfortably in front of the bowl, with a candle placed behind it so that its light reflects on the water's surface.

- Gaze into the water, focusing your eyes on the reflections and ripples.

- Allow your vision to soften and let images, symbols, or scenes appear in the water.

- Maintain a state of relaxed concentration, allowing the images to come naturally.

Interpretation:

- Pay attention to any images, feelings, or thoughts that arise during the session.

- Note the symbols or patterns you see and consider their possible meanings.

- Keep a journal to record your experiences and insights.

Crystal Ball Scrying: Techniques and Best Practices

Preparation

- Select a crystal ball made of Clear Quartz, Amethyst, or another suitable gemstone.

- Cleanse and charge the crystal ball as previously described.

- Set up your sacred space with elements that help you focus and relax.

Technique

- Sit comfortably with the crystal ball placed in front of you on a stand or a soft cloth.

- Gaze into the crystal ball, focusing your eyes on its surface and allowing your vision to soften.

- Let your mind relax and be open to any images, symbols, or scenes that appear within the crystal.

- Maintain a state of relaxed concentration, and avoid forcing any images to appear.

Interpretation

- Pay attention to any images, feelings, or thoughts that arise during the session.

- Note the symbols or patterns you see and consider their possible meanings.

- Keep a journal to record your experiences and insights.

Preparing for a Scrying Session

Proper preparation is essential for a successful scrying session. Setting the right intention, creating a sacred space, and ensuring you are grounded and centred can significantly enhance the effectiveness of your scrying practice.

Setting the Intention and Creating a Sacred Space

Setting the Intention

- **Clarify Your Purpose:** Before beginning your scrying session, take a moment to clarify your purpose. What do you hope to gain or understand from the session? Whether seeking guidance, gaining insight, or connecting with higher wisdom, having a clear intention will focus your energy and enhance the results.

- **Affirm Your Intention:** Silently or aloud, affirm your intention for the session. This can be a simple statement like, "I seek clarity on [specific issue]" or "I am open to receiving guidance and wisdom."

Creating a Sacred Space

- **Choose the Location:** Select a quiet, comfortable space where you will not be disturbed. This could be a dedicated meditation area, a quiet corner of a room, or any place where you feel relaxed and focused.

- **Set Up the Space:** Arrange items that help you create a sacred and calming environment. This can include:

  - **Candles:** Use candles to create a soft, ambient light. Candles can also represent the element of fire, adding warmth and focus to your space.

  - **Incense:** Burn incense or use essential oils to create a soothing scent. Popular choices include sage, sandalwood, frankincense, or lavender, which can help you relax and focus.

  - **Crystals:** Place additional crystals around your scrying area to enhance the energy. Stones like Clear Quartz, Amethyst, and Selenite can support clarity and spiritual connection.

  - **Comfort Items:** Include items that make you feel comfortable and grounded, such as a soft cushion, a favourite blanket, or personal mementos.

Grounding and Centering Techniques

Deep Breathing

- **Technique:** Sit comfortably and take several deep breaths. Inhale slowly through your nose, allowing your lungs to fill completely. Hold the breath for a moment, then exhale slowly through your mouth. Repeat this process several times until you feel calm and centred.

Visualisation

- **Technique:** Close your eyes and imagine roots extending from your body into the earth, anchoring you firmly. Visualise these roots growing deeper, providing stability and a strong connection to the earth. This grounding technique helps you feel centred and balanced.

Meditation

- **Technique:** Spend a few minutes in meditation to quiet your mind and centre your thoughts. Focus on your breath or use a simple mantra to maintain your concentration. Meditation helps you achieve a state of calm and openness, preparing you for the scrying session.

Enhancing the Scrying Environment

Candles

- **Placement:** Place candles around your scrying area to create a soft, ambient light. The flickering flame can help you focus and enter a meditative state. Avoid placing candles directly in front of your scrying surface to prevent glare.

Incense

- **Selection:** Choose incense that resonates with your intention. For example, sage or cedar can be used for cleansing and purification, while lavender or sandalwood can promote relaxation and focus.

- **Usage:** Light the incense and allow the smoke to waft around your scrying space, purifying the area and creating a calming atmosphere.

Quietude

- **Silence:** Ensure your scrying environment is quiet and free from distractions. Turn off electronic devices and let others in your household know you need undisturbed time.

- **Background Sound:** If complete silence is not possible or preferred, consider using gentle background sounds like soft instrumental music, nature sounds, or white noise to create a tranquil ambiance.

By setting a clear intention, creating a sacred space, and ensuring you are grounded and centred, you can significantly enhance the effectiveness of your scrying session. These preparations help you enter a focused, receptive state, allowing you to access deeper levels of insight and guidance.

Interpreting Scrying Images

Interpreting the images and symbols you see during a scrying session is a crucial part of the divination process. It requires practice, patience, and the development of your intuitive abilities. Here are some guidelines to help you interpret your scrying images effectively:

Recognizing Symbols and Patterns

Common Symbols

Animals

- Different animals can represent various aspects of life. For example, a dove might symbolise peace, while a lion could represent courage.

Shapes and Colors

- Geometric shapes and colours can also carry specific meanings. A circle might symbolise unity or completeness, while blue could indicate calmness and spirituality.

Scenes and Figures

- Seeing specific scenes or figures can provide insights into your questions. For instance, a scene of a flowing river might suggest a need for flexibility and going with the flow.

Personal Associations

Personal Symbolism

- Pay attention to what specific symbols mean to you personally. An image of a rose might remind you of love and beauty, or it could be linked to a personal memory or experience.

Emotional Responses

- Notice your emotional reactions to the images. Positive feelings might indicate affirmation or approval, while negative feelings could suggest a warning or an area that needs attention.

Developing Intuition and Psychic Abilities

Trusting Your Intuition

Inner Knowing

- Trust your initial impressions and feelings about the images you see. Your intuition is a valuable guide in interpreting scrying visions.

Practice

- The more you practise scrying, the more confident you will become in trusting your intuition and interpreting the symbols and patterns that appear.

Strengthening Psychic Abilities

Meditation

- Regular meditation can help strengthen your intuitive and psychic abilities by quieting the mind and allowing deeper insights to emerge.

Visualisation Exercises

- Practice visualisation exercises to enhance your ability to see and interpret images. Visualise symbols and scenes in your mind's eye and explore their meanings.

Keeping a Scrying Journal for Tracking Progress and Insights

Recording Sessions

Details

- After each scrying session, record the details in a dedicated scrying journal. Include the date, time, location, and your intention for the session.

Images and Symbols

- Write down the images, symbols, and patterns you saw during the session. Describe them in as much detail as possible.

Interpreting and Analysing

Initial Impressions

- Note your initial impressions and feelings about the images. What do you think they mean? How do they relate to your intention or question?

Further Analysis

- Reflect on the images over time. As you gain more experience with scrying, your interpretations may deepen and evolve. Revisit your journal entries to see if new insights emerge.

Tracking Patterns and Progress

Recurring Symbols

- Pay attention to any symbols or patterns that appear repeatedly in your scrying sessions. These recurring images can provide significant insights and guidance.

Personal Growth

- Use your journal to track your progress and growth in scrying and divination. Note any improvements in your ability to interpret images and trust your intuition.

Ethical Considerations in Divination

Practising scrying and other forms of divination comes with a set of ethical responsibilities. It's essential to use these tools with integrity, respect, and a clear intention to promote positive outcomes. Here are some key ethical considerations to keep in mind:

Respecting Privacy and Boundaries

Personal Responsibility

Consent

- Always obtain explicit consent before performing scrying or any other form of divination for another person. Respect their right to privacy and their personal boundaries.

Intentions

- Ensure that your intentions are pure and focused on providing helpful, positive insights. Avoid using divination to pry into the private matters of others without their permission.

Confidentiality

Trust

- Maintain confidentiality and respect the privacy of those you perform scrying sessions for. The information revealed during a divination session is personal and should be treated with the utmost discretion.

Responsibility

- Be mindful of the responsibility that comes with handling sensitive information. Use your insights to support and guide rather than to judge or control.

Using Divination Responsibly and Ethically

Intention and Integrity

Positive Intentions

- Approach scrying with clear, positive intentions. Your goal should be to seek guidance, provide clarity, and support personal growth and well-being.

Integrity

- Practice with integrity, honesty, and humility. Recognize the limitations of divination and avoid making absolute predictions or guarantees.

Avoiding Harm

Compassion and Support

- Use the insights gained from scrying to offer compassionate support and constructive guidance. Avoid using divination to manipulate, control, or harm others.

Constructive Feedback

- Provide feedback in a constructive and respectful manner. Be mindful of how your words and interpretations might impact the person you are reading for.

Empowering Others

Encouraging Self-Reliance - Guidance, Not Dependence

- Encourage those you read for to use divination as a tool for guidance rather than becoming dependent on it for every decision. Empower them to trust their intuition and make their own informed choices.

Personal Growth

- Support personal growth and self-awareness. Use divination to help individuals understand their own strengths, challenges, and potential paths forward.

Education and Awareness

Informed Practice

- Educate others about the responsible and ethical use of divination tools. Share knowledge about the importance of intention, respect, and ethical considerations in scrying.

Developing Skills

- Encourage those interested in scrying to develop their skills and intuition through practice, study, and self-reflection.

Balancing Scepticism and Belief

Healthy Scepticism

Questioning

- Maintain a healthy level of scepticism and critical thinking. Question the information you receive and consider multiple interpretations before drawing conclusions.

Open-Mindedness

- While scepticism is important, also remain open-minded and receptive to the insights and guidance that divination can provide.

Respect for Diverse Beliefs

Non-Judgment

- Respect the diverse beliefs and practices of others. Avoid imposing your own views or judgments on those who may have different perspectives on divination.

Cultural Sensitivity

- Be aware of the cultural significance and traditions associated with scrying and other divination practices. Show respect and appreciation for these traditions.

By adhering to these ethical considerations, you can practise scrying and other forms of divination with integrity, respect, and responsibility. This approach ensures that your practice is beneficial, supportive, and aligned with the highest good of all involved.

Combining Gemstones for Synergy

The Concept of Gemstone Synergy: Gemstone synergy refers to the combined effect of different gemstones working together to enhance and amplify their individual properties. When multiple gemstones are used in combination, their energies interact in a way that creates a more powerful and balanced effect than when used alone. This synergy occurs because each gemstone has unique vibrations and properties that can complement and support one another, resulting in a harmonious and enhanced energy field.

Benefits of Combining Gemstones for Enhanced Energy

Amplified Energies

- **Synergistic Effects:** When gemstones are combined, their energies can amplify each other, creating a stronger and more effective energy field. For example, combining Clear Quartz with any other gemstone can enhance the properties of the second stone due to Quartz's amplification abilities.

- **Increased Potency:** The combined energies of multiple gemstones can lead to increased potency in achieving specific intentions or goals, such as protection, healing, or abundance.

Balanced Energy

- **Complementary Properties:** Different gemstones have different properties that can complement and balance each other. For example, pairing grounding stones like Hematite with high-vibration stones like Amethyst can create a balanced energy that is both stabilising and spiritually uplifting.

- **Harmonized Energy Fields:** Combining gemstones with complementary energies can help to harmonise your energy field, leading to a more balanced and harmonious state of being.

Targeted Intentions

- **Specific Goals:** By selecting gemstones that align with specific intentions, you can create combinations that are tailored to your needs. For example, combining Rose Quartz, Rhodonite, and Pink Tourmaline can create a powerful set for attracting love and compassion.

- **Focused Energy:** Combining gemstones allows you to focus their combined energies on specific areas of your life, such as health, prosperity, or spiritual growth, leading to more targeted and effective outcomes.

Enhanced Healing

- **Multidimensional Healing:** Using a combination of gemstones can address multiple aspects of healing simultaneously. For instance, combining Amethyst for spiritual healing, Clear Quartz for clarity, and Rose Quartz for emotional healing can provide a comprehensive healing experience.

- **Holistic Approach:** Combining gemstones allows for a holistic approach to healing, addressing physical, emotional, mental, and spiritual aspects of well-being.

By understanding and utilising the concept of gemstone synergy, you can enhance the effectiveness of your gemstone practices. Combining different gemstones allows you to create powerful and balanced energy fields that support your intentions and promote overall well-being.

Popular Gemstone Combinations

Combining specific gemstones can create powerful synergies that enhance their individual properties and provide targeted benefits. Here are some popular gemstone combinations for various intentions:

Protection and Grounding

- **Black Tourmaline, Hematite, Smoky Quartz**

  - **Black Tourmaline:** Known for its strong protective properties, Black

Tourmaline shields against negative energy and electromagnetic radiation. It also grounds and balances the energy field.

- **Hematite:** Hematite is a grounding stone that enhances focus, concentration, and mental clarity. It also provides protection by absorbing negative energy.

- **Smoky Quartz:** Smoky Quartz is a protective and grounding stone that dispels negative energy and promotes emotional calmness.

Combining these stones creates a powerful protective barrier while grounding and stabilising your energy.

Love and Compassion

- **Rose Quartz, Rhodonite, Pink Tourmaline**

  - **Rose Quartz:** Known as the stone of unconditional love, Rose Quartz opens the heart chakra, promotes self-love, and enhances relationships.

  - **Rhodonite:** Rhodonite is an emotional balancer that nurtures love and encourages the healing of emotional wounds and scars from the past.

  - **Pink Tourmaline:** Pink Tourmaline promotes love, compassion, and emotional healing. It helps to release stress and emotional pain.

This combination fosters deep emotional healing, love, and compassion, enhancing your ability to give and receive love.

Abundance and Prosperity

- **Citrine, Green Aventurine, Pyrite**

  - **Citrine:** Known as the "Merchant's Stone," Citrine attracts wealth, prosperity, and success. It also promotes positivity and energy.

  - **Green Aventurine:** Green Aventurine is considered the luckiest of all crystals. It promotes abundance and is known to attract opportunities.

  - **Pyrite:** Pyrite is a powerful stone for manifesting wealth and abundance. It enhances willpower and determination.

Combining these stones creates a potent energy field that attracts abundance, prosperity, and opportunities.

Healing and Wellness

- **Amethyst, Clear Quartz, Rose Quartz**

  - **Amethyst:** Amethyst is a powerful healing stone that promotes spiritual awareness and intuition. It also provides emotional balance and stress relief.

  - **Clear Quartz:** Clear Quartz is known as the "Master Healer." It amplifies the energy of other stones and promotes overall healing and clarity.

  - **Rose Quartz:** Rose Quartz supports emotional healing and opens the heart to love and compassion.

This combination provides comprehensive healing, addressing physical, emotional, and spiritual well-being.

Spiritual Growth and Intuition

- **Labradorite, Lapis Lazuli, Selenite**

  - **Labradorite:** Known as the stone of transformation, Labradorite enhances intuition and spiritual awareness. It also provides protection against negative energies.

  - **Lapis Lazuli:** Lapis Lazuli is a powerful stone for spiritual growth and wisdom. It stimulates the third eye and enhances psychic abilities.

  - **Selenite:** Selenite is a high-vibration stone that promotes spiritual growth and clarity. It also cleanses and purifies the energy field.

Combining these stones enhances spiritual growth, intuition, and psychic abilities, providing a strong connection to higher realms.

By using these popular gemstone combinations, you can create powerful synergies that enhance their individual properties and provide targeted benefits for protection, love, abundance, healing, and spiritual growth.

Creating Gemstone Sets

Creating gemstone sets involves selecting complementary gemstones based on their properties and designing sets that align with specific intentions or needs. Here's how you can create effective gemstone sets:

Selecting Complementary Gemstones Based on Their Properties

Understanding Individual Properties

- Familiarise yourself with the properties and energies of different gemstones. Knowing what each gemstone offers allows you to combine them effectively.

- For example, Citrine is known for attracting abundance and positivity, while Amethyst promotes spiritual awareness and emotional balance.

Identifying Your Intention

- Determine the purpose of your gemstone set. Are you seeking protection, love, healing, abundance, or spiritual growth? Your intention will guide the selection of gemstones.

- For instance, if your intention is protection, you might choose Black Tourmaline, Hematite, and Smoky Quartz.

Matching Properties to Intention

- Select gemstones whose properties align with your intention. Ensure that the chosen stones complement each other and work harmoniously together.

- Example: For a set focused on love and compassion, you could combine Rose Quartz for unconditional love, Rhodonite for emotional healing, and Pink Tourmaline for compassion.

Designing Gemstone Sets for Specific Intentions or Needs

Protection and Grounding Set

- **Gemstones:** Black Tourmaline, Hematite, Smoky Quartz.

- **Intention:** To create a protective barrier and ground your energy.

- **Arrangement:** Place Black Tourmaline at the centre for protection, Hematite at the bottom for grounding, and Smoky Quartz around the edges to dispel negative energy.

Love and Compassion Set

- **Gemstones:** Rose Quartz, Rhodonite, Pink Tourmaline.

- **Intention:** To enhance love, compassion, and emotional healing.

- **Arrangement:** Place Rose Quartz at the centre to open the heart chakra, Rhodonite on either side for balance, and Pink Tourmaline around to promote compassion.

Abundance and Prosperity Set

- **Gemstones:** Citrine, Green Aventurine, Pyrite.

- **Intention:** To attract wealth, prosperity, and opportunities.

- **Arrangement:** Place Citrine at the centre for abundance, Green Aventurine on either side for luck, and Pyrite at the corners for manifesting wealth.

Healing and Wellness Set:

- **Gemstones:** Amethyst, Clear Quartz, Rose Quartz.

- **Intention:** To support comprehensive healing and well-being.

- **Arrangement:** Place Amethyst at the centre for spiritual healing, Clear Quartz on either side to amplify energies, and Rose Quartz around to promote emotional healing.

Spiritual Growth and Intuition Set:

- **Gemstones:** Labradorite, Lapis Lazuli, Selenite.

- **Intention:** To enhance spiritual growth, intuition, and psychic abilities.

- **Arrangement:** Place Labradorite at the centre for transformation, Lapis Lazuli on either side for wisdom, and Selenite around for spiritual clarity.

Creating gemstone sets with a clear intention and complementary properties ensures that the combined energies work harmoniously to support your goals. These sets can be used in various practices such as meditation, healing, or as part of your daily routine to enhance specific aspects of your life.

Wearing Multiple Gemstones

Layering Gemstone Jewelry for Combined Effects

Necklaces

- **Layered Look:** Wear multiple gemstone necklaces of varying lengths to keep different stones close to your heart chakra. For example, you could wear a Rose Quartz necklace for love and an Amethyst necklace for spiritual growth.

- **Coordination:** Choose necklaces that complement each other visually and energetically.

Bracelets

- **Stacking:** Stack several gemstone bracelets on one wrist to combine their energies. For instance, wearing Black Tourmaline, Hematite, and Smoky Quartz bracelets together can provide comprehensive protection and grounding.

- **Mix and Match:** Mix different textures and sizes for an aesthetically pleasing look.

Rings

- **Finger Placement:** Wear rings with different gemstones on various fingers to influence specific aspects of your life. For example, a Citrine ring for abundance on the index finger and an Amethyst ring for intuition on the middle finger.

- **Balance:** Ensure the rings are balanced in style and energy.

Tips for Harmonising Different Energies

- **Color Coordination:** Choose gemstones that complement each other visually as well as energetically. Harmonising colours can enhance the overall aesthetic and energy flow.

- **Balance and Symmetry:** Aim for balance by wearing an equal number of gemstones on both sides of your body. This can help distribute their energies evenly.

- **Intuitive Selection:** Trust your intuition when selecting gemstones to wear together. Your inner guidance can help you choose combinations that resonate with your energy and intentions.

Using Multiple Gemstones in Meditation

Placing Gemstones in Meditation Layouts

Chakra Alignment

- **Gemstone Placement:** Place corresponding gemstones on each chakra point to balance and energise your chakra system. For example, place Amethyst on your third eye chakra, Rose Quartz on your heart chakra, and Citrine on your solar plexus chakra.

- **Energy Flow:** Visualise energy flowing through each chakra, harmonising your entire system.

Circular Layouts

- **Protective Circle:** Arrange gemstones in a circle around you while meditating to create a protective and harmonious energy field. You can use stones like Black Tourmaline, Clear Quartz, and Selenite for this purpose.

- **Focused Energy:** Use a central stone to anchor the energy and support your meditation.

Visualising Combined Gemstone Energies

Energy Flow

- **Visualisation:** During meditation, visualise the energies of the gemstones flowing through your body and merging together to create a harmonious energy field. Imagine their combined vibrations enhancing your well-being and intentions.

- **Guided Imagery:** Use guided imagery to help visualise the merging and amplification of gemstone energies.

Intention Setting

- **Focused Intentions:** Focus on your specific intention while meditating with multiple gemstones. Visualise how their combined energies are working together to support and manifest your goals.

- **Affirmations:** Use affirmations to reinforce your intentions during meditation.

Creating Synergistic Crystal Grids

Designing Crystal Grids with Complementary Gemstones

Pattern Selection

- **Geometric Patterns:** Choose a geometric pattern for your crystal grid that aligns with your intention, such as a flower of life, hexagon, or spiral. Each pattern can amplify and direct the gemstones' energies in unique ways.

- **Template Use:** Use templates to ensure precision in your grid design.

Gemstone Placement

- **Complementary Stones:** Arrange complementary gemstones in the chosen pattern. For example, place Citrine, Green Aventurine, and Pyrite in a grid for abundance and prosperity.

- **Central Stone:** Use a powerful central stone to anchor the grid and set the primary intention.

Activating and Maintaining Crystal Grids

Activation

- **Using a Wand:** To activate the crystal grid, use a Clear Quartz point or your dominant hand to trace the pattern, connecting each gemstone with intention. Visualise the energy flowing between the stones, creating a powerful network of energy.

- **Intent Setting:** Speak your intention clearly and visualise it being realised.

Maintenance

- **Regular Cleansing:** Keep the grid in a clean, undisturbed space. Regularly cleanse and recharge the gemstones to maintain their potency. You can use methods like smudging, sunlight, or moonlight to keep the grid energetically vibrant.

- **Reconfiguration:** If your needs change, adjust the stones and patterns accordingly.

Introduction to Crystal Grids

What Are Crystal Grids? Crystal grids are intentional arrangements of crystals in geometric patterns designed to harness and amplify their collective energies for specific purposes. These grids utilise the combined power of gemstones and sacred geometry to create a focused and powerful energy field that can support various intentions, such as healing, protection, manifestation, and spiritual growth. The central stone, often called the "master crystal," acts as the focal point of the grid, with supporting stones arranged around it to create a harmonious and synergistic energy flow.

The Purpose and Benefits of Using Crystal Grids

Focused Intentions

- **Amplification of Intent:** Crystal grids help to amplify and focus your intentions by combining the energies of multiple stones in a deliberate pattern. This focused energy can significantly enhance the power and effectiveness of your intentions.

- **Manifestation:** By setting up a crystal grid with a clear intention, you can create a powerful tool for manifesting your desires. The grid acts as a physical representation of your goals and helps to align your energy with them.

Harmonised Energy

- **Synergy:** The arrangement of different gemstones in a crystal grid creates a synergistic effect, where the combined energies of the stones work together to produce a more potent and balanced outcome.

- **Balanced Energy Flow:** Using sacred geometry in the design of the grid ensures that the energy flows harmoniously and is evenly distributed, promoting balance and stability.

Enhanced Healing

- **Multi-Dimensional Healing:** Crystal grids can be designed to address physical, emotional, mental, and spiritual aspects of healing simultaneously. The combination of different gemstones can provide comprehensive healing support.

- **Focused Healing Energy:** By placing a crystal grid in a specific area, such as a healing room or beside a bed, you can create a focused and continuous flow of healing energy.

Protection and Clearing

- **Protective Energy Fields:** Crystal grids can create protective energy fields that shield you from negative influences and environmental stressors. This is particularly useful for personal protection or protecting a specific space.

- **Energy Clearing:** Grids can also be used to clear and purify energy in a space, removing stagnant or negative energy and promoting a positive and vibrant atmosphere.

Spiritual Growth

- **Enhanced Meditation:** Setting up a crystal grid for spiritual growth can enhance your meditation practice by providing a concentrated energy field that supports deep introspection and connection with higher realms.

- **Intuition and Insight:** Crystal grids can be designed to enhance intuition and psychic abilities, helping you to access deeper insights and spiritual guidance.

By understanding what crystal grids are and the purpose and benefits of using them, you can harness their powerful energies to support various aspects of your life. Whether you are seeking healing, protection, manifestation, or spiritual growth, crystal grids offer a versatile and effective tool for enhancing your intentions and achieving your goals.

Designing Your Crystal Grid

Creating a crystal grid involves selecting the right stones and arranging them in a way that aligns with your intentions. Here's how to design an effective crystal grid:

Selecting a Central Stone

Importance of the Central Stone:

- The central stone, or master crystal, is the focal point of your grid. It anchors the energy and sets the primary intention for the entire arrangement.

- This stone should resonate strongly with your specific goal, as its energy will be amplified by the surrounding stones.

Selection Tips:

- **Clarity and Size:** Choose a stone that is clear and of a size that stands out in your grid. Larger or more vibrant stones are often more effective as central points.

- **Alignment with Intentions:** Match the stone's properties to your goals. For example, use Clear Quartz for amplification and clarity, Amethyst for spiritual growth, or Rose Quartz for love and healing.

Choosing Supporting Stones

Harmonising Energies:

- Select supporting stones that complement the energy of the central stone and align with your intention. These stones work together to enhance the overall energy of the grid.

- Ensure the stones have compatible energies. For instance, pairing calming stones like Amethyst with grounding stones like Hematite can create a balanced energy flow.

Examples of Supporting Stones for Specific Intentions:

- **Protection:** Black Tourmaline, Hematite, Smoky Quartz.

- **Love:** Rose Quartz, Rhodonite, Pink Tourmaline.

- **Abundance:** Citrine, Green Aventurine, Pyrite.

- **Healing:** Amethyst, Clear Quartz, Rose Quartz.

- **Spiritual Growth:** Labradorite, Lapis Lazuli, Selenite.

Creating Geometric Patterns

Understanding Sacred Geometry:

- Sacred geometry involves specific shapes and patterns that are believed to have spiritual and energetic significance. Common shapes include circles, triangles, hexagons, and the flower of life.

- Using these patterns in your crystal grid can enhance the energy flow and amplify the grid's effectiveness.

Designing Your Grid:

- **Circle:** A circle is a simple and powerful shape that represents unity, wholeness, and protection. It's excellent for general healing and balancing.

- **Triangle:** A triangle can represent stability, manifestation, and the integration of mind, body, and spirit. It's effective for focused intentions and specific goals.

- **Hexagon:** The hexagon is associated with harmony and balance, often used in grids for peace and stability.

- **Flower of Life:** This intricate pattern symbolises creation and interconnectedness, ideal for spiritual growth and universal connection.

Step-by-Step Guide to Setting Up a Crystal Grid

Gather Your Materials:

- **Central Stone:** Select a central stone that aligns with your primary intention. Ensure it is cleansed and charged.

- **Supporting Stones:** Choose supporting stones that complement the central stone and enhance your intention. Cleanse and charge these stones as well.

- **Template or Design:** Decide on a geometric pattern for your grid. You can use a printed template, a cloth with a design, or create your own pattern.

Cleanse and Charge Your Stones:

- **Cleansing Methods:** Use methods such as smudging with sage, placing the stones under running water, or leaving them in sunlight or moonlight to cleanse them of any negative or residual energies.

- **Charging Methods:** Charge the stones by holding them and focusing on your specific intention. Visualise white light or energy flowing into the stones, filling them with your desired intention.

Set Up Your Space:

- **Location:** Choose a quiet, undisturbed area to set up your grid. This can be a dedicated meditation space, an altar, or any place where you can focus without interruptions.

- **Preparation:** Clear the space of any clutter and create a calm, serene environment. You may want to use candles, incense, or calming music to enhance the atmosphere.

Arrange the Stones:

- **Central Stone:** Place the central stone in the centre of your chosen pattern. This stone anchors the grid and sets the primary intention.

- **Supporting Stones:** Arrange the supporting stones around the central stone according to your chosen geometric pattern. Ensure the stones are evenly spaced and aligned with your intention.

Activate the Grid:

- **Setting Intentions:** Before activating the grid, take a moment to focus on your intention. Hold the intention clearly in your mind and visualise it being realised.

- **Using a Crystal Wand or Your Hands:** To activate the grid, you can use a crystal wand (such as a Clear Quartz wand) or your hands. Start from the central stone and move outward, connecting each stone in the pattern. Visualise energy flowing between the stones, creating a network of light and energy.

- **Affirmations:** As you activate the grid, you can also speak affirmations related to your intention. For example, if your intention is healing, you might say, "This grid is activated for healing and well-being."

Placement Tips for Maximum Energy Flow

Symmetry and Balance:

- **Symmetry:** Ensure that the stones are placed symmetrically to create a balanced and harmonious energy flow. Symmetry helps to stabilise the energy field and enhance the grid's effectiveness.

- **Balance:** Check that all stones are evenly spaced and that the pattern is visually balanced. This helps to maintain a stable and focused energy field.

Alignment with Directions:

- **Cardinal Directions:** Consider aligning your grid with the cardinal directions (north, south, east, west) to enhance the energy flow. This alignment can help to draw in universal energies and align your grid with natural forces.

- **Intentional Placement:** Place the grid in an area where it will not be disturbed. Avoid high-traffic areas or places where the stones might be moved or knocked over.

Activating Your Crystal Grid

Once you have set up your crystal grid, the next crucial step is to activate it. Activation involves charging the grid with your intention and ensuring that the energy flows harmoniously through the stones. Here's how to effectively activate your crystal grid:

Techniques for Activating and Charging a Crystal Grid

Setting Intentions and Affirmations:

- **Clear Intention:** Before activating the grid, take a moment to focus on your intention. Clearly state your goal or desire for the grid. This intention will guide the energy flow within the grid.

- **Affirmations:** Speak affirmations related to your intention. For example, if your grid is for healing, you might say, "This grid is activated for complete healing and wellness."

Using a Crystal Wand or Your Hands:

- **Crystal Wand:** Using a crystal wand (such as a Clear Quartz wand) can help direct and amplify energy. Hold the wand and start from the central stone, moving outward to connect each stone in the pattern. Visualise energy flowing through the wand and into the stones, creating a network of light and energy.

- **Hands:** If you don't have a crystal wand, you can use your hands. Hover your hands above the grid and visualise energy flowing from your hands into the stones. Move your hands in a pattern that connects each stone, similar to using a wand.

Visualisation:

- **Energy Flow:** Visualise the energy flowing through the grid, connecting each stone with light and energy. Imagine the stones glowing and the energy field becoming stronger and more vibrant.

- **Intention Visualisation:** As you connect the stones, visualise your intention being realised. See yourself achieving your goal or receiving the desired outcome.

Step-by-Step Guide to Activating a Crystal Grid

Prepare Your Space

- **Quiet Environment:** Ensure your space is quiet and undisturbed. This helps you focus and enhances the energy flow during activation.

- **Sacred Space:** Create a sacred space by lighting candles, burning incense, or playing calming music. This sets the tone for a focused and intentional activation process.

Focus on Your Intention:

- **Meditation:** Take a few moments to meditate and centre yourself. Focus on your intention and visualise the desired outcome.

- **Affirmations:** Speak your intention clearly, either silently or aloud. Use affirmations to reinforce your goal and guide the energy flow.

Activate the Grid:

- **Crystal Wand or Hands:** Begin at the central stone and use a crystal wand or your hands to connect each stone. Move in a pattern that flows naturally, such as spiralling outward or following the geometric design of the grid.

- **Energy Visualisation:** As you connect the stones, visualise energy flowing through the grid. See the stones glowing with light and your intention being infused into the grid.

Seal the Energy:

- **Final Connection:** Once all stones are connected, make a final pass over the grid to seal the energy. Visualise the grid's energy field being complete and powerful.

- **Closing Affirmation:** End with a closing affirmation to seal the activation. For example, "This grid is now fully activated and aligned with my highest good."

Maintaining and Adjusting Your Crystal Grid

To ensure that your crystal grid remains effective and continues to support your intentions, it's essential to maintain and adjust it regularly. Here's how to keep your grid energetically vibrant and aligned with your goals:

Cleansing and Recharging Your Grid

Regular Cleansing:

- **Purpose:** Cleansing removes any accumulated negative or stagnant energy from the stones, ensuring that they remain clear and effective.

- **Methods:**

  - **Smudging:** Use sage, palo santo, or incense to smudge the grid. Allow the smoke to envelop the stones and cleanse their energy.

  - **Sunlight:** Place the grid in sunlight for a few hours. The sun's rays can cleanse and recharge the stones. Be cautious with stones that may fade in sunlight, such as Amethyst.

- ○ **Moonlight:** Leave the grid under the light of the full moon overnight. Moonlight is gentle and effective for cleansing and recharging.

- ○ **Sound:** Use a singing bowl, bell, or tuning fork to cleanse the grid with sound vibrations. This method can clear and uplift the energy of the stones.

Recharging the Stones:

- **Intention:** After cleansing, recharge the stones by reaffirming your intention. Hold each stone and visualise it being filled with fresh, vibrant energy.

- **Visualisation:** Imagine a bright light or energy flowing into the stones, revitalising them and amplifying their properties.

Adjusting Stones and Patterns Based on Your Needs

Reconfiguration:

- **Changing Intentions:** If your goals or intentions change, you can reconfigure the grid to align with your new focus. Select new stones that resonate with your updated intentions and rearrange the grid accordingly.

- **Experimentation:** Feel free to experiment with different configurations and patterns. Trust your intuition to guide you in creating a layout that feels right and supports your goals.

Intuitive Adjustments:

- **Listening to Your Intuition:** Pay attention to how the grid feels energetically. If you sense that a stone needs to be moved or replaced, trust your intuition and make the necessary adjustments.

- **Subtle Shifts:** Even small adjustments can have a significant impact on the grid's energy. Regularly check in with the grid and make any subtle shifts that feel needed.

Tracking the Effects and Progress of Your Grid

Keeping a Journal:

- **Record Sessions:** After setting up and activating your grid, keep a journal to track your experiences. Note the date, intention, and any observations or feelings you have about the grid.

- **Ongoing Observations:** Regularly update your journal with any changes, insights, or manifestations that occur as a result of the grid. This helps you track the grid's effectiveness and progress.

Reflecting on Outcomes:

- **Evaluation:** Periodically reflect on the outcomes related to your grid's intention. Assess whether the grid has been effective in supporting your goals and make notes of any significant changes.

- **Adjustments:** Based on your reflections, decide if any adjustments are needed. This could involve changing stones, altering the pattern, or setting a new intention.

Feedback Loop:

CHAPTER
EIGHTEEN

Gemstone Care and Maintenance

Cleansing and Charging Techniques

Why Gemstones Need Regular Cleansing and Charging

Gemstones, like all objects, absorb and emit energy. Over time, they can accumulate negative or stagnant energies from their surroundings or from the people who handle them. Regular cleansing and charging are essential to maintaining the gemstones' optimal energetic properties and ensuring they continue to provide their intended benefits.

Energetic Buildup and Its Effects on Gemstones:

- **Diminished Effectiveness:** When gemstones accumulate negative energy, their ability to emit positive vibrations and provide their intended benefits is reduced. For example, a gemstone meant for protection may become less effective if not regularly cleansed and charged.

- **Energetic Blockages:** Energetic buildup can create blockages within the gemstone, preventing it from absorbing and transmitting energy effectively. This can hinder the flow of energy and disrupt the gemstone's ability to harmonise and balance.

- **Physical Manifestations:** In some cases, energetic buildup can even manifest physically, causing the gemstone to appear dull or lose its lustre. This physical change is often a sign that the gemstone needs to be cleansed and recharged.

- **Personal Energy:** Handling gemstones without cleansing them can transfer your own energy, including stress or negative emotions, into the stone. Over time, this can alter the gemstone's energy and impact its effectiveness.

Regular Cleansing and Charging Practices:

- **Monthly Routine:** Incorporate a monthly routine of cleansing and charging your gemstones to keep their energy clear and vibrant.

- **Intuitive Cleansing:** Pay attention to how your gemstones feel energetically. If a gemstone feels heavy or dull, cleanse and recharge it as needed, regardless of your routine schedule.

- **Special Occasions:** Cleanse and charge your gemstones before and after significant events or rituals to ensure they are energetically prepared and remain effective.

By understanding the importance of regular cleansing and charging, you can maintain the energetic integrity of your gemstones and continue to benefit from their powerful properties. This practice ensures that your gemstones remain vibrant, effective, and aligned with your intentions.

Cleansing Methods

Water Cleansing

Water is a powerful and natural cleanser for many gemstones. It can remove negative energies and refresh the stone's vibrational properties. However, it is essential to understand which gemstones are suitable for water cleansing and the various methods available.

Suitable Gemstones for Water Cleansing:

Certain gemstones can safely be cleansed with water. These include:

- **Quartz Family:** Clear Quartz, Amethyst, Citrine, Rose Quartz, Smoky Quartz

- **Agates:** All varieties of Agate

- Jasper: Red Jasper, Yellow Jasper, Green Jasper

- Tourmaline: Black Tourmaline, Pink Tourmaline, Green Tourmaline

Methods of Water Cleansing:

- **Running Water:**

  - **Process:** Hold the gemstone under running water (preferably a natural source like a stream or waterfall, but tap water works as well). Let the water flow over the stone for 1-2 minutes.

  - **Benefits:** Running water helps to wash away accumulated energies and refresh the stone's energy quickly.

  - **Frequency:** Suitable for a quick cleanse when needed.

- **Soaking:**

  - **Process:** Place the gemstone in a bowl of purified or spring water. Let it soak for several hours or overnight. You can add a pinch of sea salt to enhance the cleansing effect.

  - **Benefits:** Soaking provides a thorough cleansing, especially for stones that have absorbed a lot of energy.

  - **Frequency:** Use for a more profound cleansing, especially after intense energy work or rituals.

- **Saltwater:**

  - **Process:** Dissolve a teaspoon of sea salt in a bowl of purified water. Place the gemstone in the solution and let it soak for a few hours.

  - **Benefits:** Saltwater is particularly effective for purifying and neutralising negative energies.

  - **Frequency:** Use occasionally, as frequent saltwater cleansing can damage some stones.

Precautions for Water-Sensitive Stones:

Not all gemstones are suitable for water cleansing. Some stones can be damaged or weakened by water exposure. These include:

- Selenite: Soft and soluble in water, can deteriorate.

- Lepidolite: Contains minerals that can flake or dissolve.

- Malachite: Porous and can release toxic substances.

- Hematite: Can rust when exposed to water.

- Turquoise: Porous and can discolour or weaken.

Alternatives for Water-Sensitive Stones:

- **Smoke Cleansing:** Use Sage, Palo Santo, or incense.

- **Sound Cleansing:** Use singing bowls, bells, or tuning forks.

- **Earth Cleansing:** Bury the stones in soil for a period to absorb the earth's neutralising energies.

By selecting the appropriate cleansing method and understanding the precautions for water-sensitive stones, you can effectively maintain the energetic integrity of your gemstones without causing them harm.

Smoke Cleansing

Smoke cleansing, also known as smudging, is an ancient and widely practised method for cleansing gemstones. This method uses the smoke from sacred herbs or incense to purify and remove negative energies from the stones.

Using Sage, Palo Santo, or Incense

- **Sage:**

  - **Description:** Sage, particularly white sage, is a powerful herb used for purification. It is often used in smudging rituals to cleanse spaces, objects, and people.

  - **Benefits:** Sage smoke is believed to dispel negative energies, promote healing, and invite positive vibrations.

- **Palo Santo:**

  - **Description:** Palo Santo, also known as "holy wood," is a tree native to South America. Its wood has a sweet, fragrant aroma when burned and is used for cleansing and healing.

  - **Benefits:** Palo Santo smoke purifies and uplifts, removing negative energies and inviting peace and clarity.

- **Incense:**

- **Description:** Various types of incense can be used for smoke cleansing, such as frankincense, sandalwood, myrrh, and lavender.

- **Benefits:** Incense smoke can purify and harmonise the energy of gemstones, each type bringing its unique properties.

Step-by-Step Guide for Smoke Cleansing

- **Gather Your Materials:**

  - Sage bundle, Palo Santo stick, or your chosen incense

  - A fireproof dish or holder for catching ashes

  - A lighter or matches

  - Your gemstones

- **Prepare the Space:**

  - Find a well-ventilated area to perform the smoke cleansing. Open a window or door to allow negative energies to exit.

  - Set up your fireproof dish or holder to catch any falling ash.

- **Light the Smudging Material:**

  - Light the end of the Sage bundle, Palo Santo stick, or incense until it catches fire. Let it burn for a few seconds, then blow out the flame to produce smoke.

- **Cleanse the Gemstones:**

  - Hold the gemstone in one hand and use the other hand to guide the smoke around it. Ensure the smoke envelops the entire stone.

  - As you pass the stone through the smoke, set an intention for cleansing. You can say a prayer or affirmation, such as, "I cleanse this gemstone of all negative energies and restore its pure, positive vibrations."

  - Continue this process for each gemstone you wish to cleanse.

- **Allow the Smoke to Dissipate:**

  - Once you have cleansed all your gemstones, place the smudging material in the fireproof dish to let it burn out completely.

- Allow the smoke to dissipate and carry away any negative energies.

- **Thank the Elements:**

  - Take a moment to thank the herbs, wood, or incense for their cleansing properties. Express gratitude for the purification they have provided.

Frequency of Smoke Cleansing

- **Routine Cleansing:** Perform smoke cleansing at least once a month to maintain the energetic integrity of your gemstones.

- **Post-Usage Cleansing:** Cleanse gemstones after intense energy work, rituals, or if they have been handled by multiple people.

- **Intuitive Cleansing:** If a gemstone feels energetically heavy or dull, perform smoke cleansing as needed.

By using smoke cleansing, you can effectively remove negative energies from your gemstones and restore their positive vibrations. This method is gentle and suitable for most stones, making it a versatile option for regular gemstone maintenance.

Earth Cleansing

Earth cleansing involves burying gemstones in soil to neutralise negative energies and restore their natural vibrations. This method is effective for grounding and recharging gemstones with the earth's stabilising and nurturing energy.

Burying Gemstones in Soil

Benefits of Earth Cleansing:

- **Grounding Energy:** The earth's grounding energy helps stabilise the gemstone's vibrations and enhances its connection to nature.

- **Neutralisation:** Soil can absorb and neutralise negative energies accumulated in the gemstone.

- **Recharging:** The natural elements in the soil can recharge the gemstone, restoring its positive properties.

Step-by-Step Guide for Earth Cleansing:

1. **Select a Suitable Location:**

- Choose a safe and clean outdoor spot where the soil is free from contaminants. If you don't have access to outdoor space, you can use a pot with fresh soil.

2. **Prepare the Gemstones:**

- Cleanse the gemstones using another method (such as smoke cleansing) before burying them to remove surface energies.

3. **Bury the Gemstones:**

- Dig a small hole in the soil deep enough to cover the gemstones completely.

- Place the gemstones in the hole, ensuring they are in contact with the soil.

- Cover the gemstones with soil, gently pressing it down to secure them.

4. **Set an Intention:**

- As you bury the gemstones, set an intention for cleansing and grounding. You can say a prayer or affirmation, such as, "I return these gemstones to the earth to cleanse and ground their energies."

5. **Leave the Gemstones in the Soil:**

- Leave the gemstones buried for at least 24 hours. For a deeper cleanse, you can leave them for several days or even a week.

6. **Retrieve the Gemstones:**

- After the cleansing period, gently dig up the gemstones. Be careful not to damage them during retrieval.

- Brush off any excess soil and rinse the gemstones with water if needed.

7. **Final Blessing:**

- Hold the cleansed gemstones and express gratitude to the earth for its grounding and cleansing energy. You can say a final blessing or prayer to seal the process.

Frequency and Duration for Effective Cleansing:

- **Routine Cleansing:** Perform earth cleansing every few months to maintain the gemstone's energetic balance.

- **Post-Intensive Use:** Use earth cleansing after intense energy work or when the gemstones have been exposed to significant negative influences.

- **Duration:** A minimum of 24 hours is recommended, but longer durations (up to a week) can provide a more profound cleanse.

Precautions for Earth Cleansing:

- **Avoid Contaminated Soil:** Ensure the soil is clean and free from chemicals, pollutants, or debris that could damage the gemstones.

- **Sensitive Stones:** Be cautious with delicate or soft gemstones, as they might be damaged by prolonged contact with soil. Use alternative methods for such stones.

By using earth cleansing, you can effectively ground and neutralise negative energies in your gemstones, restoring their natural balance and enhancing their connection to the earth's stabilising energy.

Sound Cleansing

Sound cleansing is an effective method for purifying gemstones using the vibrations produced by sound. This method utilises tools such as singing bowls, bells, and tuning forks to emit sound waves that cleanse and realign the energy of the gemstones.

Using Singing Bowls, Bells, or Tuning Forks

Benefits of Sound Cleansing:

- **Vibrational Purification:** Sound waves penetrate the gemstone, breaking up stagnant or negative energy and restoring balance.

- **Non-Contact Method:** Ideal for delicate or water-sensitive stones that might be damaged by other cleansing methods.

- **Quick and Effective:** Sound cleansing is a fast method that can be done anywhere, making it convenient for regular use.

Step-by-Step Guide for Sound Cleansing:

1. **Select a Sound Cleansing Tool:**

- Choose a singing bowl, bell, or tuning fork that resonates with you. Each tool produces different sound frequencies, so select one that feels energetically aligned with your intention.

2. Prepare the Space:

- Find a quiet, peaceful area where you won't be disturbed. This will help you focus on the cleansing process.

3. Position the Gemstones:

- Place the gemstones in front of you, either on a table or a soft cloth. Ensure they are within reach of the sound vibrations.

4. Activate the Sound Tool:

- If using a singing bowl, gently strike the bowl with the mallet and then circle the rim with the mallet to produce continuous sound waves.

- If using a bell, hold the bell by the handle and gently ring it near the gemstones.

- If using a tuning fork, strike the fork against a soft surface to produce vibrations and then hold it close to the gemstones.

5. Direct the Sound Waves:

- Allow the sound waves to envelop the gemstones. Move the sound tool around the stones, ensuring the vibrations reach all sides.

- As you cleanse, set an intention for purification and energy realignment. You can say a prayer or affirmation, such as, "May these sound vibrations cleanse and restore the pure energy of these gemstones."

6. Duration:

- Continue the sound cleansing for a few minutes or until you feel the gemstones have been energetically reset. Trust your intuition to guide the duration.

7. Close the Cleansing:

- When you feel the cleansing is complete, gently stop the sound tool. Thank the instrument and the sound vibrations for their cleansing properties.

Frequency of Sound Cleansing:

- **Routine Cleansing:** Perform sound cleansing once a month to maintain the gemstone's energetic integrity.

- **Post-Usage Cleansing:** Cleanse gemstones after intense energy work, rituals, or if they have been handled by multiple people.

- **Intuitive Cleansing:** If a gemstone feels energetically heavy or dull, perform sound cleansing as needed.

Other Considerations:

- **Environment:** Ensure the environment where you perform sound cleansing is calm and free from distractions. This helps create a focused and effective cleansing session.

- **Personal Connection:** Choose a sound tool that resonates with you personally, as this enhances the overall effectiveness of the cleansing process.

By using sound cleansing, you can effectively purify and realign the energy of your gemstones. This method is gentle, quick, and suitable for all types of stones, making it an excellent choice for regular maintenance.

Other Methods

In addition to water, smoke, earth, and sound cleansing, there are other effective methods for purifying and recharging gemstones. These methods utilise natural elements such as sunlight, moonlight, and other crystals to restore the gemstones' energetic properties.

Using Sunlight and Moonlight

Sunlight Cleansing and Charging:

- **Method:** Place the gemstones in direct sunlight for a few hours. Sunlight is a powerful cleanser and charger, as it infuses the stones with vibrant, positive energy.

- **Benefits:** Sunlight revitalises gemstones, enhances their energy, and clears away negativity.

- **Precautions:** Some gemstones, such as Amethyst and Rose Quartz, can fade or become damaged by prolonged exposure to direct sunlight. Ensure the stones you choose are safe for sunlight exposure.

Moonlight Cleansing and Charging:

- **Method:** Place the gemstones under the moonlight, ideally during a full moon, for several hours or overnight. Moonlight, particularly full moon energy, is gentle and deeply cleansing.

- **Benefits:** Moonlight cleanses and recharges gemstones, promoting emotional balance and spiritual growth.

- **Frequency:** Monthly during the full moon for optimal results. Moonlight is safe for all gemstones and can be used regularly.

Utilising Other Crystals (e.g., Selenite, Clear Quartz)

Selenite Cleansing:

- **Method:** Place the gemstones on a Selenite slab or near Selenite wands. Selenite is known for its self-cleansing properties and ability to cleanse other stones.

- **Benefits:** Selenite purifies and recharges gemstones, clears negative energy, and enhances clarity.

- **Frequency:** Use Selenite cleansing as often as needed. It is a gentle and effective method suitable for all gemstones.

Clear Quartz Cleansing:

- **Method:** Place the gemstones on a Clear Quartz cluster or in a bowl with small Clear Quartz points. Clear Quartz amplifies energy and can cleanse other stones.

- **Benefits:** Clear Quartz boosts the energy of gemstones, clears negativity, and enhances their properties.

- **Frequency:** Use regularly to maintain the energetic integrity of your gemstones.

Detailed Steps for Each Method

Sunlight Cleansing and Charging:

1. **Select a Safe Location:** Choose a spot where the gemstones will receive direct sunlight without being disturbed.

2. **Place the Gemstones:** Arrange the gemstones on a natural surface, such as a stone or wooden tray.

3. **Set an Intention:** As you place the gemstones in the sunlight, set an intention for cleansing and charging. You can say a prayer or affirmation, such as, "May this sunlight cleanse and recharge these gemstones with vibrant, positive energy."

4. **Leave for a Few Hours:** Allow the gemstones to bask in the sunlight for a few hours, but avoid leaving them out for too long to prevent damage.

5. **Retrieve and Store:** After cleansing, retrieve the gemstones and store them in a safe place.

Moonlight Cleansing and Charging:

1. **Select a Safe Location:** Choose a spot where the gemstones will receive direct moonlight, such as a windowsill or outdoor area.

2. **Place the Gemstones:** Arrange the gemstones on a natural surface or cloth.

3. **Set an Intention:** As you place the gemstones in the moonlight, set an intention for cleansing and recharging. You can say a prayer or affirmation, such as, "May this moonlight cleanse and recharge these gemstones with soothing, balancing energy."

4. **Leave Overnight:** Allow the gemstones to soak in the moonlight overnight, especially during a full moon for maximum effect.

5. **Retrieve and Store:** After cleansing, retrieve the gemstones in the morning and store them in a safe place.

Selenite Cleansing:

1. **Place the Gemstones on Selenite:** Arrange the gemstones on a Selenite slab or near Selenite wands.

2. **Set an Intention:** As you place the gemstones on Selenite, set an intention for cleansing and recharging. You can say a prayer or affirmation, such as, "May this Selenite purify and recharge these gemstones with clear, positive energy."

3. **Leave for Several Hours:** Allow the gemstones to rest on the Selenite for several hours or overnight.

4. **Retrieve and Store:** After cleansing, retrieve the gemstones and store them in a safe place.

Clear Quartz Cleansing:

1. **Place the Gemstones on Clear Quartz:** Arrange the gemstones on a Clear Quartz cluster or in a bowl with small Clear Quartz points.

2. **Set an Intention:** As you place the gemstones on Clear Quartz, set an intention for cleansing and recharging. You can say a prayer or affirmation, such as, "May this Clear Quartz amplify and cleanse the energy of these gemstones."

3. **Leave for Several Hours:** Allow the gemstones to rest on the Clear

Charging Techniques

Charging gemstones is essential to amplify and maintain their energies. Utilising natural sources like sunlight, moonlight, crystal clusters, and intentional meditation ensures that your gemstones remain potent and aligned with your intentions.

Sunlight and Moonlight

Charging gemstones using sunlight and moonlight harnesses the natural energies of the sun and moon to enhance the stones' properties. Each method has its own benefits and is suitable for different types of gemstones.

Best Practices for Charging with Solar and Lunar Energy

Sunlight Charging

Best Practices:

- **Select an Appropriate Location:** Choose a spot where the gemstones will receive direct sunlight for several hours. This can be a windowsill, a garden, or any safe outdoor space.

- **Timing:** Morning sunlight is often preferred as it is less intense and more gentle on the gemstones. Avoid midday sun, especially for stones that may fade or become damaged by strong UV light.

- **Duration:** Allow the gemstones to bask in sunlight for 1-2 hours. Some stones may benefit from longer exposure, but be cautious with sensitive stones.

- **Set an Intention:** As you place the gemstones in the sunlight, set a clear intention for charging. You can say a prayer or affirmation, such as, "May this sunlight infuse these gemstones with vibrant, positive energy."

Suitable Gemstones for Sunlight Charging:

- **Citrine:** Enhances its natural abundance and positivity properties.

- **Clear Quartz:** Amplifies energy and intentions.

- **Sunstone:** Energizes and promotes vitality.

- **Carnelian:** Boosts motivation and creativity.

- **Tiger's Eye:** Strengthens confidence and protection.

Precautions:

- **Avoid Prolonged Exposure:** Stones like Amethyst, Rose Quartz, and other colourful crystals can fade with prolonged exposure to direct sunlight.

- **Check for Sensitivity:** Ensure the gemstones you choose are not prone to damage from sunlight.

Moonlight Charging

Best Practices:

- **Select an Appropriate Location:** Choose a spot where the gemstones will receive direct moonlight, such as a windowsill or an outdoor area.

- **Timing:** The full moon is the most potent time for charging gemstones, but any phase of the moon can be used, depending on the intention (e.g., waxing moon for growth, waning moon for release).

- **Duration:** Leave the gemstones under the moonlight for several hours or overnight.

- **Set an Intention:** As you place the gemstones in the moonlight, set a clear intention for charging. You can say a prayer or affirmation, such as, "May this moonlight cleanse and recharge these gemstones with calming, balanced energy."

Suitable Gemstones for Moonlight Charging:

- **Selenite:** Enhances spiritual connection and clarity.

- **Moonstone:** Boosts intuition and emotional balance.

- **Amethyst:** Calms the mind and promotes spiritual growth.

- **Rose Quartz:** Encourages love and emotional healing.

- **Labradorite:** Enhances intuition and protects against negative energies.

Benefits of Solar and Lunar Charging:

- **Sunlight:** Energizes and revitalises gemstones, enhancing their active and dynamic properties. It is especially beneficial for stones that promote confidence, motivation, and creativity.

- **Moonlight:** Provides gentle, calming energy that balances and soothes. It is ideal for gemstones used in emotional healing, intuition, and spiritual growth.

By following these best practices for charging with sunlight and moonlight, you can ensure your gemstones are energetically vibrant and ready to support your intentions. Each method offers unique benefits, allowing you to choose the most suitable charging technique for your specific needs and the properties of your gemstones.

Crystal Clusters and Geodes

Using large crystal clusters and geodes to charge smaller gemstones is an effective method to amplify and restore their energy. The natural structure and properties of clusters and geodes make them powerful tools for this purpose.

Using Large Clusters (e.g., Amethyst, Quartz) to Charge Smaller Stones

Best Practices for Charging with Crystal Clusters and Geodes

- **Select a Suitable Cluster or Geode:** Choose a large crystal cluster or geode with high vibrational energy. Amethyst and Clear Quartz clusters are commonly used for their powerful cleansing and charging properties.

- **Prepare the Cluster or Geode:** Ensure the cluster or geode is cleansed and free from any residual energy. You can cleanse it using methods such as smoke cleansing or placing it in moonlight.

- **Arrange the Smaller Gemstones:** Place the smaller gemstones on or around the cluster or geode. Ensure they are in direct contact with the larger crystal to absorb its energy effectively.

- **Set an Intention:** As you place the gemstones on the cluster or geode, set a clear intention for charging. You can say a prayer or affirmation, such as, "May this cluster/geode amplify and recharge the energy of these gemstones."

- **Leave for a Specific Duration:** Allow the gemstones to remain on the cluster or geode for several hours or overnight. The duration can vary based on how much energy the gemstones need to absorb.

Examples of Effective Crystal Clusters and Their Benefits

- **Amethyst Cluster**

  - **Benefits:** Amethyst is known for its calming and spiritual properties. It cleanses and recharges gemstones, enhancing their spiritual and emotional energies.

  - **Suitable for:** Amethyst, Clear Quartz, Rose Quartz, Citrine, and other stones needing spiritual amplification.

- **Clear Quartz Cluster**

  - **Benefits:** Clear Quartz is a versatile and powerful amplifier of energy. It can cleanse, recharge, and amplify the properties of other gemstones.

  - **Suitable for:** Any gemstone, particularly those used for amplification and clarity.

- **Selenite Geode:**

  - **Benefits:** Selenite is self-cleansing and can charge other stones. It enhances mental clarity, spiritual growth, and purification.

  - **Suitable for:** Selenite, Moonstone, Amethyst, and other stones needing clarity and spiritual enhancement.

How to Set Up and Duration for Effective Charging:

- **Setting Up:**

  - **Choose a Quiet Space:** Select a quiet and sacred space where the gemstones can remain undisturbed during the charging process.

  - **Arrange the Cluster or Geode:** Place the cluster or geode on a stable surface, such as a table or altar, where it will not be moved or knocked over.

  - **Place the Gemstones:** Arrange the smaller gemstones on or around the cluster or geode, ensuring they have direct contact.

- **Duration:**

- Short-Term Charging: For a quick boost, leave the gemstones on the cluster or geode for a few hours.

- Overnight Charging: For a more thorough charge, leave the gemstones on the cluster or geode overnight.

- Extended Charging: For deep cleansing and recharging, leave the gemstones on the cluster or geode for up to 24 hours.

Additional Tips:

- **Regular Maintenance:** Cleanse and recharge the cluster or geode regularly to ensure it remains energetically potent.

- **Rotation:** Rotate the gemstones periodically to ensure even charging and energy distribution.

By using crystal clusters and geodes for charging, you can effectively amplify and restore the energy of your smaller gemstones. This method harnesses the natural power of larger crystals to maintain the vibrational integrity of your gemstone collection.

Intentional Charging

Intentional charging involves using meditation and visualisation to imbue gemstones with specific energies and intentions. This method allows you to personalise the energy of your gemstones, aligning them with your goals and desires.

Using Meditation and Visualization to Charge Gemstones

Best Practices for Intentional Charging:

- **Create a Sacred Space:** Find a quiet, comfortable space where you won't be disturbed. Set up your space with items that promote relaxation and focus, such as candles, incense, or calming music.

- **Prepare the Gemstones:** Cleanse your gemstones using your preferred method (e.g., smoke cleansing, water cleansing) to remove any residual energies before charging.

- **Centre Yourself:** Sit comfortably and take a few deep breaths to centre yourself. Clear your mind of distractions and focus on your intention.

- **Set Your Intention:** Clearly define what you want to achieve with the gemstone. This could be anything from attracting love, protection, abundance, or healing.

Step-by-Step Guide to Intentional Charging:

1. **Hold the Gemstone:** Take the gemstone in your hands and hold it close to your heart or third eye, depending on the type of energy you wish to imbue.

2. **Visualise the Energy:** Close your eyes and visualise a bright, radiant light surrounding you. This light represents the energy you wish to charge the gemstone with.

3. **Direct the Energy:** Imagine this light flowing from your heart or third eye into the gemstone. See the gemstone glowing with this energy, becoming brighter and more vibrant.

4. **Speak Your Intention:** While visualising, speak your intention out loud or silently. For example, "I charge this gemstone with the energy of love and compassion," or "May this stone bring protection and strength."

5. **Focus and Breathe:** Focus on your breath, inhaling deeply and exhaling slowly. With each breath, feel the energy becoming stronger and more concentrated within the gemstone.

6. **Seal the Energy:** When you feel the gemstone is fully charged, visualise the energy sealing within it. Imagine a protective layer forming around the gemstone, locking in the energy.

7. **Express Gratitude:** Thank the gemstone and any spiritual guides or energies you called upon during the process. This helps to reinforce the positive energy and your connection to the stone.

Additional Tips for Intentional Charging:

- **Consistency:** Regularly charge your gemstones with intention to maintain their energetic potency. This can be done weekly or monthly, depending on how often you use the stones.

- **Personal Connection:** The more personal and specific your intention, the more effective the charging process will be. Take the time to connect deeply with your goals and desires.

- **Reinforcement:** Combine intentional charging with other charging methods, such as placing the gemstone in sunlight or moonlight after the visualisation. This can amplify the energy.

- **Energy Check:** Periodically check the energy of the gemstone by holding it and sensing its vibrational state. If it feels energetically low, repeat the intentional charging process.

By using intentional charging, you can infuse your gemstones with personalised energies that align with your specific intentions. This method enhances the connection between you and your gemstones, making them powerful tools for achieving your goals.

Storing and Handling Gemstones

Proper storage and handling of gemstones are essential for maintaining their energy and physical integrity. By storing gemstones correctly, you can protect them from damage, keep their energies clear and potent, and ensure they remain effective for their intended purposes.

Proper Storage Techniques

Storing gemstones correctly is crucial for preserving their energy and physical condition. Here are some key practices to ensure your gemstones remain in optimal condition:

Cleanse Before Storing

Always cleanse your gemstones before storing them to remove any accumulated negative energies. Use your preferred cleansing method, such as smoke cleansing, water cleansing, or sound cleansing.

Regularly Recharge

Periodically recharge your gemstones, even when they are stored, to maintain their energetic potency. This can be done by placing them in sunlight, moonlight, or on a crystal cluster.

Individual Wrapping

Wrap each gemstone individually in soft cloth or tissue paper. This prevents them from scratching each other and maintains their energy. You can also use small bags or pouches for this purpose.

Labelling

Label each wrapped gemstone with its name and properties. This helps you easily identify them and remember their specific uses.

Use of Pouches, Boxes, and Designated Crystal Shelves

Fabric Pouches

Benefits: Fabric pouches, such as those made from silk, cotton, or velvet, are soft and breathable. They protect gemstones from dust and scratches while allowing them to breathe.

Usage: Store individual gemstones or small groups of similar stones in separate pouches. This is particularly useful for travelling or keeping frequently used stones handy.

Boxes

Benefits: Wooden or gemstone boxes offer a sturdy and organised way to store gemstones. They provide protection from physical damage and environmental factors.

Usage: Use compartments within the box to separate different types of gemstones. Line the compartments with soft fabric to cushion the stones.

Designated Crystal Shelves

Benefits: Display shelves or cabinets specifically designed for crystals allow you to showcase your collection while keeping it organised and protected.

Usage: Arrange gemstones on shelves in a way that prevents them from touching each other. Ensure the shelves are stable and away from direct sunlight or extreme temperatures.

Steps for Proper Storage

Clean and Organise Storage Area

Ensure the storage area (drawer, box, shelf) is clean and free from dust and contaminants. This helps maintain the physical integrity of the gemstones.

Arrange by Type or Purpose

Organise gemstones by type (e.g., quartz family, jaspers) or by their intended purpose (e.g., healing stones, protection stones). This makes it easier to find and use them as needed.

Soft Linings

Line storage containers and shelves with soft fabric to cushion the gemstones and prevent damage.

Avoid Overcrowding

Do not overcrowd storage containers. Ensure each gemstone has enough space to avoid scratching or chipping.

Temperature Control

Store gemstones in a cool, dry place. Avoid areas with extreme temperatures or humidity, as these conditions can damage certain stones.

Additional Tips

Frequent Use

Keep frequently used gemstones in accessible pouches or boxes. This makes it easy to cleanse and recharge them regularly.

Display Stones

For gemstones that are used for display or home décor, place them on designated crystal shelves or altars. Ensure they are kept away from direct sunlight to prevent fading.

Energy Flow

Consider the flow of energy in the storage area. Keep the space energetically clean by occasionally smudging the area with Sage or Palo Santo.

Handling Gemstones

Proper handling of gemstones is essential to maintain their energy and physical integrity. Here are some key practices for handling your gemstones:

Clean Hands

Always handle your gemstones with clean hands to avoid transferring oils and dirt onto them.

Gentle Handling

Treat your gemstones with care to avoid chips and scratches. Avoid dropping or mishandling them, as this can disrupt their energy.

Regular Inspection

Periodically inspect your gemstones for any signs of wear or damage. Repair or replace them as needed to ensure they remain effective.

Respect and Intention

Handle your gemstones with respect and intention, acknowledging their power and purpose. This enhances your connection to the stones and strengthens their energy.

By following these proper storage and handling techniques, you can maintain the energy and physical integrity of your gemstones, ensuring they remain effective and vibrant for all your spiritual and healing practices.

Protection from Environmental Factors

Gemstones are sensitive to various environmental factors, including temperature, sunlight, and chemicals. Proper protection from these elements ensures that your gemstones remain in good condition and retain their energetic properties.

Avoiding Exposure to Extreme Temperatures, Sunlight, and Chemicals

Extreme Temperatures

Effect: Sudden changes in temperature can cause gemstones to crack or become damaged. Some stones are more sensitive to heat, while others may be affected by cold.

Prevention

- Store gemstones in a temperature-controlled environment, avoiding areas that experience extreme heat or cold.

- Do not leave gemstones in places where they might be exposed to direct sunlight for extended periods, such as windowsills or car dashboards.

- Avoid storing gemstones in locations prone to temperature fluctuations, such as basements or attics.

Sunlight

Effect: Prolonged exposure to direct sunlight can cause some gemstones to fade or change colour. Sunlight can also heat stones, leading to potential damage.

Prevention

- Keep light-sensitive gemstones, such as Amethyst, Rose Quartz, and Citrine, away from direct sunlight. Store them in a shaded area or a drawer.

- Use curtains or blinds to limit direct sunlight in rooms where gemstones are displayed.

- Rotate gemstones on display to minimise their exposure to sunlight.

Chemicals

Effect: Chemicals found in household cleaners, perfumes, and even body oils can damage gemstones. Some stones may react to acids, bases, or solvents.

Prevention

- Store gemstones in clean, dry containers away from household chemicals and cleaning agents.

- Avoid wearing gemstones while using harsh chemicals, cleaning, or applying lotions and perfumes.

- Clean gemstones with mild soap and water, and avoid using commercial jewellery cleaners unless they are specifically safe for your type of gemstone.

Specific Guidelines for Fragile and Light-Sensitive Stones

Fragile Stones

Examples: Selenite, Kyanite, Malachite, and Fluorite.

Protection:

- Store fragile stones separately, wrapping them in soft cloth or tissue paper to prevent scratches and physical damage.

- Avoid dropping or knocking fragile stones against hard surfaces. Handle them with care.

- Keep them in padded boxes or containers to provide extra cushioning.

Light-Sensitive Stones

Examples: Amethyst, Rose Quartz, Citrine, and Aquamarine.

Protection:

- Store light-sensitive stones in dark, cool places to prevent fading and discoloration.

- Use opaque or dark-coloured pouches and boxes to shield them from light exposure.

- Rotate displayed stones periodically to limit their exposure to light.

General Tips for Environmental Protection

Humidity Control

- Maintain a stable, low-humidity environment for storing gemstones. Excessive humidity can cause certain stones to degrade over time.

- Use silica gel packets or dehumidifiers in storage areas to control moisture levels.

Dust Prevention

- Keep gemstones in closed containers or covered displays to protect them from dust and dirt.

- Clean storage areas regularly to prevent dust accumulation.

Handling Practices

- Wash your hands before handling gemstones to avoid transferring oils and dirt.

- Use a soft cloth to handle gemstones, especially those that are delicate or prone to smudging.

CHAPTER NINETEEN

Conclusion: The Ongoing Journey with Gemstones

Understanding the Interconnectedness of Body, Mind, and Spirit

Holistic Health Concept

- **Interconnectedness:** Holistic health is based on the understanding that the body, mind, and spirit are deeply interconnected. Each aspect influences and supports the others, contributing to overall well-being.

- **Energy Flow:** Gemstones play a role in balancing the flow of energy between the body, mind, and spirit. They can help to remove blockages, enhance positive energy, and create harmony within the whole system.

Integration with Holistic Practices:

Yoga

- **Enhancing Yoga Practice:** Incorporate gemstones into your yoga practice to deepen relaxation, focus, and balance. Place stones like Amethyst or

Selenite around your mat to create a calming environment.

- **Chakra Balancing:** Use gemstones that correspond to the chakras you are focusing on in your practice. For example, place a Rose Quartz stone near your heart during heart-opening poses.

Meditation

- **Deepening Meditation:** Hold a gemstone or place it nearby during meditation to enhance your practice. Stones like Clear Quartz and Labradorite can enhance clarity and intuition.

- **Guided Visualisations:** Use gemstones as focal points for guided visualisations. Imagine the stone's energy flowing through your body, bringing healing and balance.

Herbal Medicine

- **Synergistic Healing:** Combine the use of gemstones with herbal remedies for a synergistic healing effect. Pair calming herbs like chamomile with soothing stones like Blue Lace Agate for enhanced relaxation.

- **Infusions and Elixirs:** Create gemstone-infused water or herbal elixirs to drink. Ensure the gemstones used are safe for direct contact with water or use the indirect method to infuse the water with their energy.

How Gemstones Can Complement Other Holistic Practices

Yoga

- **Enhanced Focus:** Gemstones like Fluorite and Amethyst can enhance focus and concentration during yoga, helping you to stay present in each pose.

- **Energetic Support:** Place grounding stones like Hematite or Smoky Quartz at the base of your mat to support stability and balance during your practice.

Meditation

- **Intuitive Guidance:** Use stones like Labradorite or Lapis Lazuli to enhance intuitive guidance during meditation. These stones can help you access deeper levels of consciousness and insight.

- **Emotional Healing:** Incorporate soothing stones like Rose Quartz or

Rhodonite into your meditation practice to support emotional healing and self-compassion.

Herbal Medicine

- **Complementary Energies:** Pair specific herbs with corresponding gemstones to enhance their effects. For example, use Lavender with Amethyst for relaxation or Ginger with Carnelian for vitality and energy.

- **Holistic Remedies:** Create holistic remedies that combine the healing properties of both herbs and gemstones. This can involve making herbal teas, tinctures, or baths infused with gemstone energy.

By understanding the interconnectedness of body, mind, and spirit and integrating gemstones into your holistic lifestyle, you can create a balanced and harmonious approach to well-being. Gemstones can complement and enhance other holistic practices, supporting your journey towards a healthier and more integrated self.

Balancing Physical, Emotional, and Spiritual Health

Using Gemstones to Support Overall Well-Being

Physical Health

- **Healing and Recovery:** Use gemstones like Green Aventurine and Amethyst to support physical healing and recovery. Place these stones on the affected area or incorporate them into your daily routine.

- **Energy Boost:** Carry or wear Citrine or Carnelian to boost energy levels and promote vitality.

Emotional Health

- **Stress Relief:** Use calming stones like Lepidolite and Rose Quartz to reduce stress and promote emotional balance. Hold these stones during stressful moments or place them in your environment.

- **Emotional Healing:** Work with Rhodonite and Moonstone to heal emotional wounds and foster self-compassion.

Spiritual Health

- **Spiritual Growth:** Use stones like Selenite and Amethyst to support spiritual growth and enlightenment. Incorporate them into your meditation practice or place them on your altar.

- **Intuition and Insight:** Enhance your intuition with stones like Labradorite and Lapis Lazuli. Use them during intuitive practices such as tarot readings or scrying.

Creating a Sustainable Practice

Ensuring That Your Use of Gemstones Is Sustainable and Responsible

Ethical Sourcing

- **Responsible Suppliers:** Purchase gemstones from reputable suppliers who prioritise ethical and sustainable mining practices. Ensure that the stones are sourced without causing harm to the environment or communities.

- **Supporting Fair Trade:** Choose fair trade gemstones that support the well-being of miners and their communities.

Mindful Consumption

- **Quality Over Quantity:** Focus on acquiring high-quality stones that you truly need and will use, rather than accumulating large quantities.

- **Caring for Your Stones:** Properly care for your gemstones to ensure their longevity and effectiveness. Regular cleansing and recharging can help maintain their energy.

Tips for Maintaining a Balanced and Mindful Approach to Gemstone Work

Regular Reflection

- **Self-Assessment:** Regularly assess your gemstone practices to ensure they remain balanced and aligned with your holistic lifestyle. Reflect on how the stones are impacting your physical, emotional, and spiritual health.

- **Adjustments:** Be willing to make adjustments to your practices based on your reflections and insights. This ensures that your gemstone work remains dynamic and responsive to your needs.

Integration with Daily Life

- **Seamless Integration:** Integrate gemstones into your daily life in a seamless and natural way. Use them in your morning routine, during work, and in evening rituals to maintain a consistent connection.

- **Mindfulness Practices:** Incorporate mindfulness practices such as meditation, deep breathing, and visualisation to enhance your connection with gemstones and their energies.

Cultivating Mindfulness and Presence

The Role of Mindfulness in Enhancing Your Connection with Gemstones

Focused Attention

- **Presence:** Practise being fully present when working with gemstones. Focus your attention on the stone, its energy, and your intention. This mindfulness can deepen your connection and enhance the stone's effectiveness.

- **Mindful Handling:** Handle your gemstones with care and intention. Notice their texture, weight, and energy as you work with them.

Enhanced Awareness

- **Sensory Engagement:** Engage your senses when working with gemstones. Notice their colour, shape, and feel. Pay attention to any changes in your energy or mood.

- **Intuitive Insights:** Allow yourself to receive intuitive insights during your gemstone practices. Trust your inner guidance and be open to the messages the stones may convey.

Practices for Staying Present and Fully Engaged in Your Gemstone Journey

Meditation and Breathwork

- **Mindful Meditation:** Incorporate gemstones into your meditation practice to enhance mindfulness and presence. Focus on your breath and the energy of the stone.

- **Breath Awareness:** Use breathwork techniques to stay present. Breathe deeply and rhythmically while holding or focusing on a gemstone.

Journaling and Reflection

- **Daily Journaling:** Keep a daily journal to document your experiences and reflections with gemstones. Writing can help you stay present and mindful of your journey.

- **Reflective Practices:** Set aside time for regular reflection on your gemstone practices. Consider how they are impacting your life and any adjustments needed to stay aligned with your intentions.

By embracing a holistic approach to gemstone work, integrating stones into your lifestyle, and maintaining mindfulness and presence, you can create a balanced and sustainable practice that supports your overall well-being.

The Importance of Personal Experience

Valuing Your Own Experiences and Insights in Gemstone Work

Trusting Personal Insights

- **Unique Journey:** Remember that your journey with gemstones is unique. Your experiences and insights are valuable and can guide you more accurately than external sources.

- **Empowerment:** Trusting your personal experiences empowers you to develop a deeper connection with gemstones and enhances your confidence in your practices.

Reflective Practice

- **Self-Reflection:** Regularly reflect on your experiences with gemstones. Note the physical, emotional, and spiritual effects they have on you.

- **Learning from Experience:** Treat each interaction with gemstones as a learning opportunity. Reflect on what works, what doesn't, and how different stones affect you.

Encouraging a Personal and Intuitive Approach to Exploring Gemstones

Intuitive Selection

- **Following Your Intuition:** When choosing gemstones, trust your intuition. Often, the stones you are drawn to intuitively are the ones you need most at that moment.

- **Personal Resonance:** Pay attention to how different gemstones resonate with you. Your personal attraction to certain stones can provide insights into their relevance for you.

Creative Exploration

- **Experimentation:** Don't be afraid to experiment with different gemstones and techniques. Explore new ways of incorporating them into your daily routines and spiritual practices.

- **Personalization:** Customise your gemstone practices to suit your personal needs and preferences. Your unique approach will make your practices more meaningful and effective.

Exploring New Possibilities

Staying Open to New Gemstones, Techniques, and Practices

Diverse Collection

- **Expanding Knowledge:** Continuously expand your knowledge of different gemstones and their properties. This helps you discover new stones that can enhance your practice.

- **Exploration:** Be open to exploring gemstones you haven't worked with before. Each stone offers unique energies and benefits.

Innovative Techniques

- **Learning New Methods:** Stay open to learning new techniques and practices involving gemstones. This can include advanced crystal grid designs, gemstone elixirs, or new meditation practices.

- **Adaptation:** Adapt new techniques to fit your personal style and needs. Combining traditional methods with innovative approaches can enhance your practice.

Embracing the Spirit of Curiosity and Adventure in Your Gemstone Journey

Curiosity-Driven Exploration

- **Questioning:** Maintain a spirit of curiosity in your gemstone journey. Ask questions, seek answers, and explore new ideas and concepts.

- **Adventure:** View your gemstone practice as an adventure. Embrace the unknown and enjoy the process of discovery and growth.

Continual Learning

- **Ongoing Education:** Commit to ongoing education in the field of gemstones. Attend workshops, read books, and participate in community discussions to keep your knowledge fresh and evolving.

- **Engagement:** Engage with other gemstone enthusiasts. Sharing and learning from others can provide new perspectives and inspire your practice.

Developing Your Unique Path

Crafting a Personalized Practice That Resonates with Your Individual Needs and Goals

Personal Alignment

- **Individual Needs:** Tailor your gemstone practices to align with your personal needs and goals. What works for someone else may not work for you, and that's okay.

- **Unique Expression:** Allow your practice to be a unique expression of who you are. Your individuality is a powerful component of your spiritual journey.

Goal Setting

- **Intentions:** Set clear intentions for your gemstone work. Whether it's for healing, protection, manifestation, or spiritual growth, having clear goals will guide your practice.

- **Flexibility:** Be flexible with your goals. Allow them to evolve as you grow and change. Your gemstone practice should be dynamic and adaptable.

Allowing Your Gemstone Work to Evolve and Grow Over Time

Evolving Practices

- **Growth Mindset:** Adopt a growth mindset towards your gemstone practices. Be open to change and evolution as you gain more experience and insights.

- **Continuous Improvement:** Regularly review and refine your practices. Look for ways to enhance their effectiveness and align them more closely with your evolving needs.

Adaptation and Innovation

- **Adapting Techniques:** Adapt your techniques based on your experiences and feedback. What worked initially may need adjustments as you grow in your practice.

- **Innovative Approaches:** Embrace innovative approaches to gemstone work. Experiment with new ideas and methods to keep your practice fresh and engaging.

Listening to Your Inner Guidance

Trusting Your Intuition and Inner Wisdom in Your Gemstone Practice

Intuitive Connection

- **Inner Voice:** Pay attention to your inner voice when working with gemstones. Your intuition can provide valuable guidance and insights.

- **Trust:** Trust your intuition, even if it leads you in unexpected directions. Your inner wisdom is a powerful tool in your gemstone journey.

Mindful Awareness

- **Presence:** Practice mindfulness and stay present when working with gemstones. This enhances your connection with the stones and helps you attune to their energies.

- **Awareness:** Cultivate awareness of your thoughts, feelings, and sensations during your gemstone practices. This helps you understand how the stones affect you on a deeper level.

Techniques for Enhancing Your Intuitive Connection with Gemstones

Meditation and Visualization

- **Intuitive Meditation:** Use meditation to deepen your intuitive connection with gemstones. Hold a stone during meditation and focus on its energy and the insights it may bring.

- **Visualisation:** Practice visualisation techniques to connect with the energy of gemstones. Imagine the stone's energy flowing through you and providing guidance and clarity.

Journaling and Reflection

- **Intuitive Journaling:** Keep a journal specifically for intuitive insights related to your gemstone practices. Document any intuitive messages or guidance you receive.

- **Reflective Practice:** Reflect regularly on your intuitive experiences with gemstones. This helps you build a stronger connection with your inner wisdom.

By encouraging personal discovery, embracing curiosity, and trusting your intuition, you can develop a personalised and evolving gemstone practice that resonates deeply with your unique journey.

Reflections on the Journey

Understanding Gemstone Energies

- **Hidden Energies:** Throughout the book, we've explored the hidden energies of gemstones and how they can influence physical, emotional, and spiritual well-being.

- **Scientific and Metaphysical Properties:** We've delved into both the scientific properties and the metaphysical uses of gemstones, providing a comprehensive understanding of their potential.

Techniques and Practices

- **Healing Techniques:** Detailed methods for using gemstones in healing practices, including laying on of stones, gemstone elixirs, and crystal grids.

- **Meditation and Mindfulness:** Practical advice on incorporating gemstones into meditation practices, enhancing focus, intuition, and overall mindfulness.

Integration into Daily Life

- **Holistic Lifestyle:** Guidance on integrating gemstones into a holistic lifestyle, balancing physical, emotional, and spiritual health.

- **Everyday Use:** Tips for using gemstones in various aspects of daily life, from home decor to personal accessories, creating a harmonious environment and supporting well-being.

Sustainability and Ethics

- **Responsible Sourcing:** Emphasis on the importance of ethical and sustainable sourcing of gemstones, promoting fair trade and environmental responsibility.

- **Mindful Practice:** Encouraging a mindful and balanced approach to gemstone use, ensuring that practices are respectful, intentional, and beneficial.

Reflecting on the Transformative Power of Gemstones in Your Life

Personal Growth

- **Self-Awareness:** Working with gemstones can enhance self-awareness, helping you to understand your own needs, emotions, and spiritual path more clearly.

- **Empowerment:** The practices and techniques outlined in the book can empower you to take an active role in your own healing and personal growth.

Emotional Healing

- **Stress Reduction:** Gemstones like Amethyst and Rose Quartz have been highlighted for their ability to reduce stress and promote emotional healing.

- **Emotional Balance:** Regular use of gemstones can help balance emotions, providing support during challenging times and enhancing overall emotional well-being.

Spiritual Connection

- **Deepened Intuition:** Many practices, such as meditation and chakra alignment, can deepen your intuitive abilities and spiritual insights.

- **Spiritual Growth:** Gemstones can support spiritual growth, helping you to connect with higher consciousness and explore deeper aspects of your spiritual journey.

Community and Sharing

- **Collective Wisdom:** Engaging with a community of like-minded individuals can enhance your gemstone journey, providing support, inspiration, and shared wisdom.

- **Teaching and Mentoring:** Sharing your experiences and insights with others can foster a sense of community and contribute to collective learning and growth.

By reflecting on the key insights and transformative power of gemstones, you can appreciate the depth and breadth of your journey. The knowledge and practices shared in this book aim to support your ongoing exploration and growth, enriching your life in meaningful ways.

Inspiring Quotes and Wisdom

Ancient Wisdom

- **Hippocrates:** "The natural healing force within each of us is the greatest force in getting well." This quote emphasises the innate power of self-healing, which gemstones can help to activate and support.

- **Confucius:** "When we see men of a contrary character, we should turn inwards and examine ourselves." This reflects the introspective journey that working with gemstones often entails.

Modern Insights

- **Ralph Waldo Emerson:** "The creation of a thousand forests is in one acorn." This quote symbolises the potential that lies within each gemstone to foster growth and transformation.

- **Louise Hay:** "I am in the process of positive change." This affirmation underscores the continuous journey of growth and healing supported by gemstones.

Spiritual Guidance

- **Rumi:** "The wound is the place where the Light enters you." This reminds us that healing with gemstones is not just about alleviating pain but also about finding light and wisdom through our challenges.

- **Pema Chödrön:** "Nothing ever goes away until it has taught us what we need to know." This speaks to the lessons and insights that gemstone work can reveal over time.

Gemstone-Specific Wisdom

- **Amethyst:** "Known as a stone of spiritual protection and purification, Amethyst can guard against negative energies and help maintain a calm and clear state of mind."

- **Rose Quartz:** "The stone of unconditional love, Rose Quartz opens the heart to all types of love—self-love, love of family, love of friends, and romantic love."

Encouraging Words for Continuing Your Gemstone Journey

Embrace the Journey

- **Continuous Learning:** "The path of gemstone work is one of lifelong learning and discovery. Embrace each new experience with curiosity and openness."

- **Trust the Process:** "Trust in your journey and the process of working with gemstones. Each step you take brings you closer to deeper understanding and healing."

Stay Inspired

- **Daily Affirmations:** "Incorporate daily affirmations to stay motivated and inspired. For example, 'I am open to the healing energies of the gemstones I work with.'"

- **Reflect and Celebrate:** "Take time to reflect on your progress and celebrate your achievements, no matter how small they may seem. Every step forward is a victory."

Connect with Community

- **Shared Experiences:** "Engage with a community of gemstone enthusiasts. Sharing your experiences and learning from others can provide support and deepen your practice."

- **Mentorship:** "Seek out mentors or become a mentor to others. Teaching and learning from each other can enhance your understanding and foster a sense of community."

Final Thoughts and Inspirations - Looking Ahead

The Future of Gemstone Work and Its Potential Impact on Personal and Collective Well-Being

Growing Awareness

- **Increased Interest:** The interest in gemstone work and holistic healing practices is growing as more people seek natural and complementary ways to enhance their well-being. This expanding interest paves the way for greater acceptance and integration of gemstone practices in mainstream wellness routines.

- **Educational Opportunities:** With the rise in interest, educational opportunities such as workshops, online courses, and certification programs are becoming more accessible. These resources allow for deeper exploration and understanding of gemstone work, empowering individuals to practise with greater knowledge and confidence.

Scientific Research

- **Integration of Science and Metaphysics:** As scientific research into the properties of gemstones and their effects on the human body and energy fields advances, there is potential for a greater integration of scientific and metaphysical perspectives. This can lead to a more holistic understanding of how gemstones work and why they are effective.

- **Validation of Benefits:** Ongoing research may provide more empirical evidence to support the benefits of gemstone work, leading to wider acceptance and integration into mainstream wellness practices. This scientific validation can help bridge the gap between traditional and alternative healing methods.

Technological Advancements

- **Enhanced Tools:** The development of new technologies can enhance the ways we work with gemstones. This includes advanced tools for measuring and visualising energy fields, as well as innovative ways to incorporate gemstones into daily life.

- **Accessibility:** Technology can make gemstone knowledge and practices more accessible to a global audience. Online platforms, virtual workshops, and digital resources allow for greater sharing of information and experiences, fostering a more connected and informed community.

Encouraging a Vision of a World Where Gemstones Are Used Responsibly and Ethically

Sustainable Practices

- **Environmental Impact:** Promote sustainable mining practices that minimise environmental damage and ensure the preservation of natural resources. Support initiatives and companies that prioritise eco-friendly methods and reduce the carbon footprint of gemstone extraction.

- **Ethical Sourcing:** Advocate for ethical sourcing of gemstones, ensuring that they are obtained without exploitation and that workers are treated fairly and compensated appropriately. This includes supporting fair trade initiatives and purchasing from reputable suppliers.

Community Support

- **Fair Trade:** Support fair trade practices that benefit local communities involved in gemstone mining and production. This helps to improve the quality of life for workers and their families, fostering economic growth and stability in mining regions.

- **Cultural Respect:** Honor and respect the cultural significance of gemstones in various traditions. Recognize and appreciate the wisdom and practices of indigenous cultures that have long understood the power of gemstones, and avoid cultural appropriation by learning from and supporting these communities.

Education and Awareness

- **Spreading Knowledge:** Encourage the sharing of knowledge about the ethical and responsible use of gemstones. Educate others on the importance of sustainability and fair trade in the gemstone industry, and advocate for transparency in sourcing practices.

- **Community Initiatives:** Participate in or support community initiatives that promote the ethical use of gemstones and raise awareness about the impact of our choices. This includes supporting organisations that work to improve mining conditions and protect the environment.

By looking ahead with a vision of responsible and ethical gemstone use, we can ensure that the practices we engage in are sustainable and beneficial for both individuals and the collective well-being. This approach fosters a deeper connection to the earth and a greater appreciation for the gifts it provides, creating a more harmonious and respectful relationship with the natural world.

Practical Tips for Continuing Your Gemstone Journey with Joy and Confidence

Stay Curious

- **Lifelong Learning:** Embrace the spirit of lifelong learning. Continue to explore new gemstones, techniques, and practices with curiosity and an open mind. Each new discovery can deepen your understanding and enhance your practice.

- **Experiment and Adapt:** Don't be afraid to experiment with different approaches and adapt your practices to fit your evolving needs and insights. Gemstone work is a personal journey that can grow and change over time.

Maintain Balance

- **Mindful Practice:** Practice mindfulness in your gemstone work. Stay present and fully engaged in each moment, and regularly reflect on your experiences and progress. Mindfulness can enhance your connection with gemstones and make your practices more effective.

- **Self-Care:** Ensure that your gemstone practices are balanced and integrated with other aspects of self-care and well-being. Listen to your body and mind, and adjust your practices as needed to maintain harmony and balance.

Final Thoughts on the Enduring Value of Gemstones in Enhancing Life and Promoting Well-Being

Timeless Wisdom

- **Ancient Practices:** Gemstones have been used for healing and spiritual practices for thousands of years. Their enduring value lies in the timeless wisdom they carry and their ability to connect us to the natural world.

- **Modern Relevance:** While rooted in ancient traditions, gemstone work continues to be relevant in modern times, offering tools and insights that can enhance contemporary lifestyles and promote holistic well-being.

Personal Transformation

- **Empowerment:** Gemstones have the power to support personal transformation, helping individuals to heal, grow, and thrive. By working with gemstones, you can access deeper layers of your being and unlock your full potential.

- **Community and Connection:** The journey with gemstones is also about connecting with others who share similar interests and values. By fostering a sense of community and shared learning, we can collectively enhance our well-being and create positive change.

CHAPTER TWENTY

Thank You

Thank you for taking the time to explore the fascinating world of gemstones and their secret energies with me. Your journey through these pages reflects a deep curiosity and appreciation for the wonders of the natural world. If this book has enriched your understanding, inspired you, or sparked new ideas, I would be truly grateful if you could share your thoughts by leaving a review. Your feedback not only helps other readers discover this work but also encourages the ongoing exploration of these ancient mysteries. Thank you for your support!

Printed in Great Britain
by Amazon

48794708R00218